SINGAPORE & MALAYSIA

● AT COST ●

A TRAVELLER'S GUIDE

SINGAPORE & MALAYSIA

• AT COST •

A TRAVELLER'S GUIDE

LITTLE HILLS PRESS

(c) Photographs — Singapore Tourist Promotion Board
Tourist Development Corporation Malaysia

Typeset by Colorcraft, Hong Kong
Printed in Hong Kong

Little Hills Press Pty. Ltd.,
Tavistock House, 34 Bromham Road,
Bedford MK40 2QD,
United Kingdom.

Regent House, 37-43 Alexander Street,
Crows Nest, NSW, 2065, Australia.

Distributed in the USA and Canada by
The Talman Company, Inc.
150 Fifth Avenue,
New York, N.Y. 10011

ISBN 0 949773 89 1

All rights reserved. No part of this publication may be reproduced, stored in a retrieval system, or transmitted in any form or by any means, electronic, mechanical, photocopying, recording or otherwise, without the prior permission in writing of the publishers.

Maps © Directorate of National Mapping Malaysia, pages VI, 52-53, 80, 88, 98, 108-109, 134-135, 146, 156, 160-161, 176, 188, 206-207, 216-217, 226-227.

© Survey Department, Republic of Singapore, p 8-9

DISCLAIMER
Whilst all care has been taken by the publisher and author to ensure that the information is accurate and up to date, the publisher does not take responsibility for the information published herein. The recommendations are those of the author, and as things get better or worse, places close and others open, some elements in the book may be inaccurate when you get there. Please write and tell us about it so we can update in subsequent editions.

CONTENTS

SINGAPORE (Introduction, History, Population, Language, Religion, Festivals, Entry and Exit Regulations, Embassies, Money, Communications, Miscellaneous)	1
Travel Information (How to Get There, Accommodation, Local Transport, Food, Entertainment)	15
Shopping and Sightseeing	25
Tours	39
Sport and Recreation	47
MALAYSIA (Introduction, History, Climate, Population, Language, Religion, Festivals, Entry Regulations, Embassies, Money, Communications, Miscellaneous, Do's and Don'ts)	55
Travel Information (How to Get There, Accommodation, Local Transport, Food, Shopping, Natural Attractions)	71
Kuala Lumpur	79
Negeri Sembilan	99
Melaka	107
Penang	125
Perlis	143
Kedah	147
Perak	157
East Coast	175
Terengganu	187
Negeri Pahang Darul Makmur	197
Johor	205
Sabah and Sarawak	215
Hill Resorts of Malaysia	231
National Parks of Malaysia	247
Index	264

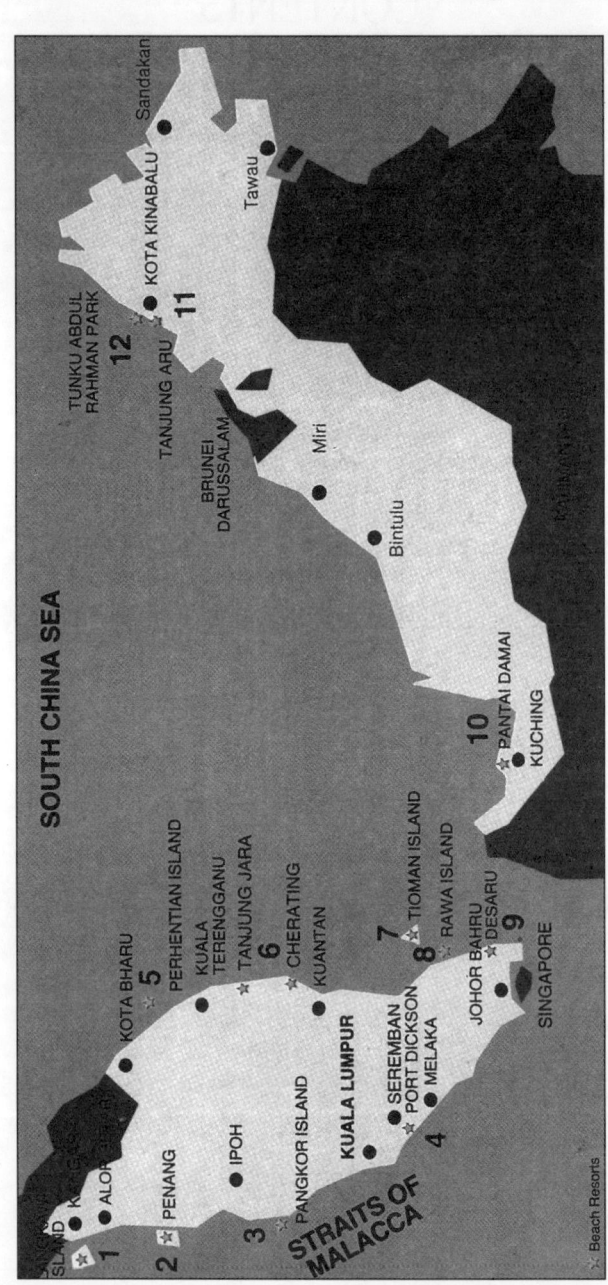

SINGAPORE

A small tropical island of only 617 km² (238 sq. miles) with 57 smaller islets, lying just 1 deg. north of the Equator, Singapore is the world's busiest port. Hundreds of ships ride at anchor at this crucial junction of the Indian and Pacific Oceans, or glide in and out of her bustling container wharves. Giant oil refineries tower over the scattered islands of her harbour, making her the world's third biggest refining centre after Rotterdam and Houston.

Singapore is the clearing house for the region's wealth. Her port trades in tin, rubber, coconut, oil, rice, timber, jute, spices and coffee. Her banking system is one of the world's key financial centres. Her shipyards and dry docks repair everything from island traders to vast tankers.

Changi International Airport is served by over 40 of the world's major airlines, with 10 million passengers passing through every year.

To the north, a 1 km-long causeway links Singapore with Peninsular Malaysia at Johore Bahru. It is a vital artery for road traffic and a railway system which leads 1,923 km (1,192 miles) to Bangkok.

HISTORY

In the 7th century AD Singapore was known as Temasek or "Sea Town", a trading centre of Sumatra's ancient Sri Vijayan Empire. By the 13th century she had become one of its three kingdoms. According to legend, the island was renamed Singa Pura or "Lion City" after a visiting prince, Sang Nila Utama, saw an animal he mistook for a lion, but which was more probably a native tiger.

The 14th century saw the empires of Java and Siam struggling for regional dominance with the Chinese Imperial Fleet under Admiral Cheng Ho. Within the next hundred years the great city of Singa Pura would be destroyed and reclaimed by the jungle.

Throughout the 16th century the Dutch, Portuguese and British sailed by. In 1811, a hundred Malays from Johore led by the local chief, the Temenggong, settled at the mouth of the Singapore river.

Sir Thomas Stamford Raffles signed a treaty on February 6, 1819, and Singapore became a trading post for the British East India Company. Although Raffles spent only nine months in Singapore, he laid the principles for the city's development as a free port, and the giant international marketplace of Southeast Asia. By the time he died in 1827, the Sultan of Johore had ceded full sovereignty to Britain.

In 1832 Singapore became the centre of government for the Straits Settlements of Penang, Malacca and Singapore. The opening of the Suez Canal in 1869 and the advent of the telegraph and steamship increased Singapore's importance as a centre for expanding trade between East and West.

For many years, Singapore was considered Britain's strategic defence base in the Far East, but the myth of the island's impregnability was shattered when it fell to the Japanese in a matter of weeks during the Second World War in 1942. The Japanese occupation lasted until September 1945.

Post-war Singapore became a Crown Colony, and the growth of a national identity led to self-government in 1959. The transition from colonialism was achieved without bitterness.

In 1965, Singapore became an independent republic.

POPULATION

Because Singapore lacks natural resources, its strength lies in its hardworking, adaptable and resilient population of 2.5 million, comprising 76% Chinese, 15% Malays, 7% Indians and Pakistans and 2% others. The original inhabitants were Malay fishermen, but after the arrival of Sir Stamford Raffles and the establishment of a British trading post, Singapore became a magnet that drew hundreds of thousands of migrants and merchants.

Each racial group has retained its own cultural identity while developing as an integral part of the Singapore community.

LANGUAGE

Although Chinese Singaporeans have traditionally spoken their own dialects, the government actively encourages the use of

Mandarin. There are four official languages in Singapore: Mandarin, Malay, Tamil and English.

English is the language of business and administration, and is widely spoken and understood, as most Singaporeans are bilingual, and speak their mother tongue as well as English.

RELIGION

Singapore enjoys freedom of worship. The main religions are Buddhism, Taoism, Islam, Hinduism and Christianity. Mosques sit near churches, while Chinese and Indian temples can be found throughout the island.

The majority of Singapore's national monuments listed for preservation are houses of worship.

FESTIVALS

Every year Singapore celebrates its diversity in feasts and festivals. Check with the Singapore Tourist Promotion Board for venues, ph 339 6622.

Thaipusam

Hindu penitents pierce their bodies, foreheads, cheeks and even tongues with sharp skewers and weighted hooks and walk in a trance-like state from the Sri Perumal Temple in Serangoon Road to the Chettiar Tank Road Temple.

Access to both the Sri Perumal and Chettiar temples is free of charge and you can take photographs. Shoes must, however, be removed within the temple courtyards, and visitors should expect large crowds there.

Chinese New Year

The streets of Chinatown are lit and decorated for a month before this festival as shoppers crowd the area for traditional goods. The idea is that by the eve of New Year, houses would have been cleaned and redecorated and all debts paid. The first day of the New Year is set aside for paying respects to relatives, and giving the children lucky red envelopes containing money (hong bao).

Chingay Parade

Held shortly after the New Year, this is Chinese in origin. The procession, with decorated floats, stilt-walkers, acrobats, lion and dragon dancers and stunning displays by men carrying giant flags, attracts thousands of spectators.

Birthday of the Monkey God
Spirit mediums representing the mischievous Monkey God star in these celebrations (held twice a year), piercing their bodies and entering a trance before giving out special charms to devotees. Performances of Chinese opera or wayang are also held in temple grounds.

Ching Ming (Qing Ming) Festival
During this festival Chinese honour and remember their ancestors. Families go to the cemeteries along Lornie Road, Upper Thomson Road and Lim Chu Kang Road to tidy the graves of their ancestors and to lay offerings of food and incense.

Songkran Festival
Thai Buddhist temples in Singapore celebrate the Thai water festival by bathing images of Buddha in holy water. Worshippers and visitors are also likely to be splashed with water — considered a blessing in Thailand where the festival takes place during the hottest season of the year.

Good Friday
Christians commemorate the day Christ died to save mankind. Singapore's Catholics follow an effigy of Christ in a solemn candlelight procession around the grounds of St. Joseph's Church in Victoria Street.

Ramadan
The fasting month when Muslims abstain from food and drink between the hours of sunrise and sunset as an act of faith. Part of Geylang Serai district is daily decorated and lit up with dozens of stalls selling seasonal specialities for the feast that celebrates the end of Ramadan.

Vesak Day
A holy day for Buddhists, who celebrate the birth, enlightenment and death of Buddha. Prayers are held at Buddhist temples throughout the island.

Hari Raya Puasa

Hari Raya Puasa marks the end of Ramadan, the fasting month. Singapore's Muslims pray in mosques; then dressed in new clothes, visit friends and relatives for a seemingly endless round of feasting and celebration.

Dragon Boat Festival

Exciting races with competitors from Asia, Australasia, Europe and the USA are the main features of this festival, which also includes the eating of special meat-filled dumplings. The festival honours an ancient Chinese poet, Ch'u Yuan, who drowned himself in protest against the evils of corruption. In an attempt to save him, fishermen raced out to sea beating drums and thrashing the water to try to scare away fish that might attack him. On the anniversary of his death, rice dumplings were thrown into the water to appease his spirit.

Birthday of the Third Prince

Spirit mediums demonstrate their powers during this festival which commemorates the birth of the Third Prince of the Lotus, a child god who carried a magic bracelet in one hand and a spear in the other.

Hari Raya Haji

A celebration of the Haj or pilgrimage to Mecca in fulfilment of one of the five obligations of Muslims. Singapore's Muslims gather in mosques early in the day, and later animals are ritually slaughtered and the meat distributed to the needy.

National Day

Singapore celebrates its independence on August 9, with a procession and displays of cultural dances (lion and dragon dances, acrobatic performances, traditional Indian and Malay dances). Military bands, groups of students, girl pipers, and others all contribute to the display.

Festival of the Hungry Gods (Market Festival)

During the seventh month of the lunar calendar, stall holders from markets all over Singapore combine to lay out displays of food for the spirits of the dead, which are thought to roam the earth at this time. Prayers, the burning of incense and performances of Chinese opera go further towards keeping the spirits happy.

Navarathri Festival

Nine nights of classical Indian music, dance and song recitals are staged between 7pm and 10pm in the Chettiar Temple hall in Tank Road, in homage to the consorts of the gods making up the Hindu trinity.

Moon Cake Festival

On the night of the year when the moon is believed to be at its fullest and most beautiful, Chinese celebrate the overthrow of the Mongol dynasty in China by eating mooncakes - large circles of dough enfolding lotus nuts, sweet red bean paste and even salted egg yolk. Processions of paper lanterns, each with a flickering candle inside, turn parts of Singapore into a fairyland.

Thimithi (Fire Walking) Festival

A spectacular demonstration of faith takes place when Hindu devotees of the goddess Draupadai walk across a pit of burning coals in fulfilment of their vows.

Deepavali

This joyous Hindu celebration, the Festival of Lights, is associated with legends telling of the victory of good (light) over evil (dark). In the weeks before Deepavali 'Little India' is a fairyland of lights and decorations as shops and temples prepare to welcome the festival.

Kusu Island Pilgrimage

Throughout the 9th lunar month Chinese Taoists flock to Kusu Island off the south of Singapore to pray at the sacred temple devoted to Do Bo Gong (Tua Pek Kong). Visits are also made to a Malay shrine on the island, an example of religious respect that resulted from the legend that a pair of shipwrecked Chinese and Malay fishermen, rescued by a turtle, lived together happily on Kusu for the rest of their lives.

Festival of the Nine Emperor Gods
The 9th day of the 9th lunar month, regarded as one of the most auspicious days of the year, is devoted to honouring the 9 Emperor Gods who are believed to cure ailments and bring luck and longevity. Highlight of the celebration is a procession of the images of the gods, borne in sedan chairs, followed by crowds of worshippers bearing yellow flags.

Maulud Nabi
On this day when Muslims celebrate the birth of the prophet Mohammed, prayers are offered and stories of his life and achievements are retold in mosques throughout Singapore.

Christmas
Orchard Road is totally transformed with masses of lights and beautiful decorations as hotels and shopping centres prepare for Christmas. A public holiday in Singapore, Christmas Day is celebrated by Christians and non-Christians alike, with exchanges of gifts and feasting.

ENTRY REGULATIONS

Anyone travelling to Singapore must have a valid passport or an internationally recognised travel document.

Citizens of British Commonwealth countries and The Netherlands do not require a visa, whether visiting for social purposes or for employment. Citizens of the United States only require a visa if the visit is for employment and residence, while those from France and West Germany do not require a visa if the visit is for social purposes for a stay not exceeding 3 months.

Health Regulations
Vaccinations are not required for smallpox or cholera, and yellow fever vaccination is only required if the person has passed through any country which is either partly or wholly endemic for yellow fever, within the preceding six days.

Customs Allowance
Each incoming traveller (except when coming from Malaysia) is allowed duty-free: 1 bottle (1 litre) of spirits; 1 bottle (1 litre) of

8 SINGAPORE AND MALAYSIA AT COST

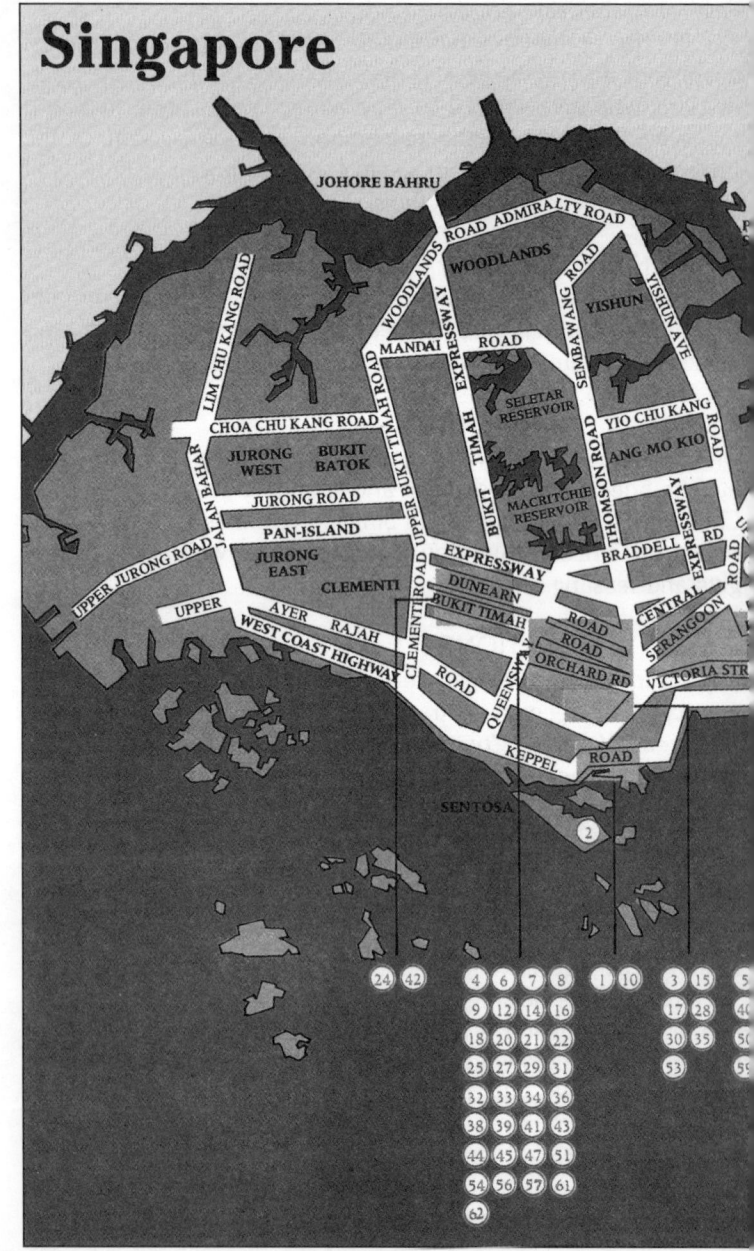

SINGAPORE 9

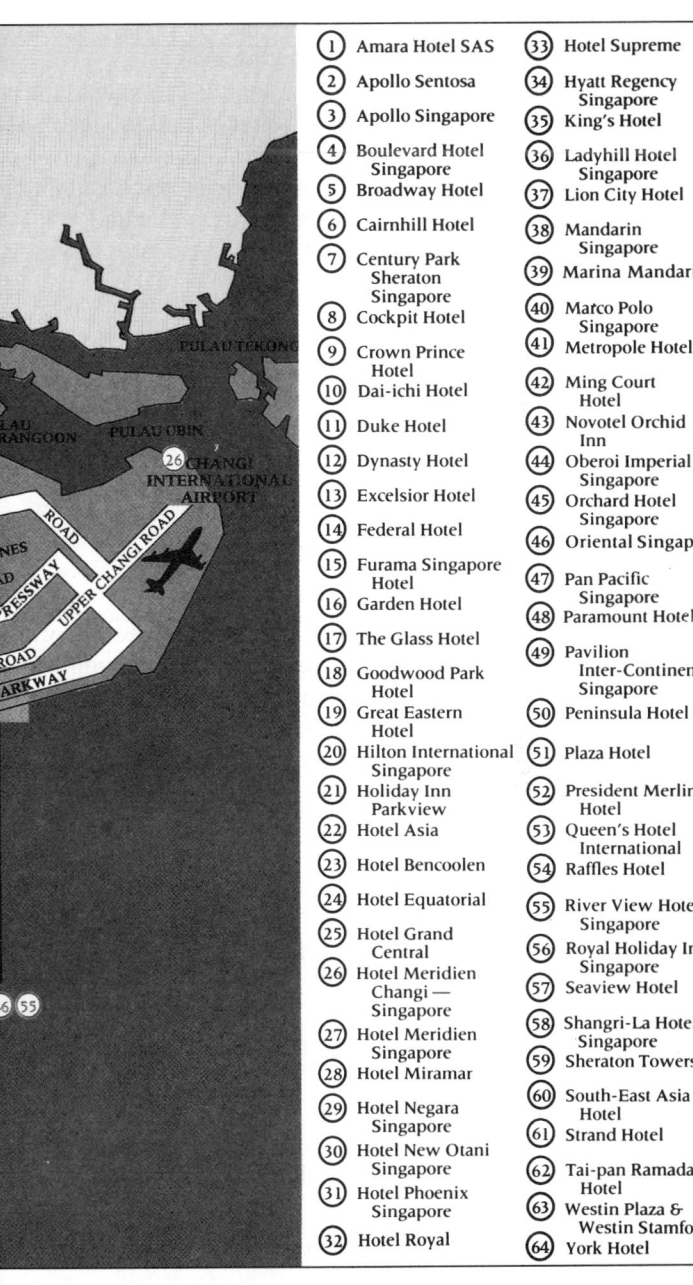

1. Amara Hotel SAS
2. Apollo Sentosa
3. Apollo Singapore
4. Boulevard Hotel Singapore
5. Broadway Hotel
6. Cairnhill Hotel
7. Century Park Sheraton Singapore
8. Cockpit Hotel
9. Crown Prince Hotel
10. Dai-ichi Hotel
11. Duke Hotel
12. Dynasty Hotel
13. Excelsior Hotel
14. Federal Hotel
15. Furama Singapore Hotel
16. Garden Hotel
17. The Glass Hotel
18. Goodwood Park Hotel
19. Great Eastern Hotel
20. Hilton International Singapore
21. Holiday Inn Parkview
22. Hotel Asia
23. Hotel Bencoolen
24. Hotel Equatorial
25. Hotel Grand Central
26. Hotel Meridien Changi — Singapore
27. Hotel Meridien Singapore
28. Hotel Miramar
29. Hotel Negara Singapore
30. Hotel New Otani Singapore
31. Hotel Phoenix Singapore
32. Hotel Royal
33. Hotel Supreme
34. Hyatt Regency Singapore
35. King's Hotel
36. Ladyhill Hotel Singapore
37. Lion City Hotel
38. Mandarin Singapore
39. Marina Mandarin
40. Marco Polo Singapore
41. Metropole Hotel
42. Ming Court Hotel
43. Novotel Orchid Inn
44. Oberoi Imperial Singapore
45. Orchard Hotel Singapore
46. Oriental Singapore
47. Pan Pacific Singapore
48. Paramount Hotel
49. Pavilion Inter-Continental Singapore
50. Peninsula Hotel
51. Plaza Hotel
52. President Merlin Hotel
53. Queen's Hotel International
54. Raffles Hotel
55. River View Hotel Singapore
56. Royal Holiday Inn Singapore
57. Seaview Hotel
58. Shangri-La Hotel Singapore
59. Sheraton Towers
60. South-East Asia Hotel
61. Strand Hotel
62. Tai-pan Ramada Hotel
63. Westin Plaza & Westin Stamford
64. York Hotel

wine; 1 bottle (1 litre) of beer, stout, ale or porter; and 200 cigarettes or 50 cigars or 250g (8oz) of tobacco.

Visitors below 18 years of age are not entitled to any liquor or tobacco duty-free privileges. Liquor, cigarettes and tobacco specially marked for export with the legend "Singapore Duty Not Paid" and cigarettes with prefix "E" are restricted to consumption outside Singapore and their re-importation is prohibited.

The penalties for drug trafficking and abuse are severe in Singapore.

Currency Regulations
There is no limit on the import or export of foreign currency notes, travellers' cheques and other instruments of payment, stocks and bonds. Imports and exports of gold must be declared to the Trade Development Board.

EXIT REGULATIONS

Customs
There is no export duty. Export permits are required for arms, ammunition, explosives, animals, gold in form, platinum, precious stones and jewellery (except personal effects, within limits), poisons and drugs. Any goods in excess of reasonable personal effects are to be declared at exit points and an Outward Declaration prepared, if necessary.

Airport Tax
To Brunei and Malaysia: S$5; to other countries: S$12. For convenience tourists can pre-purchase their Airport Tax coupons from most hotels, TAS and Airline Offices in town.

EMBASSIES
Australia:	Australian High Commission, 25 Napier Road, ph 737 9311.
N.Z.:	N.Z. High Commission, 13 Nassim Road, ph 235 9966.
Canada:	Canadian High Commission, 230 Orchard Road, ph 737 1322.
U.K.:	British High Commission, Tanglin Road, ph 473 9333.

U.S.A.:	US Embassy, 30 Hill Street, ph 338 0251.
Netherlands:	541 Orchard Road, #13-01, Liat Towers, ph 737 1155.
Germany:	545 Orchard Road, #14-01, Far East Shopping Centre, ph 737 1355.

MONEY

The monetary unit is the Singapore Dollar (S$) and 1S$ = 100 cents. Notes come in the following denominations — $1, $5, $10, $20, $50, $100, $500, $1,000, $10,000; coins — 1c, 5c, 10c, 20c, 50c, $1.

Exchange rates, roughly, are as follows:
A$ = S$1.60
NZ$ = S$1.25
CAN$ = S$1.55
US$ = S$1.90
UK£   = S$3.50
Gl   = S$0.98
DM   = S$1.10

Banks are open from 10am to 3pm, Mon-Fri, 9.30am to 11.30am Sat. Branches of the Development Bank of Singapore stay open till 3pm on Sat.

Apart from banks and hotels, money can be changed wherever the sign "Licensed Money Changer" is displayed. Most shopping complexes have a licensed money changer. Visitors are recommended not to change money through anyone not licensed.

COMMUNICATIONS

Singapore has 24-hour telex, telephone and telegram services to all parts of the world.

Long Distance Calls
Visitors can speak directly from their hotel rooms to most principal cities in the world.

Newspapers
Locally, there are Chinese, Malay and Tamil papers, an English language paper, *The Straits Times* (morning), and a business

daily, *Business Times*. International editions of foreign newspapers are available in major hotels and newsagents.

Post
Most hotels provide postal services at the front desk. The GPO and Telecom's Customer Services Centre at Exeter Road, are both open 24 hours daily. The rates for sending postcards by airmail are as follows:

Australia — 25 cents
New Zealand — 40 cents
U.K. & Europe — 40 cents
U.S.A. — 55 cents
Canada — 55 cents

Aerogrammes to all parts of the world cost 35 cents.

MISCELLANEOUS

Airport Facilities
A baggage storage service is available at the arrival hall and both the east and west wings of the departure level within the passenger terminal.

Other facilities include shops, duty-free emporiums, snack bars, restaurants, bank offering 24-hour money exchange service, post office, police station, pay phones, information, car hire, hotel reservation counters, private reception room, VIP room and airfreight for unaccompanied baggage.

Credit Cards
Major credit and charge cards are widely accepted by establishments in Singapore. Should any shop insist on adding a surcharge, do not tolerate it and contact the card company involved.

Drinking Water
The water from the tap (faucet) is clean and safe to drink.

Electricity
The voltage is 220–240 volts AC, 50 cycles. Most hotels have a transformer to reduce the voltage to 110–120 volts, 60 cycles, when necessary.

Jaywalking

Pedestrians crossing a road within 50m of a pedestrian crossing, an overhead pedestrian bridge or an underpass, risk a S$50 fine.

Health

Singapore's medical facilities are very good. Pharmaceuticals are available from numerous outlets including supermarkets, department stores, hotels and shopping centres. Registered pharmacists work from 9am to 6pm; some shops open until 10pm. Most hotels have their own doctor on 24-hour call. Contact the Front Office or Room Service. Other doctors are listed under "Medical Practitioners" in the Yellow Pages of the Singapore phone book. Dentists are listed under "Dental Surgeons". For ambulance, dial 995.

Tipping

Tipping is not a way of life in Singapore. It is prohibited at the airport and discouraged in hotels and restaurants that have a 10% service charge.

TRAVEL INFORMATION

HOW TO GET TO SINGAPORE

By Air
Changi International Airport is served by over 40 of the world's major airlines, including Air Canada, Air India, Air New Zealand, Air Niugini, Alitalia, British Airways, Cathay Pacific Airways, Garuda Indonesia, Japan Air Lines, Qantas Airways, Singapore Airlines and United Airlines.

British Airways have 6 flights a week Australia/Singapore, daily flights London/Singapore and 1 flight a week Auckland/Singapore.

Singapore Airlines have daily flights Australia/Singapore, Auckland/Singapore, San Francisco/Singapore, New York/Singapore, London/Singapore, Toronto/Singapore and Montreal/Singapore.

Qantas Airways have daily flights Sydney/Singapore, Melbourne/Singapore, Hobart/Singapore, 4 flights a week Adelaide/Singapore, Perth/Singapore and daily flights Auckland/Singapore and London/Singapore.

Air New Zealand have 4 flights a week Auckland/Singapore and Christchurch/Singapore, and 3 flights a week Wellington/Singapore.

By Sea
The following is a list of ships which call at Singapore:
Canberra — departing from UK — once a year.
Coral Princess — departing from Hong Kong, Singapore — November and December.
Orient Princess — departing from Singapore — January to December.
Pearl of Scandinavia — departing from Bangkok, Singapore, Hong Kong — January, February, March, April.
Queen Elizabeth 2 — departing from UK — annual round world cruise (January–April) Translantic cruise after world cruise.
Rotterdam — departing from US — once a year.

Royal Viking Star — departing from Hong Kong — once in November and once in March.
Sagafjord — departing from Port Everglades — once a year.
Sea Princess/Pacific Princess/Royal Princess — departing from Australia/United Kingdom/United States — once a year.

By Bus from Malaysia
From Johore Bahru to Rochor Road Terminus — S$1
　　　　　　　　　to Queen Street or Bukit Timah Road — 80c.
From Mersing to New Bridge Road Fringe Car Park Terminus — S$11
From Malacca to New Bridge Road Fringe Car Park Terminus — S$11
From Kuala Lumpur to New Bridge Road Fringe Car Park Terminus — S$17.
From Butterworth to New Bridge Road Fringe Car Park Terminus — S$30.
From Kuantan to New Bridge Road Fringe Car Park Terminus — S$16.

By Train
The railway takes travellers from Bangkok in Thailand, through Butterworth and Kuala Lumpur in Malaysia, to Singapore.
　The fares, in an air-conditioned coach, are —
Bangkok to Singapore — S$175.60 (1st Class) S$80.30 (2nd Class)
Butterworth to Singapore — S$50
Kuala Lumpur to Singapore — S$28

ACCOMMODATION

As Singapore is conveniently situated for a stop-over to break the long flights to Great Britain and Europe, there are a lot of accommodation packages available through the various airlines. Listed below are details of accommodation offered by Cathay Pacific. These prices are for twin share and include transfers to/from Changi Airport and breakfast.

York Hotel, 21 Mt. Elizabeth, ph 737 0511: 1st night US$37.10, extra night US$19.10.
Boulevard Hotel, 200 Orchard Boulevard, ph 737 2911: 1st night US$37.60, extra night US$19.60.
Royal Holiday Inn, 25 Scotts Road, ph 737 7966: 1st night US$38.40, extra night US$20.50.
Orchard Hotel, 442 Orchard Road, ph 734 7766: 1st night US$39.10, extra night US$21.20.
Ming Court, Tangin Road, ph 7371133: 1st night US$38.40, extra night US$20.50.
Century Park Sheraton, 16 Nassim Hill, ph 732 1222: 1st night US$43.90, extra night US$25.90.
Park View Holiday Inn, 11 Cavenagh Road, ph 737 8333: 1st night US$45.40, extra night US$27.40.
Marco Polo, 247 Tanglin Road, ph 474 7141: 1st night US$46.30, extra night US$28.30.
Hyatt Regency, 10–12 Scotts Road, ph 733 1188: 1st night US$46.30, extra night US$28.30.
Hilton International, 581 Orchard Road, ph 737 2233: 1st night US$46.70, extra night US$28.80.
Westin Stamford, 2 Stamford Road, ph 338 8585: 1st night US$45.80, extra night US$27.80.
Oriental, 6 Raffles Boulevard, ph 338 0066: 1st night US$52.00, extra night US$34.10.
Shangri-La, Orange Grove Road, ph 737 3644: 1st night US$61.10, extra night US$43.10.

LOCAL TRANSPORT

Buses

Regular bus services operate from 6am–11.30pm, with fares ranging from 40c to a maximum of 80c, except for Services 3 and 168 (air-conditioned) which begin at 60c, with a maximum of S$1.20. The Singapore Explorer ticket allows holders to enjoy unlimited use of the local bus service for either 1 day (S$5) or 3 days (S$12). All major places of interest may be reached by bus. An Explorer Bus Map indicating these places along the routes is issued together with the Explorer ticket.

Trishaws

The trishaw — bicycle with side car — is a fascinating way to explore the city, especially the narrow alleys of Chinatown. Visitors are advised to use only trishaws organised through a hotel or any travel agent, as there is no standardised fare structure.

MRTS

Singapore Mass Rapid Transport System (signposted MRTS for visitors) is only partly completed, but it is already able to take passengers from Orchard Road to the river area for as little as 50c in a matter of minutes. The coaches are air-conditioned, and the walkways have become a tourist attraction in themselves, featuring acres of polished marble, paintings by local artists and plenty of greenery. Total completion is scheduled for 1990.

Taxis

There are more than 10,000 metered taxis for hire in Singapore. All of them are fitted with electronic taximeters and almost all are air-conditioned. Each taxi is allowed a maximum of 4 passengers.

Fares recorded on the meter are S$1.60 for the first 1.5km or part thereof; 10c for every subsequent 300m thereafter or less, up to 10km; 10c every 250m thereafter or less, after 10km; 10c every 45 second of waiting time.

Charges not recorded on the meter: an additional 50c for each passenger in excess of 2 (babies excluded), 3 children under 12 years old = 2 adult passengers; an additional S$1 for each piece of luggage (other than hand luggage); a surcharge of 50% of the metered fare between midnight and 6am.

A surcharge of S$3 per taxi has to be paid by passengers taking a taxi from Changi Airport, but there is no surcharge on trips to the airport. The fare from the airport to hotels in the Orchard Road area should be between S$9–S$12 (excluding surcharge). From the harbour, the fare will be between S$8 and S$9, depending on where the ship is berthed.

There is also a CBD (Central Business District) surcharge of S$1 for taking a taxi from the Restricted Zone during weekdays from 4–7pm and on Saturdays from noon–3pm.

Before starting off ensure that the driver knows the exact destination, that the meter is flagged, and that the fare on the meter reads S$1.60.

Written complaints and commendations (together with taxi registration number, the date and the time of the incident) should be directed to the Registry of Vehicles, Sin Ming Drive, or the Singapore Tourist Promotion Board, Raffles City Tower #36-04, 250 North Bridge Road.

Central Business District (CBD)
Under the Area Licence Scheme, designed to alleviate traffic congestion, cars (including taxis) entering the CBD during the morning peak hours (7.30am–10.15am, Mon–Sat, except Public Holidays) are required to purchase and display Area Licences. A car or taxi carrying 4 or more persons, including the driver, is exempted from this requirement.

The Daily Area Licence costs S$5 (S$2 for taxis) and this fee is payable by either the taxi driver or the passenger. If neither wishes to pay the licence fee, the driver can refuse to drive the passenger into the CBD, or the passenger can agree to one of the following:
share the taxi with 2 other passengers.
allow the driver to take a longer route to avoid the CBD (this does not apply, however, when hotels and other destinations are located within the CBD itself).

Passengers need not pay for an Area Licence if the taxi already displays one.

Every taxi journey originating in the CBD between 4pm–7pm on weekdays and between noon–3pm on Saturdays is subject to a S$1 surcharge (except Public Holidays). For further information visitors should contact the Registry of Vehicles (ph 459 4222) or the Automobile Association (ph 737 2444).

Car Rentals
Ace Tours & Car Rentals, ph 235 3755/235 4433; Avis Rent A Car, ph 737 9477; Blue Star Car Rentals & Tours, ph 253 4643/253 4661; City Car Rentals & Tours, ph 733 2145; Elpin Tours & Limousine Services, ph 235 3111/734 1333; Friendly Tour Corporation, ph 373 2292; Happy Car Rentals & Tours, ph 235 9902; Keng Soon Credit, ph 337 7533/337 2517; Negara Tourist Service,

ph 737 2080; NG Transport & Tourist Service, Ph 250 9588; Orchard Motors, ph 475 9466/474 8897; San's Tours & Car Rentals, ph 734 9922; Sime Travel, ph 224 5454; Singapore Tourist Transport Service, ph 298 4968/294 6059; Sintat Thrifty Rent-A-Car, ph 273 2211; Sunrise Car Rentals, ph 336 0626/336 0629; Z-Car Rental & Travel Service, ph 338 6901/338 8122.

Car Rental Rates (air-conditioned)

Chauffeur-driven — hourly: from S$40 minimum 3 hours.
daily: S$210–S$420 (8 hours).

Self-driven — daily: S$60–S$200.
weekly: S$360–S$1,200.
(mileage charge from 60c per km).

NB. Rates will vary from company to company. Prices quoted are to be used only as a guide.

FOOD

Singapore caters adequately for a variety of cuisines and tastes, but we hope you like Chinese. Here are listed a few restaurants we suggest you try.

Chinese (Hokkien)
Beng Thin Hoon Kee, OCBC Centre, Chulia Street, ph 533 7708; Beng Hiang, 20 Murray Street, ph 221 6695; Prince Room, Selegie Complex, Selegie Road, ph 337 7021.

Chinese (Peking)
Eastern Palace, Supreme House, Penang Road, ph 337 8224; Pine Court, Mandarin Hotel, Orchard Road, ph 737 4411.

Chinese (Teochew)
Hung Kang, 38 North Canal Road, ph 221 3305; Swatow Teochew, Centrepoint, Orchard Road, ph 235-4717.

Chinese (Hakka)
Moi Kong Hakka, 22 Murray Street, ph 221 7758; Plum Village, 16 Jalan Leban, off Upper Thomson Road.

Chinese (Hainanese)
Swee Kee, 51/53 Middle Road, ph 337 0314; Yet Con, 25 Purvis Street, two blocks down Beach Road from Raffles Hotel.

Chinese (Szechuan)
Golden Phoenix, Hotel Equatorial, Bukit Timah Road, ph 732 0431; Ming Jiang, Goodwood Park Hotel, 22 Scotts Road, ph 737

7411; Omei, Hotel Grand Central, Cavenagh/Orchard Roads, ph 737 9944.

Chinese (Vegetarian)
Fut Sai Kai, 147 Kitchener Road, ph 298 0336; Happy Realm Vegetarian, Pearl Centre, next to People's Park, ph 222 6141.

Chinese (Cantonese)
Fatty Weng Seong, 102 Guillemard Road, ph 348 2332; Majestic, 31-37 Bukit Pasoh Road, ph 223-5111; Shang Palace, Shangri-La Hotel, Orange Grove Road, ph 737 3644; Tung Lok Sharksfin, Liang Court, 177 River Valley Road, ph 336-6022.

Malay/Indonesian
Arumanis Indonesian, Far East Plaza, 14 Scotts Road, ph 733-2526; Aziza's, 36 Emerald Hill Road, ph 235 1130; Kintamani Indonesian, Apollo Hotel, Havelock Road, ph 733 2081; Rendezvous, 4/5 Bras Basah Road, ph 337 6619.

Northern Indian
Moti Mahal, 18 Murray Street, ph 221 4338; Omar Khayyam, 55 Hill Street, ph 336 1505; Rang Mahal, Oberoi Imperial Hotel, Jalan Rumbia, ph 737 1666; Tandoor, Holiday Inn Park View, 11 Cavenagh Road, ph 733 8333.

Southern Indian
Banana Leaf Apollo, 56 Race Course Road, ph 293 5054; Jubilee, 771/3 North Bridge Road, ph 298 8714; Komala Vilas, 76 Serangoon Road, ph 293 6980.

Nonya
Bibi's, Peranakan Place, Emerald Hill Road, ph 732 6966; Keday Kopi, Peranakan Place, 180 Orchard Road, ph 732 6966; Rumah Melaka, Far East Plaza, 14 Scotts Road, ph 733 2797.

International
  All the large international hotels have first class dining rooms.

Food Centres
Often referred to as hawkers' stalls, after the mobile food carts that once plied the streets of Singapore, the new food centres house a collection of stalls offering all kinds of inexpensive and tasty local dishes. They are generally clean.

  Food centres offer visitors the opportunity of sampling a range of ethnic dishes. All types of Chinese, Malay, Indonesian, Indian and Nonya food are offered, as well as fresh fruit and drinks.

In addition, prices of dishes are clearly marked. The Rasa Singapura, next to the Singapore Handicraft Centre, houses stall-holders selected by a special tasting committee following up on public recommendations. Here some of Singapore's most highly regarded food is served.

Other popular food centres include —
Cuppage Centre, next to Centrepoint in Cuppage Road.
Funan Centre, in the air-conditioned shopping complex.
People's Park, Eu Tong Sen Street, right on the edge of Chinatown.
Newton Circus, at Scotts/Bukit Timah/Newton Roads intersection.
Satay Club, Queen Elizabeth Walk near Connaught Road by the Pandang.
Lagoon Food Centre, on the East Coast Parkway next to the Lagoon and right on the beach.
Botanic Gardens, just across from main gate in Cluny Road.

ENTERTAINMENT

Nightclubs
Taiwanese singers, plush and opulent surroundings, lavish meals are the hallmarks of most Chinese nightclubs. But if you prefer a less sedentary way of life, then try a hostess nightclub, where you can dance the calories away.

Private Clubs
A number of major hotels have clubs with private membership as well as membership for hotel guests. A variety of games such as backgammon and chess can be enjoyed, as well as drinks and dancing. The social directors will perform introductions if asked.

Theatre-Restaurants
Dine well on subtle Cantonese cuisine while enjoying the show at The Neptune, the largest theatre restaurant in this region. Stars from Hong Kong and Taiwan provide entertainment at the Lido Palace.

Wayang (Chinese Street Opera)
Spend your evening at the opera — in the streets. Chinese opera is an unforgettable experience. Performed during temple celebra-

tions and festivals, wayang is actually meant for the gods and spirits; but less-than-divine eyes are also free to enjoy this stunning spectacle of glittering costumes and painted faces.

At the Singapore Handicraft Centre a weekly wayang is performed on Saturdays and Sundays from 7.30–9.30pm.

Cultural Shows
There are many shows designed for the tourist who's interested in a more comprehensive glimpse of Singaporean culture.

ASEAN Night (Mandarin Hotel)
Potpourri of songs and dances from Singapore, Malaysia, Thailand, Indonesia, Brunei and the Philippines is presented nightly at the poolside (except Monday). A marvellous taste of South East Asia.
Dinner begins at 7pm and showtime is at 7.30pm.
Admission: S$36+ per adult (with dinner), S$18+
(without dinner)
S$23+ per child (with dinner), S$15+
(without dinner)

Cultural Show (Raffles Hotel)
Dinner is served at 7pm in the Long Bar or from the a la carte menu at the Palm Court. Then at 8pm you can enjoy the colourful show as you sip a long cool drink at the Long Bar verandah.
Admission: S$30 per adult (dinner/show)
S$14 per adult (dinner/drink) (inclusive of tax).

Instant Asia Culture Show
For 45 minutes, a part of Singapore's rich heritage comes alive in song and dance. The show starts with the lion dance, then willowy dancers evoke images of lotus blossoms and fairies. Malay and Indian dancers perform their traditional dances, and then to the haunting notes from a snake-charmer's pipe a sinuous python hypnotically sways. After the performance the audience is encouraged to go on stage to meet the slithering star.

Showtime is at 11.45am daily at Raffles Hotel (Ballroom), Beach Road.

Admission: S$10 per adult
S$5 per child (inclusive of two-way shuttle service)

Malam Singapura (Hyatt Regency)
An entertaining evening combining dinner and a 45 minute cultural show at the poolside (except on Sunday). The show begins at 8pm.
Admission: S$38 per adult (with dinner)
S$18 per adult (without dinner)
S$22 per child (with dinner)
S$12 per child (without dinner) (inclusive of tax)

Peranakan Cultural Evening (Bibi's Restaurant)
Enjoy a Peranakan meal before settling down to a 45 minute cultural show. The highlight is a traditional Peranakan wedding. Begins at 7.30pm every Tuesday and Thursday.
Admission: S$45 per person, inclusive of buffet dinner.

SHOPPING AND SIGHTSEEING

Singapore is a shopper's paradise, overflowing with all the exciting and exotic treasures of the East, and fashionable luxuries of the West. Few countries in the world can match the variety of goods sold in Singapore, nor can they match the prices, for just about everything is duty-free. In fact, many goods sell at a lower price than in their country of origin!

Shops are open seven days a week from around 10am till at least 9pm, and visitors should look for shops with the Associate Membership emblem — a red decal with a gold Merlion. Wherever displayed, this emblem symbolises fair pricing, quality products and services.

Always compare prices before buying. Price lists for cameras and electrical goods are available on demand in shops and department stores.

Obtain written confirmation of any instructions given to shops to post parcels abroad.

Be sure to check for correct voltage and cycle. Countries such as Singapore, UK, Australia, NZ and Hong Kong use 220–240 volts, 50 cycles. Countries such as the US, Canada, Japan, Indonesia and the Philippines use 110–120 volts, 60 cycles. Some of the equipment is universal and can be used in any country. Special adaptors or transformers are available if required.

Get a Warranty Card for cameras, watches and electrical goods, and a receipt for all purchases except when buying from small tradesmen.

Don't listen to touts and unlicensed tourist guides. If approached, ask to see their official Singapore Tourist Promotion Board guide badge and licence.

If you have any complaints you should forward them in writing to: Tourism Services, Singapore Tourist Promotion Board, Raffles City Tower #36-04, 250 North Bridge Road, Singapore 0617, or the Consumer's Association of Singapore, Trade Union House, Shenton Way, Singapore 0106.

26 SINGAPORE AND MALAYSIA AT COST

Major Shopping Areas
Although shopping complexes contain a very wide range of specialty stores, there are certain areas of Singapore that tend to concentrate on particular items. The main shopping areas of Singapore and their specialties are:

Arab Street
Batik fabric and readymade clothing, basketware, cane, luggage and Malay jewellery are the best buys in this traditional area.

Change Alley
Strings of hanging beads, brightly-coloured batik garments, reptile goods, French perfume, luggage of all shapes and sizes compete for attention in this old bazaar. You will be hustled by salesmen, but remember to indulge in some good-natured bargaining before buying their wares.

This atmosphere prevails in Change Alley Aerial Plaza, a modern extension which links Collyer Quay and Raffles Place. Here you will find souvenir T-shirts, real and costume jewellery, fruits, flowers, cakes.

North Bridge Road/High Street/Coleman Street
Specially for photographic equipment, watches and textiles. Nearby in Stamford Road are stores selling reptile skin goods and cane furniture.

Orchard Road
The greatest concentration of shopping complexes in Singapore, with the emphasis on boutiques and department stores. The hotel shopping arcades in Orchard Road, Tanglin Road and Scotts Road are renowned for their luxury goods. This area also has several Chinese emporiums.

Raffles Place/Collyer Quay
Among the towering highrises of banks and offices are Clifford Centre and The Arcade — mazes of little shops offering electrical goods, cameras, watches, jewellery, toys, stationery.

Singapore's Business Centre

Thoipresom Festival

St. Paul Hill Fort, Malacca

Serangoon Road
All types of Indian handicrafts, particularly fabrics and jewellery. Spices can also be purchased here.

SIGHTSEEING

CULTURAL DISTRICTS

Arab Street is the heart of the old Muslim district of Singapore, and is within earshot of the Sultan Mosque in North Bridge Road. This street is famous for its batik fabrics and basketware. Prayer rugs, Malay jewellery, perfume essences and other interesting items can also be found here. (Bus 13 from Orchard Road, alight at Victoria Street and walk to Arab Street — 40c)

Chinatown is the area roughly bounded by South Bridge Road and New Bridge Road, between Kreta Ayer Road and Mosque Street. The architecture, trades and lifestyles of China can be seen in this fascinating part of town where the houses, shops, markets, stalls and temples offer an intriguing glimpse of the past. Best explored on foot or by a trishaw tour. (Bus 124, 143, 173, 174 from Orchard Road, alight in front of the Indian Temple at South Bridge Road — 50c)

Serangoon Road is often referred to as "Little India", as this street is full of sights, sounds and smells of India. Saris, spices, garlands, peacock feathers, a fortune teller whose bird selects the fortune card, vegetarian and other Indian food, are all part of this colourful district. (Bus 64, 106, 111 from Orchard Road — 50c and Bus 65, 92–40c)

MONUMENTS AND LANDMARKS

The ARMENIAN CHURCH, Hill Street, was constructed in 1835. This beautiful old church is Singapore's oldest, and is still used for regular services. It has been preserved as a national monument.

The HOUSE OF TAN YEOK NEE (Chen Xu Nian), cnr. Clemenceau Avenue and Penang Road, is a fine example of a wealthy merchant's house built in 1885 in the style then popular in Southern China. Designated a national monument, the house is now the headquarters of the Salvation Army.

MERLION PARK, at the mouth of the Singapore River, has the 8m high Merlion (half lion, half fish), the symbol of Singapore. It is well lit at night, and makes a good subject for photography.

The NATIONAL MUSEUM AND ART GALLERY, in Stamford Road, is a fine Victorian building housing an interesting display of the ethnology, art and history of Singapore and South East Asia. Displays of particular interest include the Haw Par Jade Collection, one of the largest of its kind in the world; the History of Singapore Gallery, with 20 dioramas depicting the development of Singapore; and the Straits Chinese Gallery, with its ornate furniture and artefacts. Open Tues-Sun, 9am–4.30pm (Art Gallery closes at 5.30pm), there are free guided tours Tues-Sat (except Public Holidays) in English at 11am. Admission to the Museum is S$1 adult; 50c children (6–16).

RAFFLES HOTEL, Beach Road, was built in the French Renaissance style in 1886. This famous old hotel was the haunt of the social elite throughout the colonial era. In the words of Somerset Maugham, one of many writers who stayed there, Raffles "stands for all the exotic fables of the East". Today visitors can enjoy sipping a Singapore Sling (created by a Raffles barman more than 60 years ago) in the Palm Court, or relaxing under a ceiling fan. (Bus CBD1, 7, 14 or 16 in Orchard Road — 40c)

SIR STAMFORD RAFFLES LANDING SITE, behind Parliament House. A copy of the original bronze statue of Sir Stamford Raffles, founder of modern Singapore, has been erected on the bank of the Singapore River at the spot where he is believed to have first stepped ashore in 1819. The original statue stands in front of the Victoria Theatre.

The SUPREME COURT AND CITY HALL, in St. Andrew's Road, stand on one side of the Padang or open green. These impressive buildings with Corinthian columns house the seats of justice and government.

SHOPPING AND SIGHTSEEING 29

THONG CHAI MEDICAL INSTITUTION (Tong Ji Yi Yuan), Wayang Street, was built in 1892 as a free dispensary, and is now preserved as a national monument. This building houses a company selling all types of Chinese arts, handicrafts and curios.

The WAR MEMORIAL, Memorial Park, Beach Road, has four tapering white columns reaching almost 70m high, symbolising the four cultures of Singapore, and is a memorial to the civilians who lost their lives during the Japanese occupation of World War II.

PLACES OF WORSHIP

AL ABRAR MOSQUE, Telok Ayer Street. Built by Southern Indian Muslims from 1850–55, it is sometimes known as Koochopillay or Indian Mosque.

CATHEDRAL OF THE GOOD SHEPHERD, Queen Street. This historic monument was constructed in the 1840s and is one of the places of worship for Singapore's Roman Catholics.

CHETTIAR TEMPLE, Tank Road. This ornate temple is the finishing point for the annual Thaipusam procession, and site of traditional Indian songs and dances during the 9-day Navarathri festival.

HAJJAH FATIMAH MOSQUE, Beach Road. The leaning minaret of this small mosque has Gothic overtones. It was built between 1845 and 1946, financed by a wealthy Muslim woman, after whom it is named.

JAMAE MOSQUE, Telok Ayer Street. Built in 1830–55 by Chulia Muslims from the southwest coast of India, this mosque is also known as the Chulia Mosque.

NAGORE DURGHA SHRINE, Telok Ayer Street. An intriguing blend of Eastern and Western architectural styles, this shrine was built around 1828–1830 in veneration of an Indian Muslim.

ST. ANDREW'S CATHEDRAL, Coleman Street. A fine Gothic-style Anglican cathedral, built between 1856 and 1863 to replace an earlier cathedral which was twice struck by lightning.

SIONG LIM TEMPLE (Shuang Lin Si), Jalan Toa Payoh. The largest Buddhist temple in Singapore, built between 1898 and 1908 with many ornate and interesting features.

SRI MARIAMMAN TEMPLE, South Bridge Road. The flamboyantly decorated entrance of Singapore's oldest Hindu temple, built in 1827–1843, is covered with polychromed gods and goddesses. This temple is the site of an annual fire-walking ceremony.

SULTAN MOSQUE, North Bridge Road. Singapore's largest mosque, with fine Oriental rugs carpeting the entrance and a vast crystal chandelier adorning the simple, airy prayer hall.

TAN SI CHONG SU TEMPLE (Chen Shi Zong Ci), Magazine Road. A small but beautiful ancestral temple and hall built for the Tan clan in 1876.

TEMPLE OF 1,000 LIGHTS, Race Course Road. Dominated by a 15m high statue of Buddha, and surrounded by countless electric lights, this temple houses a number of Buddhist relics.

THIAN HOCK KENG TEMPLE (Tian Fu Gong), Telok Ayer Street. A wonderfully ornate temple with pillars, stonework and carvings imported from China, built in 1840. This is Singapore's oldest Chinese temple, where newly arrived migrants offered prayers of thanksgiving for safe passage to their new homes. Its name means "Temple of Heavenly Happiness".

PARKS AND GARDENS

BOTANIC GARDENS, Napier/Cluny Roads. A peaceful retreat with palms, tropical and subtropical trees, shrubs and flowers, and an interesting orchid pavilion. Free open-air concerts every Sunday at 5.30pm (weather permitting). Open Mon–Fri 5am–11pm. Weekends and Public Holidays 5am-midnight.

SHOPPING AND SIGHTSEEING 31

BUKIT TIMAH NATURE RESERVE, Upper Bukit Timah Road. Birds, butterflies and the occasional monkey can be seen in this reserve, where well-marked trails lead through jungle. The initial hill is steep, so walking shoes and a reasonable degree of fitness are required.

CHINESE GARDEN (Yu Hwa Yuan), off Yuan Ching Road, Jurong. A classical Chinese garden of 13ha, based on the style of the Song dynasty. Pagodas, curved bridges, bamboos, lotus blooms and water lilies make it reminiscent of Peking's Summer Palace. A white bridge links it to the Japanese Garden. Open Mon–Sat 9am–7pm, Sun and Public Holidays 8.30am–7pm. Admission S$2 adult, S$1 child and 50c per camera.

JAPANESE GARDEN (Seiwaen), off Yuan Ching Road, Jurong. The Japanese name of this garden, Seiwaen, means "Garden of Tranquility" and this is an apt description. This is one of the largest classical gardens ever built outside Japan. Open Mon–Sat 9.30am–6pm, Sun and Public Holidays 8.30am–6pm. Admission S$1 adult, 50c child and 50c camera.
Admission for both gardens — S$2.50 adult, S$1.20 child, 50c per camera.

FORT CANNING PARK, Fort Canning Rise/Clemenceau Avenue. This park covers old Government Hill, the site of Singapore's first Government House, and once known to Malays as Forbidden Hill. Here are the remains of an old Christian cemetery, a scared Malay grave, a squash court complex and restaurant, and the entrance to an old British fort.

MACRITCHIE RESERVOIR, Lornie Road. A popular spot with joggers, this large jungled park surrounds the reservoir.

SELETAR RESERVOIR, Mandai Road. Scenic reservoir park with observation tower.

MANDAI ORCHARD GARDEN, Mandai Lake Road, near Zoological Gardens. A commercial orchid garden where a whole hillside is covered with brilliant blooms of the most exotic orchids. There is also a Water Garden containing rare tropical plants. Open daily 9am–5.30pm. Admission S$1 adult, 50c child.

MT FABER, off Kampong Bahru Road. The highest point on this part of the island (115m), Mt Faber offers good views of the city harbour, southern islands and islands of Indonesia's Rhio archipelago. Telescopes are provided. It is also the point where cable cars to Sentosa commence.

QUEEN ELIZABETH WALK, Connaught Drive. A promenade between the Satay Club and Merlion Park.

BIRD AND ANIMAL SANCTUARIES

JURONG BIRD PARK, Jalan Ahmad Ibrahim, Jurong. This huge beautifully landscaped garden is home to more than 3,500 birds Highlights are the 2ha Walk-In Aviary, the world's largest, a Nocturnal House and a spectacular Bird Show. Open daily 9am–6pm. Showtime: 10.30am and 3.30pm daily. Extra show: 1.30pm Sun and Public Holidays. Free Flight Show at 10.30am, Parrot Circus at 10.30am. Admission S$3.50 adult, S$1.50 child, 50c per camera. Tramcar: S$1 adult, 50c child.

Bird Park Road Runner. Journey Express from Orchard Road Hotels to Birdpark — S$6.50 (one way) twice daily — excluding admission tickets — ph 339 7738.

ZOOLOGICAL GARDENS, Mandai Lake Road. More than 1,600 animals, half of which are from South East Asia, live here in a natural setting. One of the world's greatest naturalistic animal shows is held in a multipurpose amphitheatre. It is also the only zoo in the world where you can have breakfast or tea with an orang-utan. Open daily 8.30am–6pm. Showtime: 10.30am, 11.30am, 2.30pm and 3.30pm daily. Feeding time: 9am–5pm. Admission S$3.50 adult, S$1.50 child, 50c per still camera S$2 per movie camera.

The twice-daily Zoo Express picks up at 7 convenient points in the Orchard Road vicinity. Return trip, including entrance to Zoo S$15 adult, S$9 child.

SHOPPING AND SIGHTSEEING 33

FOR FUN, SUN AND SEA

EAST COAST PARK, East Coast Parkway. A series of attractions are situated in this popular recreational area that stretches 8.5km (5 miles) along the east coast.

The Singapore Tennis Centre, ph 442 5966, has 14 tennis courts and 2 squash courts for hire. Golfers can practise their swing at the Parkland Golf Driving Range, ph 440 6726, while the East Coast Sailing Centre, ph 449 5118, has sailboards for hire, and provides coaching.

Safe swimming can be enjoyed at the beaches along the park, or in the huge Swimming Lagoon. A Bicycle Hire Centre, situated next to the open-air Lagoon Food Centre, hires out bicycles by the hour.

Restaurants, changing rooms and other amenities make this park a pleasant place to relax for half a day or more.

CN WEST LEISURE PARK, Japanese Garden Road, Jurong. A large aquatic centre with a boating pool, wave pool, children's wading pools and giant water slide. Open Tues–Fri 12noon–6pm, weekends and Public Holidays 9.30am–6pm. Admission Tues–Fri S$4 adult, S$1.50 child, weekends and Public Holidays S$3 adult, S$1 child.

SENTOSA. An island resort lying close to the south coast of Singapore with a wide range of attractions and recreational facilities. These include Fort Siloso, a 19th century British fort; the Pioneers of Singapore Galleries and Surrender Chambers which feature 89 life-sized figures in tableaux of these historic events; a Maritime Museum; a Coralarium with more than 2,500 seashells from around the world and a coral cave; an Insectarium with about 4,000 insects on display; an Art Centre; a Musical Fountain with spectacular evening displays; and a unique Rare Stone Museum, with some 3,000 specimens.

Transport on Sentosa is provided by a monorail that runs along a 6km track, passing the sea, forest and various attractions of the island.

Musical Fountain Displays: 7.30pm, 8.30pm and 9pm nightly with extra shows at 9.30pm on eve of Public Holidays.

Travelling to Sentosa:
Ferries leave the World Trade Centre Ferry Terminal and Sentosa at 15 minute intervals from 7.30am–11pm, Mon–Thurs, and from 7.30am–midnight on Fri, Sat, Sun and the eve of Public Holidays and Public Holidays. The trip takes 6 minutes.

Cable cars operate from the top of Mt Faber, via Jardine Steps and across to Sentosa (1.8km) from 10am–7pm Mon–Sat, and 9am–7pm Sun and Public Holidays. The round trip costs S$6 adult, S$3 child.

Admission: There are three types of admission tickets —
Normal Ticket: S$4.50 adult, S$2.50 child under 12 years. Covers admission to Musical Fountain shows, Swimming Lagoon, Fort Siloso, Nature Walk, Maritime Museum, unlimited monorail and bus rides, return ferry trip, jogging, playgrounds, beaches and other facilities. Valid for the whole day from 8.30am–10pm (closing time).

After 5pm Ticket: S$3 adult, S$2 child under 12 years. Similar to the normal ticket, except Maritime Museum, but valid only from 5pm–10pm.

All-Inclusive Ticket: S$7 adult, S$3.50 child under 12 years. Similar to the normal ticket but also includes admission to Pioneers of Singapore and Surrender Chambers and Coralarium.

For further enquiries, contact: Public Relations Unit, Sentosa Development Corporation, ph 473 4388; Sentosa Information Office, World Trade Centre, ph 270 7888/9.

SOUTHERN ISLANDS. Singapore's southern islands are ideal for a day of swimming and lazing in the sun. Several of these islands have safe swimming lagoons, jetties, sun shelters, changing facilities and toilets. The most popular island is Kusu, which also has a Chinese temple and hillside Malay shrine. Nearby is the lovely tree-shaded island of St. John's. Both these islands can be reached by regular ferry service from the World Trade Centre. The others are accessible via hired boats from Jardine Steps (next to the World Trade Centre) or Clifford Pier.

SHOPPING AND SIGHTSEEING 35

Kusu/St. John's Ferry Timetable — Ferry Departure Times

	World Trade Centre	Kusu Island	St. John's Island
Mon–Sat	10.00am	10.45am	11.15am
	1.30pm	2.15pm	2.45pm
Sun & Public Holidays	9.00am	10.00am	10.20am
	10.00am	11.00am	11.20am
	11.20am	12.20pm	12.40pm
	12.20pm	1.20pm	1.40pm
	1.40pm	2.40pm	3.00pm
	2.40pm	3.40pm	4.00pm
	4.00pm	5.00pm	5.20pm
	5.00pm	6.00pm	6.20pm
	7.20pm	8.00pm	8.20pm

WATERSKIING. Enthusiasts of this sport will find conditions off the north coast of Singapore, in the Johor Straits, ideal. Furthermore, there are attractive islands nearby for relaxation, Skis, a power boat and driver can be hired for S$55 an hour from the Ponggol Boatel, 207-J 17th Avenue, Ponggol Point, ph 481 0032.

WET'N'WILD, East Coast Lagoon. An aquatic centre with thrilling water chutes. Open weekdays 10am–6pm, weekends 10am–7pm. Admission S$3 adult, S$2.50 child Mon–Fri, S$4 adult, S$3 weekends and Public Holidays.

OTHER PLACES OF INTEREST

BIRD SINGING, Tiong Bahru/Seng Poh Roads. Bird fanciers bring their feathered pets in beautifully made bamboo or wicker cages for an informal concert outside a coffee shop each Sunday morning around 8am.

CHANGING OF THE ISTANA GUARDS, corner of Orchard Road and Clemenceau Avenue. On the 1st Sunday of the month, at 6pm, this ceremony is held, with a drill performed to the music of a military band, at the entrance to the Istana or Presidential palace.

CROCODILE FARM, 790 Upper Serangoon Road. Crocodiles, alligators, snakes and lizards are bred in tanks. Their skins made into all kinds of fashion accessories and sold at very moderate prices. (Remember that some countries consider skin goods to be prohibited imports.)

CROCODILARIUM, 730 East Coast Parkway. A conveniently located reptile breeding and manufacturing centre which sells the finished products at competitive prices. Open 9am–5pm daily. Feeding time — Tues and Thurs 11am.

HAW PAR VILLA (Tiger Balm Gardens), Pasir Panjang Road. A fantasy in stone, with colourful and wonderful statues and stone carvings depicting Chinese myths and legends. Witness fire and brimstone in a Chinese hell; meet Madam White Snake and other legendary characters; explore stone grottoes. Open daily 8am–6pm. Admission Free.

KRANJI WAR MEMORIAL, off Woodlands Road. A tribute to the Allied Forces who fought to defend Singapore in World War II.

NEW MING VILLAGE, 32 Pandan Road. Demonstrations of the art of Chinese pottery making are given. Copies of Ming dynasty blue and white porcelain are produced and sold here. Open daily 9am–5.30pm.

PERANAKAN PLACE, corner of Emerald Hill and Orchard Road. The unique culture of the Peranakans, descendents of an interesting blend of Chinese, Malay and local settlers is featured in this series of restored shophouses, open from 9am daily. Gifts, antiques and food are available. Guided tours of the Show House are given daily.

THE SINGAPORE EXPERIENCE, Changi Airport Transit Lounge. The story of Singapore, from its beginnings as a fishing village in 1819 up to the present, is told in a 35 minute multiscreen presentation.

SINGAPORE MINT COIN GALLERY, 249 Jalan Boon Lay, Jurong. Minting operations can be viewed here. There is also a display of coins, medals and medallions from Singapore and around the world. Coins and souvenirs are on sale. Open Mon–Fri 9.30am–4.30pm.

SINGAPORE RIVER. A walk along the banks of the Singapore River provides glimpses of Singapore's interesting past. Old shophouses and warehouses contrast dramatically with soaring skycrapers. Beyond Read Bridge, old warehouses that once held sacks of rice, rubber and spices unloaded from lighters that came up the river, bear silent witness to the past.

SINGAPORE SCIENCE CENTRE, off Jurong Town Hall Road. Close to 500 exhibits related to Life Sciences, Physical Sciences and Aviation are displayed in four halls. Audio visual presentations add further interest. Visitors are encouraged to play with the "hands-on" exhibits to see how things work. Open Tues–Sun 10am–6pm (open Monday if a Public Holiday). Admission S$2 adult, 50c child.

VAN KLEEF AQUARIUM, River Valley Road. The aquarium houses more than 4,000 specimens of fish, coral and marine life, with everything from a shark to a seahorse. Open daily 9.30am–9pm. Admission 60c adult, 40c child.

Cathedral of the Good Shepherd.

TOURS

The following provides an indication only of tour content and cost. Itineraries will vary with the different agencies, as will the prices.

Tour bookings can be arranged through any travel agent, at the tour desk at your hotel, or through the agents specified in the itineraries below —
Eastwind ph 533 3432, Elpin Tours ph 235 3111, Holiday Tours & Travel ph 737 0533, RMG ph 298 3944, Siakson ph 336 0288, Singapore Sightseeing ph 737 8778, Tour East ph 220 2200.

The Singapore Tourist Promotion Board has produced an interesting guide for tourists wishing to draw up their own itineraries. This is called Tour-It-Yourself and is available on arrival in Singapore.

TOURS WITHIN SINGAPORE

DAY TOURS
City Tour (daily) — S$21 adult, S$11 child — coach.
Coach ride passing Elizabeth Walk, Supreme Court, City Hall, Singapore River and Merlion Park; proceed towards Chinatown; stop at Sri Mariamman Temple; proceed to Haw Par Villa; watch the Instant Asia Cultural Show; drive past Queenstown Housing Estate; and proceed to Botanic Gardens where tour ends. Duration 3–3.5 hours.
Tour starts 9am and 2.30pm. (Siakson — only 9am).
Operators: Tour East, RMG, Siakson, Singapore Sightseeing.

East Coast Tour (daily) — S$16 adult, S$9 child — coach.
Coach ride to Temple of a Thousand Lights and Dragon Mountain Temple; stop at Changi Prison Chapel, Changi Village and Crocodilarium. Duration 3–3.5 hours.
Tour starts 2pm.
Operators: RMG, Siakson, Singapore Sightseeing.

East Coast & Rural Tour (daily) — S$19 adult, S$9 child — coach.
Coach ride passing Katong and Bedok areas to see the contrast of old shophouses, modern bungalows and the massive public housing estates; stop at a Malay kampong, Temple of Kuan Yin, Changi Prison Chapel, Changi Village and Crocodilarium. Duration 3–3.5 hours.
Tour starts 2.30pm
Operator: Tour East.

Footsteps of Raffles (daily) — S$25 adult, S$12 child — coach.
Coach ride to National Museum; proceed to "Little India" in Serangoon Road; stop at Raffle Hotel for the 50 minute "Raffles Experience"; stop at Raffles Landing Site at Singapore River, Thian Hock Keng Tample, Mt Faber and Botanic Gardens. Duration 3.75 hours.
Tour starts 9am
Operator: Tour East.

Harbour Day Cruise (daily) — S$20 adult, S$10 child — coach/junk.
Coach ride to Clifford Pier; board the Chinese junk; sail along the harbour; stop at Kusu Island; cruise around Pulau Terkukor and Sentosa Island. Duration 2.5 hours.
Tour starts 10.30am, 3pm and 4pm.
Operators: Eastwind, Watertours (wholesalers) Tour East, RMG (retailers).

Heritage Tour (daily) — S$19 adult, S$9 child — coach.
Coach ride through the city to Arab Street; stop at some shops, see Sultan Mosque; proceed to "Little India" in Serangoon Road; stop at Raffles Landing Site at Singapore River; view some of the old warehouses; proceed to Thian Hock Keng Temple; last stop at National Museum. Duration 3.5 hours.
Tour starts 9.30am and 2.30pm.
Operator: RMG.

Historic Site Tour (daily) — S$19 adult, S$10 child — coach.
Coach ride passing Raffles Landing Site at Singapore River; stop

at "Little India" in Serangoon Road; stop at the Temple of A Thousand Lights and the Dragon Mountain Temple. Drive past Mountbatten Road and East Coast Parkway to Crocodilarium; stop at some unique shops at Arab Street; last stop is National Museum. Duration 3.25 hours.
Tour starts 9am
Operator: Siakson.

Jurong Bird Park Tour (daily) — S$22 adult, S$12 child — coach.
Coach ride to Jurong Bird Park; watch the 25 minute bird show; stop at Chinese Garden; proceed to Jurong Industrial Town and Garden of Fame at Jurong Hill. Duration 3–3.5 hours.
Tour starts 9am and 2pm.
Operators: Tour East, RMG, Siakson, Singapore Sightseeing.

Sentosa Tour (daily) — S$30 adult, S$15 child — coach/ferry.
Coach ride to World Trade Centre's ferry terminal; ferry ride (10 minutes) to Sentosa Island; monorail ride to Coralarium, Pioneers of Singapore, Surrender Chambers, Fort Siloso, Maritime Museum; cable car ride to Mt Faber. Duration 3.5 hours.
Tour starts 9am and 2pm
Operators: Tour East, RMG, Siakson, Singapore Sightseeing.

Sentosa Discovery (daily) — S$19 adult, S$14 child — car/ferry.
Transportation to Mt Faber Cable Car Station and take the cable car to Sentosa Island; monorail ride, and then visits to Coralarium, Wax Museum, Fort Siloso, Maritime Museum and Musical Fountain; take the ferry back. Duration 3.5 hours.
Tour starts 9am, 2pm and 7pm.
Operators: Elpin Tours & Limousine Services.

Island Picnic (daily except Mon & Thurs) — S$45 adult, S$25 child — coach.
Coach ride to Clifford Pier; board bumboat; stop at Pulau Sakeng to see a Malay Village, Kusu Island to see the shrines, and Sisters' Island for picnic lunch, sunbathing, fishing and snorkelling. Duration 7.5 hours.
Tour starts 9am.
Operator: Tour East.

42 SINGAPORE AND MALAYSIA AT COST

Round Island Tour (Mon/Wed/Fri) — S$56 adult, S$28 child — coach/boat.
Coach ride to Haw Par Villa; proceed to Jurong's hill top lookout-point; proceed to Lim Chu Kang, the rural area of Singapore to see vegetable and poultry farms; stop at an orchid farm; proceed to Admiralty House for lunch; stop at a typical public housing apartment, proceed to Kwong Min San or Bright Hill Temple; stop at Changi Point to board a boat to see a fish farm and kelongs; last stop at Crocodilarium. Duration 8.5 hours.
Tour starts 9am.
Operator: Tour East.

Shopping Tour (daily except Sun and Public Holidays) — S$17 adult, S$8 child — coach.
Coach ride to Arab Street; shop for sarong, songket, rattan and other items; walk through Change Alley; stop at the batik items and pewterware; last stop at Lim's Handicraft in Holland Village. Duration 3.5 hours.
Tour starts 2.30pm.
Operator: Tour East.

Sunday Special (Singapore & Johor) — S$64 adult, S$32 child — coach.
Coach ride to National Museum to see the Haw Par jade collection; drive past the waterfront and Raffles Place; walk through Chinatown and "Little India" in Serangoon Road; proceed to Kwong Min San (Bright Hill Temple); stop at Mandai Orchard Garden; cross the Causeway to Johor to have lunch; stop at a Malay kampong, Abu Bakar Mosque, a bazaar and the Sultan's palace. Duration 6 hours.
Tour starts 9am.
Operator: Tour East.

Contrasting Cultures (Mon, Wed, Fri, Sun) — S$29 adult, S$15 child — coach.
Coach ride to "Little India"; walk along the streets; sample Indian tidbits; stop at shops selling Indian spices and flower garlands. Proceed to Kwong Min San Temple — the largest Buddhist complex outside India and China; see the 400 murals and the big

Raffles Hotel, Singapore

Sultan Abdul Samad Building, Kuala Lumpur

marble statue of Kuan Yin with 15 heads and 1,000 hands; stop at Peranakan Place; tour its museum and sample the Nonya cakes at its shops. Duration 3.5 hours.
Tour starts 9am.
Operator: Singapore Sightseeing.

Zoo and Mandai Orchard Tour (Tues, Thurs, Fri) — S$21 adult, S$12 child — coach.
Coach ride to Singapore Zoological Gardens; ride on an electric tram to tour the zoo; watch "Animal Showtime"; stop at Mandai Orchid Garden and on the return journey, a brief stop at the Seletar Reservoir. Duration 3.5 hours.
Tour starts 2pm.
Operator: Siakson.

Zoo Special (Mon, Wed, Fri) — S$30 adult, S$15 child — coach.
Coach ride to Singapore Zoological Gardens,; watch "Animal Showtime" and have tea with the orang-utans. Duration 3.5 hours.
Tour starts 2.30pm
Operator: Tour East

Breakfast at the Zoo (Tues, Wed, Sat) — S$30 per person — coach.
Coach ride to zoo, have breakfast (lunch) with an orang-utan; tour zoo on tram; watch "Animal Showtime". Duration 3 hours.
Tour starts 8.30am & 1pm.
Operator: Holiday Tours & Travel.

Zoo Express (daily) — S$16 adult, S$10 child.
Transportation to zoo; watch "Animal Showtime", take photos with the animals and see them being fed. Duration 3 hours.
Tour starts 9am & 2pm.
Operator: Elpin Tours & Limousine Services.

NIGHT TOURS
Singapore By Night (daily) — S$39 adult, S$29 child — coach.
Coach ride to Newton Circus Hawker Centre for dinner,; drive in the city area to see Singapore by night; stop at Mt Faber and

proceed to Raffles Hotel for a Singapore Sling. Duration 3.5 hours.
Tour starts 7pm.
Operator: Singapore Sightseeing.

Nightlife Spectacular (daily) — S$58 adult (inclusive of dinner, cocktail, cover charge) — coach.
Coach ride through "Little India" and Chinatown; visit a satellite town and community centre; enjoy a seafood dinner, and then proceed to a nightclub. Duration 4 hours.
Tour starts 7.30pm.
Operator: Elpin Tours & Limousine Services.

Trishaw Tour (daily) — S$35 per person.
Coach ride to Waterloo Street carpark; ride on a trishaw to Cross Street; walk in Chinatown; and proceed to Raffles Hotel for Singapore Sling. Duration 1.5 to 2 hours.
Tour starts 7pm.
Operators: Tour East, Singapore Sightseeing.

Twilight/Dinner Cruise (daily) — $33 adult, S$17 child — coach/junk.
Coach ride to Clifford Pier, board the Chinese junk; sail along the harbour, cruise around Kusu Island, Pulau Terkukor and Sentosa Island. This cruise includes a Singapore style buffet dinner on board the junk. Duration 3 hours.
Tour starts 6pm
Operators: Tour East, RMG.

Starlite Dinner Cruise (daily) — S$36 adult, S$18 child — junk.
Sunset cruise along the harbour and around the islands in a Chinese junk; dinner on board; return to Clifford Pier after sundown (view of lighted harbour). Duration 3 hours.
Tour starts 6pm.
Operator: Eastwind — wholesalers.

TOURS OUTSIDE SINGAPORE

Johor Bahru Tour (daily) — S$21 adult, S$10 child — coach.
Coach ride to Johor Bahru; stop at the grounds of Istana Besar,

Bukit Serene and Sultan Abu Bakar Mosque; see the sarong weaving factory and rubber plantation; and stop at Kranji War Memorial on the return journey to Singapore. Duration 3 to 3.5 hours.
Tour starts 9am & 2pm.
Operators: Tour East, RMG, Siakson, Singapore Sightseeing.

Kukup Tour (Mon, Wed, Fri, Sun) — S$59 adult, S$29 child — coach.
Coach ride into Johor; stop at rubber, oil palm, cocoa, coffee and pineapple plantations; proceed to Kukup for lunch; and an optional fishing boat ride to the kelongs. Duration 8 hours.
Tour starts 8am
Operators: Tour East, RMG, Siakson, Singapore Sightseeing.

Malacca Tour (daily) — S$68 adult, S$48 child — coach.
Coach ride into Johor; stop at pottery factory, pineapple plantation and typical Malaysian kampong; proceed to Malacca; climb St. Paul's Hill; stop at Porta De Santiago, Bandar Hilir, "antique row" of Jonker Street, Cheng Hoon Teng Temple and St. Peter's Church. Duration 12 hours.
Tour starts 7.30am.
Operators: Tour East (Mon, Wed, Fri), Siakson and Singapore Sightseeing (Tues, Thurs, Sat), RMG (Sun only).

Desaru (Mon, Tues, Fri) — S$147 adult (based on twin sharing), S$85 child — coach.
Coach ride to Desaru, travelling pass oil palm and rubber trees. Arrive at the Village of Casuarinas. Stay overnight. Depart for Singapore on Day 2. Duration 2 days/1 night.
Tour starts 9am.
Operator: Siakson.

Plantation Tour (Wed only) — S$58 adult, S$29 child — coach.
Coach ride to Johor; stop at pineapple, coconut and oil palm plantations; proceed to Abu Bakar Mosque and the estate of Ulu Tiram to see oil palm being harvested. The tour includes a Malaysian-style buffet lunch with a special drink called the Planter's Punch. Minimum 15 persons. Duration 6 hours.

46 SINGAPORE AND MALAYSIA AT COST

Tour starts 9am.
Operator: Tour East.

Malacca/Kuala Lumpur Tour (Sat only) — S$585 adult (based on twin sharing) — by coach.
Coach ride to the West Coast of Malaysia; stop at a kampong and a pineapple plantation; stay overnight in Malacca town; proceed to Kuala Lumpur for a city tour and overnight stay; return to Singapore by air. Duration 3 days/2 nights.
Tour starts 7.30am.
Operator: Tour East.

Round Malaysia Tour — S$1,495 (inclusive of accommodation, based on twin-sharing).
Take a more comprehensive look at Malaysia. Starting from Singapore, travel to Malacca and then to Malaysia's capital, Kuala Lumpur. Cool off at Cameron Highlands, a hill resort, before continuing to Penang. Move on to explore the east coast, stopping at Kota Bahru, Tanjong Jara and finally, Kuantan, before heading back to Singapore. Duration 9 days.
Tour starts 7.30am.
Operator: Tour East.

Exotic Islands and Beaches — S$817 per person (inclusive of accommodation, based on twin-sharing).
The tour leaves from Singapore and takes you to Kuantan. Here you will visit a fishing village and a weaving centre. Between June and September you may be able to catch a glimpse of the giant female leatherback turtle laying her eggs. From Kuantan, journey to Mersing where a ferry will take you across to Pulau Tioman — an exotic island ideal for snorkelling, fishing or just lazing in the sun. Then fly from Pulau Tioman to Singapore. Duration 5 days.
Operator: Tour East.

SPORT AND RECREATION

Singapore's idyllic weather is perfect for a wide variety of sports and recreation activities. The facilities are excellent, and the prices are reasonable. Following are a few examples.

Archery
Archery Club of Singapore, 5 Binchange Walk, ph 258 1140.

Athletics
National Stadium at Kallang, where the regional South East Asian Games are staged. For information contact the Singapore Sports Council, ph 345 7111 ext 399.

Boat Hire
Ponggol Boatel, 17th Avenue, Ponggol, ph 481 0031.
Jardine Steps & Clifford Pier — motorised bumboats for hire at wharf.

Bowling
Jackie's Bowl (Katong), 542B East Coast Road, ph 241 6519 — S$2.20 per game before 6pm weekdays, S$2.80 per game weekends and after 6pm weekdays.
Jackie's Bowl (Orchard), 8 Grange Road, ph 737 4744, S$2.70 per game before 6pm weekdays, S$3 per game weekends and after 6pm weekdays.
Kallang Bowl, 5 Stadium Walk, ph 345 0545, S$2 per game before 6pm weekdays, S$2.50 per game weekends and after 6pm weekdays (with computerised scoring S$2.70 and S$3).
Kallang Bowlers Drome, Stadium Walk, ph 345 0545, S$2.20 per game 10am to 6pm weekdays, S$3 per game weekends and after 6pm weekdays.
Pasir Panjang Bowl, 269 Pasir Panjang Road, ph 775 5555, S$2 per game before 5.30pm weekdays, S$2.50 per game weekends and after 5.30pm weekdays.
Plaza Bowl, 8th floor, Textile Centre, Jalan Sultan, ph 292 4821,

S$2.50 per game before 6pm weekdays, S$3 per game weekends and after 6pm weekdays.

Canoeing
East Coast Parkway, along the beach from the Lagoon Food Centre — S$3 single-seater, S$5 double-seater per hour.
Sentosa Lagoon, near the swimming lagoon, S$3 single-seater, S$4 double-seater.

Cricket
Singapore Cricket Club, The Esplanade, ph 338 9271.

Cycling
East Coast Bicycle Centre, Bicycle Hire, next to the Food Centre. — 80c per hour, S$1 per hour for BMX.

Flying
Republic of Singapore Flying Club, East Camp Building, 140B Seletar Airbase, ph 481 0502/481 0200. Joy ride for 3 people at S$250 per hour. Training flights from S$190 to S$250 (non-members), S$150 to S$230 (members).

Golf
Changi Golf Club, Netheravon Road, ph 545 1298 — S$30 Green fee (weekdays), S$50 weekends (if no competition, with minimum of 3 players and handicap cards). Caddy fee: S$13 (1st class), S$11 (2nd class).
Jurong Country Club, Jurong Town Hall Road, ph 560 5655 — S$50 per game on weekdays, S$100 on weekends and public holidays. S$50 Green fee. Caddy fee: S$16 (A class), S$13 (B class), S$10 (C class).
Keppel Club, Bukit Chermin, 18-hole, par 72 course, ph 273 5522 — S$50 per player Tues–Fri, S$80 weekends and public holidays. Caddy fee: S$14 (A class), S$12 (B class).
Parkland Golf Driving Range, 920 East Coast Parkway, 48 Bays, 200m range, ph 440 6726, Proshop and coaching, ph 345 1470 — 4.5kg of balls — 7.30am–3.30pm (S$5), 5.30pm–10pm (S$6).
Sembawang Country Club, 17km (10.5 miles) Sembawang Road, ph 257 0642, Locked bag service 1, Sembawang Post Office,

Singapore 9175 — S$30 per game weekdays, S$80 weekends. Caddy fee: S$16 (A class), S$14 (B class), S$12 (C class).

Sentosa Golf Club, Sentosa Island, ph 472 2722 — S$50 whole day on weekdays, S$100 per game weekends and public holidays. Caddy fee: S$15. Golf clubs: S$15.

Singapore Island Country Club, Upper Thomson Road, ph 459 2222 — S$100 per person for whole day on weekdays only. Caddy fee: S$18 (1st class), S$15 (2nd class), S$12 (trainee).

Tanglin Golf Courses, Minden Road, ph 473 7236 — S$5 per game weekdays, S$7 weekends, S$3 for half-set bag. Caddy carts: 50c.

Warren Golf Club, Folkestone Road, 9-hole, par 70 course, ph 777 6533 — S$50 per player weekdays only. Caddy fee: S$15 (A class), S$14 (B class), S$13 (C class).

Horse Racing
Singapore Turf Club, Bukit Timah Racecourse, ph 469 3611 — Admission S$5.

Horse Riding
Bukit Timah Saddle Club, c/- Singapore Turf Club, Bukit Timah Road, ph 469 3611, ext 295.

Sailing
Changi Sailing Club, Netheravon Road, ph 545 2876.

Scuba Diving
Singapore Club, Aquanaut, c/- 20 Bideford Road #11–05, Wellington Building, ph 737 0673.

Squash
Alexandra Park, Royal Road off York and Bedford Roads, ph 473 7230 — S$3 per hour per court.

Changi Squash Courts, Gosport Road, ph 545 2941 — S$3 per hour per court.

East Coast Recreation Centre, East Coast Parkway, ph 449 0541 — $4 per hour per court daily (during offpeak hours), S$6 per hour per court daily (during peak hours). Glass courts: S$12 at all days and times.

Farrer Park, Rutland Road, ph 251 4166 — S$1.50 per half hour per court.
National Stadium, Kallang, ph 348 1258 (bookings 10am–4pm weekdays) — S$2 per half hour per court.
Singapore Squash Centre, Fort Canning Rise, ph 336 0155 — S$4–5 per hour per court depending on day and time of day.

Tennis
Alexandra Park, Royal Road, off York and Bedford Roads, ph 473 7236 — S$2 till 7pm.
Changi Tennis Courts, Gosport Road, ph 545 2941 — S$3 per hour per court (members), S$4–5 per hour per court depending on time of day (public).
Farrer Park Tennis Courts, Rutland Road, ph 251 4166 — S$3 per hour per court.
Kallang Squash & Tennis Centre, Kallang, ph 345 1291 (bookings 10am–4pm weekdays) — S$3–5 per hour per court depending on day and time of day.
Seletar Tennis, The Oval, off Jalan Kayu, 3 Parklane, Seletar Base, ph 481 4745 — S$3 per hour per court depending on day and time of day.
Sembawang Tennis Centre, Deptford Road, ph 257 1147 — S$2–4 per hour per court depending on day and time of day.
Singapore Tennis Centre, East Coast Parkway, ph 442 5966 — S$14 whole day (unlimited hours).
Tanglin Tennis Courts, Minden Road, ph 473 7236 — S$3–5 per hour court depending on day and time of day.

Waterskiing
Ponggol Boatel, Ponggol, 17th Avenue, ph 481 0031 — S$60 per hour for ski boat with ski equipment.

Windsurfing (Board Sailing)
East Coast Sailing Centre, 1210 East Coast Parkway, ph 449 5118 — S$45 4-hour course (1pm–5pm) daily, S$80 2-day basic course (3 hours each day). Rental of sailboard: S$10 per hour. Open 9.30am–6.30pm daily.

Malaysia

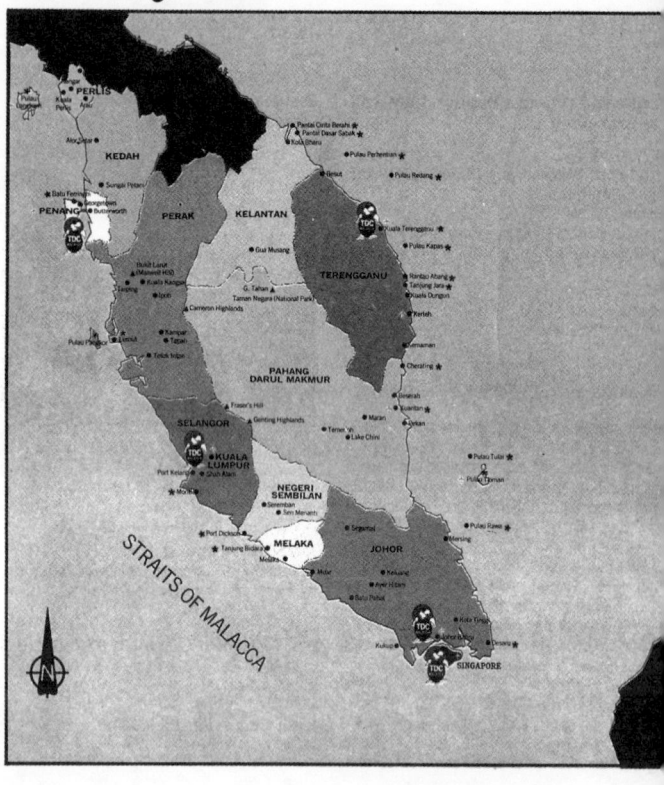

★ BEACH RESORT
▲ HILL RESORT/MOUNTAIN
✈ AIRPORT/AIRSTRIP
Pulau ISLAND
🛡 TDC OFFICE

SPORT AND RECREATION 53

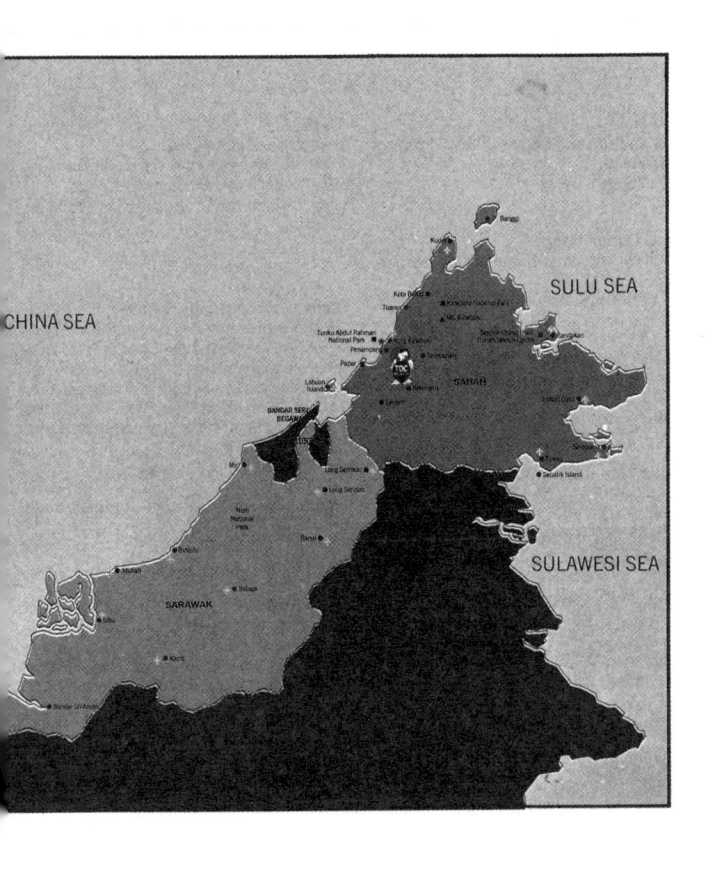

MALAYSIA

Malaysia is situated in the central part of Southeast Asia, just north of the Equator. To the north are Burma, Thailand, Laos, Kampuchea and Vietnam, to the south are Singapore and Indonesia, and to the east are the islands of the Philippines.

The land mass of Malaysia is made up of two parts, the Malay Peninsula and the states of Sabah and Sarawak on the island of Borneo. The total land area is 330,434km^2 (127,548 sq. miles) with 131,587km^2 (50,793 sq. miles) in Peninsular Malaysia and 198,847km^2 (76,755 sq. miles) in Sabah and Sarawak.

Malaysia is divided into thirteen states, eleven in Peninsular Malaysia, and the two on the island of Borneo. Nine of these states have hereditary rulers. The Supreme Head of State is the Yang di-Pertuan Agong (King) who is elected every five years from among the nine Rulers. The thirteen states are listed below with their capitals.

Perlis — Kangar
Kedah — Alor Setar
Penang — Georgetown
Perak — Ipoh
Negeri Selangor Darul Ehsan — Shah Alam
Negeri Sembilan — Seremban
Melaka — Melaka
Johor — Johor Bahru
Negeri Pahang Darul Makmur — Kuantan
Terengganu — Kuala Terengganu
Kelantan — Kota Bharu
Sabah — Kota Kinabalu
Sarawak — Kuching.

The head of government is the Prime Minister, who must be a member of the Dewan Rakyat (House of Representatives). The Parliament itself comprises two houses: The Dewan Rakyat, which is fully elective, and the Dewan Negara (Senate) to which members are nominated by the King from among citizens who have rendered distinguished public service, or have achieved distinction in the professions, or are representatives of racial minorities, or are capable of representing the interests of the aborigines.

As Head of Government, the Prime Minister heads the Cabinet, which is made up of the various Ministers of Government. Each of the thirteen states also has its own Chief Minister, or Menteri Besar, who is also elected to office, and its own (elected) State Assembly.

Malaysia is among the world's largest producers of tin, rubber and palm oil. Other major products: Petroleum (the exploration and production being under the supervision of the national oil corporation, Petronas), timber and pepper. A number of agencies have also been set up to speed up industrialisation, and the implemention of the New Economic Policy (NEP).

Transportation is a fast-growing industry, with Malaysian Airline System (MAS) leading the field in air services. Tourism is yet another growing and important industry and a special agency, The Tourist Development Corporation (TDC) has been set up to promote tourism. TDC has offices in Singapore, Bangkok, Hong Kong, Tokyo, Sydney, Frankfurt, London and Los Angeles.

The national flag of Malaysia has 14 horizontal stripes of equal width representing the equal membership of the 13 States and the Federal Government. The dark blue canton in the top corner nearest to the flagstaff stands for the unity of the people. The crescent is the symbol of Islam and the 14 point star represents the unity of the 13 States and Federal Government. Yellow is the royal colour of the Rulers.

Malaysia's national flower is Bunga Raya — the hibiscus. Although there are many varieties of this flower, the one selected is red in colour with five petals, and is found in profusion in the country.

HISTORY

Because of its strategic position between the Indian Ocean and the South China Sea, Malaysia has long been a meeting place for traders and travellers from West and East. Hence its history is one of continual interaction with foreign powers and influences.

The earliest known kingdom in Malaysia was the Kingdom of Kedah, mentioned in Chinese and Sanskrit records as early as

600 to 700AD. Hindu-Buddhist influence was strong in the centuries before the coming of Islam. By 1400, when the Malacca Malay Kingdom was at the height of its power, Islam had become a major influence. By 1511, however, Malacca (Melaka) had fallen to the Portuguese.

Hard on the heels of the Portuguese came their trading rival, the Dutch. With the help of Johor and Naning Malays, the Dutch attacked and defeated the Portuguese in 1641. Melaka was under Dutch control until 1824, when under the Anglo-Dutch Treaty of that year Melaka was exchanged for Bencoolen, the English-held territory on the other side of the straits.

The first English ship to arrive in Malayan waters was the Edward Bonaventure commanded by Edward Lancaster. She anchored off Penang from June to August 1592 to take on fresh provision. Thereafter came Francis Light and Stamford Raffles, of Singapore fame, who stayed in Melaka in the early 1800s when Dutch power fell to Napoleon's armies. By the time the English officially occupied Melaka, they had two other ports under their control. Francis Light had founded Penang for the East India Company, and Stamford Raffles had established Singapore. From these three ports the English penetrated inland. Through friendly treaties, relentless persuasion and negotiations with powerful Thailand in the north, the English slowly extended their control over all the states of the Malay Peninsula.

Sarawak, once part of the Sultan of Brunei's Empire, had been ruled since 1841 by a British adventurer, James Brooke and his descendants. In 1888 Sarawak and North Borneo (Sabah) became British protectorates. By the 1920s all the states that eventually comprised Malaysia were under English control. The first stirrings of Malaysian nationalism were felt as early as the 1930s, and following the end of World War II, the momentum of nationalism resumed, culminating in independence for the Federation of Malaya in 1957.

In 1963 Malaysia was formed, bringing together the States of Malaya, Singapore, Sabah and Sarawak. Singapore however left the federation in 1965.

Today Malaysia is a member of the six-nation Association of South East Asian Nations (ASEAN). This association, comprising Malaysia, Thailand, Indonesia, Singapore, Brunei Darussalam and the Philippines, was formed to promote greater economic, social and cultural co-operation among these nations.

CLIMATE
There are no distinct seasons and temperatures vary little the year round, ranging from 21C to 32C (70F to 90F), with cooler temperatures in the hill resorts. Average annual rainfall varies from 2,000 to 2,500mm (80 to 100 ins). Humidity is high all year round.

November to February is the rainy season for the east coast of Peninsular Malaysia, the north-eastern part of Sabah and the western part of Sarawak. In some years rainfall is concentrated in short periods and flooding can occur. During the months of April, May and October, the west coast of the peninsula experiences occasional thunderstorms in the afternoons. Showers are heavy but they clear up as quickly as they come. And, some consolation, the showers are warm.

POPULATION
Malaysia is a multi-racial country with a population of 15.6 million, 12.9 million in Peninsular Malaysia and 2.7 million in Sabah and Sarawak. Malays, Chinese, Indians and the indigenous people of Sabah and Sarawak form the majority of the population, however the Malays who are largely Moslem dominate government and the bureaucracy.

All schools in Malaysia follow a common curriculum and syllabus.

LANGUAGE
Bahasa Malaysia (Malay) is the national and official language of the country, and is the medium of instruction in all schools. English is widely used all over the country, especially in business, and is a compulsory subject in school. Other languages used are Chinese (Mandarin) and Tamil.

Here are some words and phrases which might come in handy. Pronunciation guide — a as in far, c as in chip, sy as in shut, g as in girl.

Greetings

Welcome	Selamat datang
Hello	Hello
How do you do?	Apa khabar?
Good morning	Selamat pagi
Good afternoon	Selamat petang
Good night	Selamat malam
Good bye	Selamat tinggal
Fine	Baik

Pronouns

I	Saya
You	Anda, awak, Encik (Mr), cik (Miss), Puan (Mrs)
We	Kami
He/She	Dia
They	Mereka

Questions

Can you help me?	Bolehkah encik tolong saya?
How do I get there?	Bagaimanakah saya boleh ke sana?
How far?	Berapa jauh?
How long will it take?	Berapa lama?
How much?	(price) Berapa Harganya?
What is this/that?	Apakah ini/itu?
What is your name sir?	Siapa nama encik?
When?	Bila?
Where?	Di mana?
Why?	Mengapa?

Useful Words and Expressions

A little	Sedikit
A lot	Banyak
Beach	Pantai
Beef	Daging lembu
Chicken	Ayam
Cold	Sejuk
Crab	Ketam
Drink	Minum

Do not have	Tiada
Eat	Makan
Excuse me	Maafkan saya
Female	Perempuan
Fish	Ikan
Fruit	Buah
Have	Ada
Hot	Panas
I am sorry	Saya minta maaf
Meat	Daging
Money	Wang/duit
Mutton	Daging Kambing
No	Tidak
Please	Tolong/Sila
Pork	Daging babi
Prawn	Udang
Salt	Garam
Shop	Kedai
Sugar	Gula
Thank you	Terima kasih
Toilet	Tandas/bilik air
Trishaw	Beca
Wait	Tunggu
Want	Mahu
Water	Air
Yes	Ya

Numbers

One	Satu
Two	Dua
Three	Tiga
Four	Empat
Five	Lima
Six	Enam
Seven	Tujuh
Eight	Lapan
Nine	Sembilan
Ten	Sepuluh
Eleven	Sebelas
Twelve	Dua belas

Twenty	Dua puluh
One hundred	Seratus
Directions	
Go up	Naik
Go down	Turun
Turn	Belok
Right	Kanan
Left	Kiri
Front	Hadapan
Behind	Belakang
North	Utara
South	Selatan
East	Timur
West	Barat

RELIGION

Islam is the official religion of the country, but freedom of worship is guaranteed. Consequently it is not uncommon to see mosques, temples and churches sharing a common neighbourhood. Buddhism, Taoism, Hinduism and Christianity are among other religions practised in Malaysia.

FESTIVALS

Malaysia celebrates many festivals. Each of the different racial communities has its own customs, traditions and festivals. Public holidays only are shown here.

National Public Holidays

February 17 and 18 (for Kelantan and Terengganu only February 17)	Chinese New Year
May 1	Labour Day
May 17 and 18	*Hari Raya Puasa
May 30 (except for Federal Territory of Labuan)	Wesak Day
June 1	Yang Dipertuan Agong's Birthday
July 24	*Hari Raya Haji
August 14	Maal Hijrah

August 31	National Day
October 23	Prophet Muhammad's Birthday
November 8 (except for Sabah, Sarawak and FT of Labuan)	Deepavali
December 25	Christmas

State Public Holidays

January 1 (except Johore, Kedah, Kelantan, Perlis and Terengganu)	New Year's Day
January 17 (only for Kedah)	Kedah Sultan's Birthday
February 1 (Kuala Lumpur and FT of Labuan)	Federal Territory Day
February 2 (Negeri Sembilan, Perak, Penang and Selangor)	Thaipusam
February 24 (Johore only)	Hol Day (Almarhum Sultan Ismail)
March 8 (Selangor only)	Selangor Sultan's Birthday
March 16 (Kedah and Negri Sembilan only)	Israk and Mikraj
March 21 (Terengganu only)	Terengganu Sultan's Installation
March 30 and 31 (Kelantan only)	Kelantan Sultan's Birthday
April 1 (Sabah and Sarawak only)	*Good Friday
April 8 (Johore only)	Johore Sultan's Birthday
April 18 (Johore only)	*1st Day of Ramadhan
April 19 (Perak only)	Perak Sultan's Birthday
April 29 (Terengganu only)	*Terengganu Sultan's Birthday
May 4 (Kelantan, Melaka, Perak, Perlis, Selangor and Terengganu)	Nuzul Quran
May 7 (Pahang only)	Hol Day
May 30 and 31 (FT of Labuan and Sabah only)	Harvest Celebrations
June 2 and 3 (Sarawak only)	Dayak Day

June 8 (Melaka only)	Governor of Malacca's Birthday
July 17 (Sarawak only)	Governor of Sarawak's Birthday
July 16 (Penang only)	Governor of Penang's Birthday
July 19 (Negeri Sembilan only)	Yang Di-Pertuan Besar of Negeri Sembilan's Birthday
July 25 (Kedah, Kelantan, Pahang, Perlis and Terengganu)	*Second Day of Hari Raya Haji
September 14 (Perlis only)	Raja of Perlis' Birthday
September 16 (Sabah only)	Governor of Sabah's Birthday
October 24 (Pahang only)	Pahang Sultan's Birthday

*Subject to change.

A major event each year is Hari Raya Puasa to mark the end of the Muslim fasting month. It starts with day-break visits to the cemetery, followed by thanksgiving prayers at all mosques. Adults and children alike are dressed in their Sunday best. Malaysian muslims hold "open-house" where relatives and friends call on one another. A variety of local dishes are served throughout the day. Tourists are welcome at Seri Perdana, the Prime Minister's residence during its open-house on Hari Raya.

Chinese New Year is another major festival and this too means the exchange of gifts, visits to the temples and holding "open-house" for relatives and friends. Children at this time look forward to the "ang pow" — the gift of money in bright red envelopes.

Malaysia's Indian community celebrates Deepavali. The name means "festival of lights", and the homes are decorated with candles and oil lamps. Like the other major festivals the Hindus too visit relatives and friends at this time.

Christmas is celebrated with a difference in Malaysia. Apart from the usual carolling and thanksgiving, Malaysian Christians celebrate the occasion by having "open-house" for relatives and friends. The "open-house" concept to celebrate the main communal or religious festivals in Malaysia is common to all.

ENTRY REGULATIONS

Visitors to Malaysia must be in possession of a valid national passport or other internationally recognised travel document endorsed for travel to Malaysia.

Citizens of Australia, Canada, West Germany, The Netherlands, New Zealand, United States or United Kingdom do not need a visa to visit Malaysia for social or business reasons.

No vaccinations are required for Cholera or Smallpox, and Yellow Fever vaccinations are only required if you are arriving from an infected area or endemic zone. It is wise, however, to check with your local doctor about the advisability of some type of Malaria protection.

Items such as cameras, watches, pens, lighters, cosmetics, perfume and portable radio cassette players are duty free in Malaysia. Visitors bringing in dutiable goods such as video equipment may have to pay a deposit for temporary importation, refundable when they leave. This is normally up to 50% of the value. You are advised to carry the receipt of purchase. If you have to pay any tax or deposit, please ensure you are given an official receipt. If in doubt ask to see a senior officer who is always on duty.

The importation of illegal drugs into Malaysia carries the death penalty.

International airports in Malaysia are staffed by customs officers and normal checks of baggage are made on all international arrivals. Standard security checks are also in operation at all Malaysian airports.

Airport tax is collected at all airports. For domestic flights the tax is M$3, for flights to Singapore and Brunei the tax is M$5, while for all other international flights the tax is M$15.

EMBASSIES

Australia: Australian High Commission, 6 Jalan Yap Kwan Seng, Kuala Lumpur, ph 03-242 3122.

N.Z.: N.Z. High Commission, 193 Jalan Tun Razak, 16-01, Kuala Lumpur, ph 03-486 422.

Canada: Canadian High Commission, Plaza MBF, 172 Jalan Ampang, Kuala Lumpur, ph 03-261 2000.

U.K.:	British High Commission, Wisma Damansara, Jalan Senantan, Kuala Lumpur, ph 03-254 1533.
U.S.A.:	376 Jalan Tun Razak, ph 03-248 9011.
Germany:	3 Jalan U Thant, Kuala Lumpur, ph 03-242 9825.
Netherlands:	4 Jalan Mesra (off Jalan Damai/Jalan Ampang) ph 03-243 1143.

MONEY

The unit of currency is the Malaysian Ringgit, or dollar, which is divided into 100 sen or cents. Currency notes are issued in denominations of $1, $5, $10, $20, $50, $100, $500 and $1,000. Coins are issued in 1 sen, 5 sen, 10 sen, 20 sen and 50 sen. Coins of $1 denominations also exist and they are legal tender, but they are commemorative issues and are seldom seen in circulation.

Approximate rates of exchange are:

A$	=	M$2.30
NZ$	=	M$1.70
CAN$	=	M$2.15
US$	=	M$2.50
UK£	=	M$4.70
Gl	=	M$1.30
DM	=	M$1.50

COMMUNICATIONS

Telephones
Public telephone booths are available in most towns. Coin operated phones can be found in supermarkets and at post offices. You will need 10c coins for local calls. Long distance calls are best made from your hotel.

Telegrams and Telexes.
Telegrams and telexes may be sent from your hotel or from main telegraph offices.

Newspapers
Local newspapers in English are readily available. Foreign newspapers and magazines can be obtained at main newsstands and bookstalls.

Post

There are certain regulations governing the transmission of certain dutiable items. Listed below are the postal rates of postcards and aerogrammes. Please check with the postal authorities for further enquiry.

Postcards — to Australia and New Zealand — 30 sen.
              to US and Canada — 55 sen.
              to UK and Europe — 40 sen.
Aerogrammes — to all countries — 40 sen.

Radio and Television

There are four government radio networks broadcasting in the various languages, including English. In Kuala Lumpur a visitor can tune into the Federal Capital radio station.

There are two government-run TV Channels. Apart from locally produced programmes some popular American and British series are also shown. A third channel is run by a commercial TV station.

MISCELLANEOUS

Credit Cards

Most large establishments in Malaysia will accept internationally-known credit cards.

Opening Hours

Generally shops are open from 9.30am–7pm, while supermarkets and department stores operate from 10am–10pm. In Johor, Kedah, Perlis, Kelantan and Terengganu, the public holiday is Friday instead of Sunday, so some shops may be closed.

Government Offices — Mon–Thurs, 8am–12.45pm, 2pm–4.15pm.
                        Fri, 8am–12.15pm, 2.45pm–4.15pm.
                        Sat, 8am–12.45pm
In Johor, Kedah, Perlis, Kelantan and Terengganu government offices are open from 8am–12.45pm Thurs, and closed Fri.

Banks — Mon–Fri, 10am–3pm.
          Sat, 9.30am–11.30am.

For Kedah, Perlis, Kelantan and Terengganu banks are open 9.30am–11.30am Thurs, closed Fri.

There are more than 40 commercial banks operating in Malaysia with 580 branches throughout the country.

Electricity

Mains voltage in Malaysia is 220 volts. If you are planning to bring any electrical equipment with 110 volts, please pack a converter.

Health

Private clinics are easily found even in the smallest towns. In major cities medical centres offer the best facilities. It is very inexpensive to visit a private doctor, and they dispense medicine on the spot. Approximate fee for a private medical visit to a clinic is M$20 including medicine. There are government hospitals throughout the country, but apart from emergencies they are more geared to serve the local population.

Spectacles and contact lens practitioners produce excellent products. Spectacle frames from France, Germany and other countries are available at a much lower cost than in their countries of origin. Most opticians are trained overseas. Visitors from many countries often take the opportunity to buy spectacles or contact lenses in Malaysia.

Chemist shops (drug stores) abound in Malaysia and apart from western medicine they also dispense traditional Chinese medicine. Chemist shops are open during normal trading hours and even on Sundays in supermarkets.

Laundry and Dry Cleaning

Most major hotels offer same-day service for laundry, cleaning and dry cleaning. Laundrettes are not easily accessible but local laundry and dry cleaning shops can be easily found in most towns. They are inexpensive but the visitor may have to wait 2 or 3 days.

Time

Malaysia is 8 hours ahead of GMT and 16 hours ahead of the US Pacific Standard Time.

Clothing

Light weight clothing is worn all year round. Informal dress is the order of the day with emphasis on comfort. This does not mean that a pair of "Stubbies" (shorts) is all that is required, you are expected to wear something on your torso. For more formal occasions however, more formal clothing is expected. Gentlemen usually put on jackets and ties while ladies appear in dresses. Alternatively, batik, a local fabric, may be worn. Batik is favoured even for formal occasions because of its comfort in tropical climate.

Tipping

A service charge of 10% is added automatically to restaurant and hotel bills, plus a 5% government tax, so tipping is unnecessary unless service is exceptionally good.

FRIENDLY DOs AND DON'Ts

Compiled by a seasoned "Mat Salleh" (colloquial: white-man).

Dress Code

On the beach — bikinis the limit, beyond that you're in trouble, and that goes for guys as well.

In the "pasat" (market) or "pekan" (town) — dress as you would when visiting a favourite rich old aunt you can't afford to offend. The key phrase is: "Nothing showing, nothing shocking!".

In the mosque — all covered up except your feet, ie take off your shoes before entering. As for guys, the catch word is "clean" locks, you know what I mean!

Gestures

Thumbs up and V-signs are universally accepted.

Don't point with your toe or pointer; try the local way, with your thumb.

When meeting — no pecking of cheeks or kissing, friendly handshakes or a nod and smile go a long way.

When saying farewell — the same applies, waving with open palms also universally accepted.

Abrupt actions should be avoided.

Petting and kissing in public is offensive.

Speech
Applicable everywhere: "Keep your temper, nobody wants it."
Whenever you want to take a photo of someone don't say "cheese", say "please..."

Miscellaneous
When invited to a home for a meal, a small gift or a bag of fruits to the host speaks volumes.
Remember to remove your shoes at the bottom of stairways or doorways.
On the beach or islands, coconuts are not for the plucking.
Don't litter and take heed:
DRUG TRAFFICKING IS ILLEGAL AND CARRIES THE DEATH PENALTY.

Finally enjoy and relax, if you require any directions or information just ask.

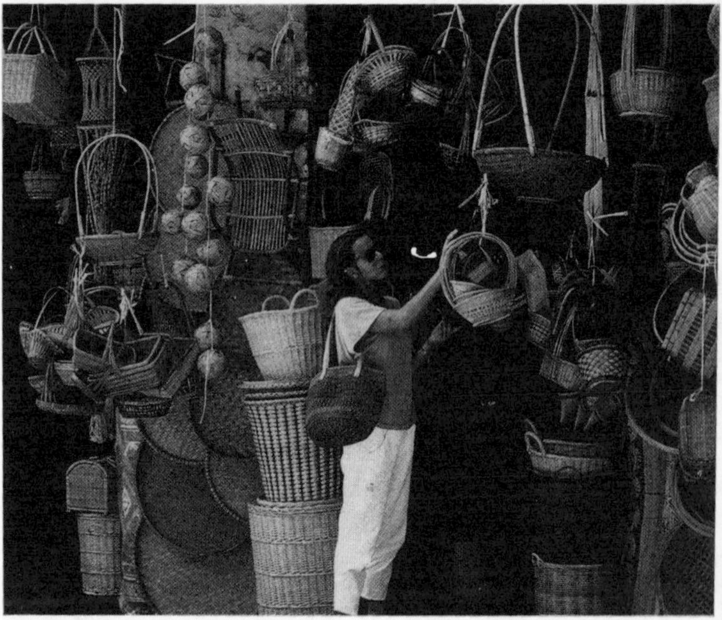

TRAVEL INFORMATION

HOW TO GET THERE

By Air
More than 23 international airlines fly in and out of Malaysia. Airports at Kuala Lumpur, Penang, Kuantan, Kota Kinabalu and Kuching cater for international flights.

By Sea
There are passenger terminals at Penang, Port Kelang, Kuantan, Kuching and Kota Kinabalu.

By Road
A road network from Singapore to Thailand means you can drive, or catch a bus, from either of these points into Malaysia.

By Rail
Train services extend from Singapore to Padang Besar at the Thai border, linking up with Thai Railways to Bangkok in Thailand.

ACCOMMODATION

Malaysia offers accommodation in international class hotels, as well as simpler hotels, rest houses and hostels. What you won't find are motels, caravan or camping sites, bed-and-breakfast or private self-catering holiday apartments.

Hotels
Hotels in Malaysia have not been officially classified, but there are international chains such as Hilton, Regent, Holiday Inn and Hyatt, offering luxurious accommodation. Local or regional chains such as the Merlin, the Ming Court and the Shangri-La are to be found in major cities. They are also luxurious and their charges lie in the same range as the international chains. First class hotels are numerous and charge around M$120 for a double room, whereas the budget hotels charge around M$35 for a double room.

Government Rest Houses

Although government rest houses exist in most main towns, they are primarily for government officers on transit. Visitors are able to stay if accommodation is available, but they are fully booked during school holidays. Advance booking can be rather difficult. The best bet is to inquire on the spot. Rates ranging from M$20–M$50 are quite reasonable.

Hostels

The Malaysian Youth Hostel Association operates a number of youth hostels around the country. Youth hostels are available at the following locations:

Kuala Lumpur — 2
Penang — 1
Port Dickson — 1
Fraser's Hill — 1
Cameron Highlands — 2
Kuantan — 1
Kota Bharu — 1
Kota Kinabalu — 1
Pangkor Island — 1.

LOCAL TRANSPORT

There are various ways of travelling within Malaysia. You can get to your destination either by air, train, bus, taxi or even trishaws.

Planes

MAS provides special fares for travel within Malaysia.

Trains

Malayan Railways or Keretapi Tanah Melayu (KTM) provide a comfortable and economical rail service. There are two main lines being operated for passenger service. One runs along the west coast. From Singapore, this line runs northwards through Kuala Lumpur and Butterworth and meets the Thai railways at the border. The other line branches off from the west coast line at the town of Gemas and travels up to the north-eastern part of the peninsula near Kota Bharu. This line also meets the State Railway of Thailand line at the border.

For foreign tourists, KTM offers a Railpass which entitles the holder to unlimited travel in any class and to any destination for a period of 10 days or 30 days. The Railpass costs M$85 for 10 days and M$175 for 30 days. The cost of the pass does not include sleeping berth charges.

Ferries

Introduced in August 1986, Feri Malaysia operates cruise Muhibah, a holiday cruise ship, between Singapore, Kuantan, Kuching and Kota Kinabalu. The ship offers air-conditioned cabins and comfortable suites for accommodation, as well as facilities such as restaurants, cafeteria, discotheque, gymnasium, cinema, swimming pool and golf putting green. Stopover packages and shore excursions are available and further information can be obtained by contacting Feri Malaysia Sdn. Bhd. Ground Floor, Menara Utama UMBC, Jalan Sultan Sulaiman, 50000 Kuala Lumpur, ph 03-238 8899, TX FM KUL MA 20176.

Outstation Taxis

Malaysia also offers the budget conscious traveller long distance taxis which travel from one state to another. It operates on a shared cost basis. Each person is charged a flat rate. As soon as the taxi driver gets four passengers going to the same destination, off he goes. The rates are very reasonable.

You can also "charter" a whole taxi by paying four times the fare. For example, the fare per person from Kuala Lumpur to Butterworth is M$25. If you charter the taxi you pay the driver M$100.

Buses

There are three types of buses that operate in Malaysia. The non-aircon buses plying between the states, the non-aircon buses that provide service within each state and the aircon express buses connecting major towns in Malaysia. Prices are reasonable though at times they do not adhere strictly to timetables. Like the outstation taxis, travelling by bus is relatively cheap.

Trishaws

These are the best way to move around short distances, but are not available in every town. They are pedal cycles with carriages either at the side or in front of the driver. It costs about M$1 per km, but make sure you agree on the price before boarding.

Car

The roads are good in Malaysia, there is a network of approximately 30,000km (18,600 miles) of roads and highways, and this is definitely the best way of getting around.

From the causeway connecting Singapore and Peninsular Malaysia, the main road runs up the West Coast to the Thai border. From this road, two highways cross the peninsula to the East Coast. In the north the East-West Highway connects Butterworth with Kota Bharu, while in the central part the Kuala Lumpur-Karak Highway cuts through the main range and joins a road leading to Kuantan on the East Coast. In Sabah and Sarawak motorable roads run along the coast connecting major towns.

Car Rentals

Rental cars are available on unlimited mileage basis. The daily rates on this basis vary from M$120 for economy cars to M$300 for cars in super luxury class. Weekly rates are also available.

An International Driving Licence is required by the tourist who wishes to drive in Malaysia. Driving is on the left hand side of the road, and international traffic signs are used, as well as a few local ones. Some local signs —

AWAS = CAUTION
IKUT KIRI = KEEP LEFT
KURANG-KAN LAJU = SLOW DOWN
JALAN SEHALA = ONE WAY in direction of the arrow
UTARA = NORTH
SELATAN = SOUTH
TIMUR = EAST
BARAT = WEST

The speed limit in built-up areas is 50kmh (30mph), and outside towns the familiar speed limit signs are displayed where limits have been imposed. The wearing of seat belts by drivers and front seat passengers is compulsory. A fine of up to M$200 or imprisonment not exceeding 6 weeks can be imposed on those who fail to wear seat belts.

For safety, local drivers have developed a few signals of their own. The driver in front flashing his Right Indicator is signalling "Do Not Overtake". Flashing of Left Indicator signals "Overtake With Caution". A driver flashing his headlamps is claiming the right of way. At round-abouts or traffic circles, the driver on the right has the right of way.

Petrol is around 92 sen a litre and petrol stations are found in or at the edge of most towns. Make sure you fill up your tank by 6pm or 7pm, as very few stations have 24 hour service.

FOOD

If variety is the spice of life, when it comes to eating Malaysia has few equals. Each state in the country has its own distinctive flavour, with Malay food being on the spicy side. Chinese food in its endless variety is available almost everywhere. Indian food from both north and south India is widely available. Outside hotels, European food from the sizzling steaks to the fast foods from the US can be obtained in the larger towns, although you may have to search and ask around.

Tropical fruit such as durian (you'll either love it or hate it), ciku, mangosteen, rambutan, guavas, watermelons, papayas and bananas, can be bought from fruit stalls along highways as well as in towns. Around cinemas and other entertainment areas there are also fruit-sellers with a variety of fruits which have been cut up and stored in cool display cases. Try them. They are delicious.

SHOPPING

One popular pastime all travellers enjoy in Malaysia is shopping because the things you can buy are unique to Malaysia. Whether you shop at supermarkets, department stores or open markets, you'll delight in the range of pewter, batik, jewellery, pottery and antiques.

There are small duty-free shops at Kuala Lumpur and Penang airports, as well as in city centres. Cameras, watches, pens, lighters, cosmetics, perfume and electronic goods are duty-free in Malaysia.

Giant kites can be bought in kit form, and miniature tops are available.

In the markets, bargaining is still popular. So if a stall-holder offers an item and you think it is too expensive, you could try making an offer. In department stores, however, 'fixed price' is a general rule, so bargaining is not possible there.

BEACHES

If it is beautiful, empty beaches you are seeking, then Malaysia has them.

There are aproximately 700km (434 miles) of beaches on the East Coast, including the one which turtles swim to, to lay their eggs between May and September every year. Islands off the East Cost also offer magnificent beaches.

On the West Coast the mainland does not have good beaches except for stretches in Port Dickson and Malacca. The islands off-shore however, are better provided. Pulau Pangkor and Penang have fine beaches, as do Pulau Langkawi, Pantai Rhu and Pantai Tengah.

NATIONAL PARKS

The tropical rain forests of Malaysia are very, very old. While other areas were subjected to the ravages of the Ice Age and climatic changes which destroyed their vegetation, the Malaysian rain forests, as represented by the national parks, have become storehouses of flora and fauna which have long vanished elsewhere.

The more popular national parks are the Taman Negara in Peninsular Malaysia, Niah National Park in Sarawak and Kinabalu National Park in Sabah. Each offers its own unique attractions. Taman Negara is particularly favoured for its fishing and animal observation hides. Niah National Park has caves ranking among the largest in the world, and Kinabalu National Park has Mount Kinabalu which can be climbed by the average, healthy man, woman or teenager.

More detailed information on these parks is found in a later chapter.

SPORT AND RECREATION

International sports such as golf, tennis, horse racing, motor racing, soccer, cricket and squash are enjoyed by locals and visitors alike. Local sports such as sepak takraw, giant top spinning and kite flying are undertaken seriously and demand an enormous amount of skill. These sports are exciting to watch as well as photograph.

KUALA LUMPUR

This region is a popular tourist destination with an immense variety of interests catered for. It encompasses the Federal Territory of Kuala Lumpur and the states of Selangor Darul Ehsan, Negeri Sembilan and Melaka.

KUALA LUMPUR — FEDERAL TERRITORY

Kuala Lumpur is the hub of Malaysia. As a former colonial headquarters, it is the home of the independence movement, and the centre of policy making.

Colourful KL, as it is known, is a bustling cosmopolitan city with a rich mix of architectural styles from Moorish to Tudor. It is a modern city, but yet preserves a charm from another era, and the two are in accord. KL's main street has magnificent Moorish buildings on one side, with arches, domes and spires, and a playing field with a Tudor-styled clubhouse in the background.

Further down the road are the railway station and railway administration buildings, both in quaint Moorish style again. The delightful part about all these buildings is that they are still in use as their builders meant them to be.

HOW TO GET THERE

By Air
Subang Airport, 24km (15 miles) from town, is the gateway to Kuala Lumpur. A total of 23 airlines have flights to this airport, including Air New Zealand, British Air, Qantas and Lufthansa.

The fare by taxi (coupon system) to the town centre (railway station) is M$15.60.

By Rail
From either Singapore or Butterworth the fare by Second Class air conditioned coach to KL is M$28. Taxis are available from the railway station to any part of town.

80 SINGAPORE AND MALAYSIA AT COST

K.L. AND ENVIRONS

By Bus

The main bus terminal in KL is Pudu Raya Terminal on Jalan Pudu. For Kota Bharu and the East Coast, a fleet of buses also arrives and departs from Medan Tuanku on Jalan Tuanku Abdul Rahman. The fares quoted here are for air conditioned buses. The fare for non-air conditioned buses is slightly lower —

Singapore/Kuala Lumpur — M$17
Butterworth/Kuala Lumpur — M$15.50
Kota Bharu/Kuala Lumpur — M$25.

By Out-Station Taxi
Kuala Lumpur is also accessible by out-station taxis from Johor Bahru and most major towns in Peninsular Malaysia. Enquire at the nearest tourist information office, or your hotel, as to the cost.

TOURIST INFORMATION
Tourist Development Corporation, 25th Floor, Menara Dato Onn, Putra World Trade Centre, Jalan Tun Ismail, 50480 Kuala Lumpur, ph 03-293 5188.
Tourist Information Counter, Level 2, Putra World Trade Centre, Jalan Tun Ismail, 50480 Kuala Lumpur, ph 03-291 4247.
KL Visitors' Centre, 3 Jalan Sultan Hishamuddin, 50050 Kuala Lumpur, ph 03-230 1369.
Open Mon–Fri 8am–4.15pm, Sat 8am–12.45pm. Closed Sunday.

ACCOMMODATION
Kuala Lumpur has a wide range of hotels, including most of the top international chains. Prices quoted here are for a double room, are in Malaysian Dollars, and of course are subject to change. The Telephone Area Code is 03.

International Standard
Federal Hotel, 35 Jalan Bukit Bintang, ph 248 9166 — $125; Holiday Inn on the Park, Jalan Pinang, ph 248 1066 — $120; Hotel Equatorial, Jalan Sultan Ismail, ph 261 2022 — $145; Hotel Grand Continental, Jalan Belia/Jalan Raja Laut, ph 292 26144 — $110; Kuala Lumpur Hilton, Jalan Sultan Ismail, ph 242 2122 — $160; Merlin Hotel, Jalan Sultan Ismail, ph 248 0033 — $133; Ming Court Kuala Lumpur, Jalan Ampang, ph 261 8888 — $160; Pan Pacific KL, Jalan Putra, ph 442 5555 — $150; Prince Hotel, Jalan Imbi, ph 243 8388 — $145; Shangri-La Hotel, 11, Jalan Sultan Ismail, ph 232 2388 — $160; The Regent of Kuala Lumpur, Jalan Imbi, ph 242 5588 — $160.

SINGAPORE AND MALAYSIA AT COST

Good Tourist
Apollo Hotel, 106-110 Jalan Bukit Bintang, ph 242 8133 — $59; Fortuna Hotel, 87, Jalan Berangan, ph 241 9111 — $95; Furama Hotel, Kompleks Selangor, Jalan Sultan, ph 230 1777 — $60; Grand Central, Jalan Putra, ph 292 3011 — $91; Grand Pacific Hotel, Jalan Tun Ismail/Jalan Ipoh, ph 298 2177 — $70; Holiday Inn City Centre, Jalan Raja Laut, ph 293 9233 — $95; Hotel Emerald, 166 Jalan Pudu, off Jalan Bukit Bintang, ph 242 9233; Hotel Imperial, 76-80 Jalan Hicks, ph 242 2377; Hotel Malaya, Jalan Hang Lekir, ph 232 7722 — $79; KL International, Jalan Raja Muda, ph 292 9133 — $72; KL Mandarin, 2-8 Jalan Sultan, ph 230 3000 — $78; Malaysia Hotel, 67-71 Jalan Bukit Bintang, ph 242 8033; Mirama Hotel, Jalan Maharajalela, ph 248 9122 — $88; PuduRaya Hotel, 4th Floor, PuduRaya Station, Jalan Pudu, ph 232 1000 — $55; South East Asia Hotel, 69, Jalan Haji Hussein, Off Jalan Tuanku Abdul Rahman, ph 292 6077 — $76; Sungai Wang Hotel, 74-76 Jalan Bukit Bintang, ph 248 5255 — $84; The Lodge, Jalan Sultan Ismail, ph 242 0122 — $88; The Plaza Hotel, Jalan Raja Laut, ph 298 2255 — $82.

Budget
City Hotel, 366, Jalan Raja Laut, ph 292 4466 — $38; Dashrun Hotel, 285, Jalan Tuanku Abdul Rahman, ph 292 9314 — $45; KL Station Hotel, Bangunan Stesen Keretapi, Jalan Sultan Hishamuddin, ph 274 7433 — $30; Palace Hotel, 46-1 Jalan Masjid India, ph 298 6122 — $39; Shiraz Hotel, 1 & 3, Jalan Medan Tuanku, ph 292 0159 — $35; Wisma Belia, 40, Jalan Syed Putra, ph 274 4833 — $20.

YMCA of Kuala Lumpur, Jalan Brickfield, ph 274 1439 — $10.

LOCAL TRANSPORT
Kuala Lumpur has an efficient network of taxi and bus services enabling visitors to get around the city quickly and conveniently.

Taxis
Taxis can be hired either from taxi stands or hailed by the roadside. If a request for taxi is made by phone, the fare will be calculated from the taxi stand from where the vehicle has to

come to pick the passenger. All taxis are fitted with fare meters and the rates are as indicated below (correct at time of printing).

By Distance
For the first 1.6km (1 mile) or part thereof — 70 sen (non-air conditioned) $1 (air conditioned).
For every additional 0.8km (0.5 mile) — 30 sen (air conditioned or non-air conditioned).
For each 8 minutes waiting time — 30 sen.

By Time
For the first hour or part thereof — $6 (non-air conditioned) $12 (air conditioned)
For every additional quarter hour — $1.50 (non-air conditioned) $4 (air conditioned).

Extra Charges
Between 12am–6am a 50% surcharge on the rates is applicable.
A charge of an additional 10 sen for each passenger in excess of two is applicable for the entire journey.
A charge of 10 sen per piece of luggage except hand luggage is applicable for the entire journey.

Fares for outstation taxis are usually calculated by the distance. Generally, taxi drivers understand English. It is advisable to inform the driver of your destination before boarding the vehicle, and to ensure that the fare meter is working.

Passengers who require taxi services from Kuala Lumpur International Airport to any destinations within the city or the suburbs have to purchase taxi coupons in advance from the booth located at the airport concourse, and use the coupons for their trips instead of paying cash. The price of the coupons varies according to destination. The coupons should be given to the taxi driver only at the end of the journey.

Bus
Bus fares are calculated at the rate of 20c for the first km and 5c for each additional 2km. When travelling by bus, particularly in peak hours, it is advisable to have loose change ready or the exact fare if you know it.

The city's bus service is supplemented by mini buses. All mini buses plying round the city charge a standard fare of 50c to any destination within their routes.

The bus service to the airport operates from 6am daily and runs every hour. Board S.J. Kenderaan bus No. 47 at Jalan Sultan Mohammad. The fare to the terminal is $1.20, and the travelling time is 45 minutes.

Car Rental

A number of car rental services are available in Kuala Lumpur. Most of them have their offices in the leading hotels of the city. The following are the leading hire and drive car agencies —
Mayflower-Acme Tours, Angkasa Raya Buildings, 123, Jalan Ampang, ph 248 6739.
Avis Rent-A-Car, 40, Jalan Sultan Ismail, ph 274 3057, 241 0561.
Sintat Rent-A-Car, Holiday Inn, Jalan Pinang, ph 274 3028.
National Rent-A-Car, 78, Jalan Ampang, ph 248 9188.
Express Rent-A-Car, G-02, Wisma Stephens, Jalan Raja Chulan, ph 242 3682.
Hertz Rent-A-Car, 52, Jalan Ampang, ph 232 9125.
Toyota Rent-A-Car, Lot 5, Ground Floor, Federal Hotel, Jalan Bukit Bintang, ph 438 8387, 438 142, 438 273.
SMAS Rent-A-Car, Ground Floor, Pernas Building, Jalan Raja Laut, ph 293 6233.
Budget Rent-A-Car, Wisma MCA, 163, Jalan Ampang, ph 261 1122.

EATING OUT

There is no shortage of good food and service in Kuala Lumpur. There are wayside stalls and restaurants serving a variety of Malay, Chinese, Indian and Western food.

Eating in the open air is a distinctive Malaysian experience. A number of car parking areas are turned into colourful eating areas at night. If you are interested in visiting a typical open air food stall, you will find a large concentration of stalls at Jalan Brickfields, Jalan Bukit Bintang, Jalan Imbi, off Jalan Raja, Jalan Kampung Baru, and on the top floor of Central Market.

For those who prefer to dine in comfort there are a number of air-conditioned restaurants that serve local and western food.

Some of the restaurants even have Malaysian cultural shows to entertain their dinner guests.

Most of the international hotels in the city also have restaurants, and some of them serve Japanese, European or Chinese cuisine.

Following are some recommended restaurants.

Malay
Sri Yazmin Restaurant, 6, Jalan Kia Peng, ph 241 5655; Warong Rasa Sayang, Jalan Raja Muda Musa, ph 292 3009; Sate Ria, 9, Jalan Tuanku Abdul Rahman, ph 291 1648; Kampung Restoran, Jalan Tun Perak, ph 243 7113; Satay Anika, Bukit Bintang Plaza, Jalan Bukit Bintang, ph 248 3113; Rasa Ultara, Bukit Bintang Plaza, Jalan Bukit Bintang, ph 243 8324.

Indian and Pakistani
Bilal Restaurant, 33, Jalan Ampang, ph 232 0804; Simla Restaurant, 95, Jalan Ampang, ph 232 8539; Shiraz, Medan Tuanku Abdul Rahman, ph 291 0035; Bangles Restaurant, 60-C, Jalan Tuanku Abdul Rahman, ph 298 3780.

Chinese
Marco Polo Restaurant, 1st Floor, Wisma Lim Foo Yong, Jalan Raja Chulan, ph 242 5595; Regent Court, Jalan Sultan Ismail, ph 242 232; The Pines, 297, Jalan Brickfields, ph 274 1194; Rasa Sayang Seafood, Jalan Imbi, ph 243 9890; Shang Palace, Shangri-La Hotel, Jalan Sultan Ismail, ph 232 2388.

Western and Local
The Ship, 40/1, Jalan Sultan Ismail, ph 241 8805; L'Espresso, G22, 23 & 24, Wisma Stephens, Jalan Raja Chulan, ph 241 4669; Decanter, No. 7, Jalan Setiakasih Lima, Damansara Height, ph 255 2507; Esquire Kitchen, Sungel Wang Plaza, Jalan Sultan Ismail, ph 248 4506; Le Coq D'Or, 121, Jalan Ampang, ph 242 9732; Fima Rantel (Malaysian) Sdn. Bhd., Jalan Damansara, Kawasan Museum, ph 274 7951; Bullock Cart Restaurant, Pub & Lounge, 53, Jalan Hicks, ph 242 9129; Castell Sdn. Bhd., (Pub of Grill) 81, Jalan Bukit Bintang, ph 242 8328; Suasa Brasserie, The Regent of Kuala Lumpur, Jalan Sultan Ismail, ph 242 5588.

Siamese
Sri Chiengmai, 14, Jalan Perak, ph 248 2927; Seri Pattaya, 93, Jalan Maharajalela, ph 242 3901; Restaurant Sri Thai, Wisma Selangor, Jalan University, Petaling Jaya, ph 756 3535.

Taiwanese
Goldleaf Lontong, 44, Jalan Bukit Bintang, ph 248 0803.

Korean
Arirang, 144-146, Jalan Bukit Bintang; Koryo-Won, Komplek Antarabangsa, Jalan Sultan Ismail, ph 242 7655.

Japanese
Edogin Japanese Restaurant (M) Sdn. Bhd, 207A, Jalan Tun Razak, ph 241 0807.

ENTERTAINMENT

When the sun sets Kuala Lumpur comes alive with entertainment as the nightclubs, discos and cabarets open for business. There is an abundance of places of entertainment to suit varied tastes.

Cinemas
Cinemas are open daily, the first show normally starting at about 1pm, with the last show at 9.15pm. There is usually a midnight show on Saturdays. Tickets range from M$2 to M$3 per show.

Nightclubs and Cabarets
Kira's Nite Club, Bangunan Angkasaraya, ph 242 0556.
Paddock, Kuala Lumpur Hilton, Jalan Sultan Ismail, ph 242 2222.
Pertama Cabaret, Pertama Complex, Jalan Tuanku Abdul Rahman, ph 298 2533.
Shangri-La Night Club, Bangunan Hentian Puduraya, ph 232 1174.
Sky Swan Nightclub, 22, Jalan Tong Shin, ph 242 0233.
Campbell Nightclub and Music Hall, Jalan Campbell, ph 292 9655.
Toppan Club, Wisma Stephens, Jalan Raja Chulan, ph 248 9304.

Discos
Tin Mine, Kuala Lumpur Hilton, Jalan Sultan Ismail, ph 242 2222.
Pink Coconut, Hotel Malaya, Jalan Hang Lekir, ph 238 7655.

Federal Club, Federal Hotel, Jalan Bukit Bintang, ph 248 9166.
Pyramid Club, 3rd Floor, Wilayah Shopping Complex, Jalan Munshi Abdullah, ph 292 3092.
Sapphire, Plaza Yow Chuan, Jalan Tun Abdul Razak, ph 243 0043.
Starship Disco, Wisma Central, Jalan Ampang, ph 242 7581.
High Voltage, Massdisco LB29, Lower Basement 2, Sungai Wang Plaza, ph 242 1220.

SHOPPING
There are a number of interesting shopping areas in KL where a wide range of goods, including local handicraft, are available.

Pasar Minggu (Sunday Market)
Literally meaning Sunday Market, the Pasar Minggu located in the heart of Kampung Baru is where you can shop at leisure. The open air bazaar occupies an area where, particularly on Saturday evenings, a concentration of shops and stalls sell a variety of local foodstuffs and handicraft. If you happen to be in KL during weekdays you can still visit the Pasar Minggu to shop for souvenirs as some of the shops are open for business.

Aked Ibu Kota
Located in the busy shopping centre of Jalan Tuanku Abdul Rahman, the arcade houses a variety of goods to cater for the needs of visitors. Local handicrafts such as woodcarving, coppertooling, batik and songket are available here. The arcade opens for business daily, 9am–6pm, except Sundays and public holidays.

Chinatown
One of the busiest and most colourful parts of the city is Chinatown in Petaling Street. With open markets selling textiles, herbs, household goods, fruit, flowers, cakes and vegetables, it is a major attraction for the local population. Some stalls are open during the day but around dusk, the daytime streets are transformed into a brightly-lit night-time bazaar.

CITY CENTRE

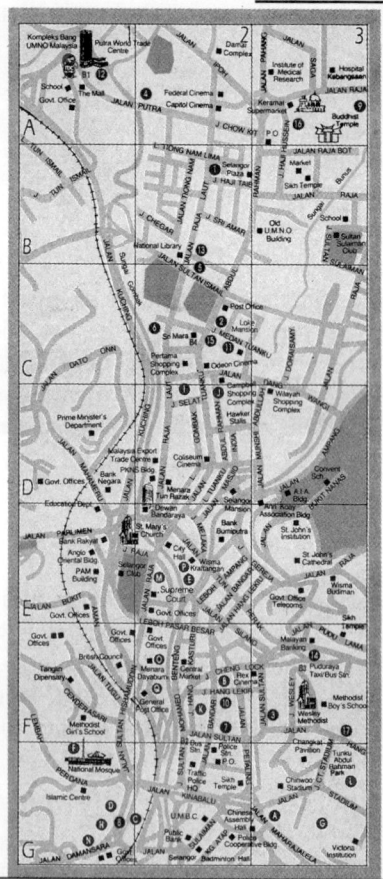

● PLACES OF INTEREST

A. CHAN SEE SHU YUEN TEMPLE G3
B. CHINATOWN F2
C. KUALA LUMPUR RAILWAY STATION G2
D. MALAYAN RAILWAY ADMINISTRATION HQ G1
E. MASJID JAME' E2
F. MASJID NEGARA G1
G. MERDEKA STADIUM G3
H. NATIONAL ART GALLERY G1
I. PASAR TANI (FARMERS' MARKET) D2
J. SELANGOR PEWTER SHOWROOM D2
K. SRI MAHAMARIAMMAN TEMPLE, F2
L. STADIUM NEGARA G3
M. SULTAN ABDUL SAMAD BUILDING. E2
N. K.L. VISITORS CENTRE/ K.L.T.A. OFFICE G1
O. INFOKRAF MALAYSIA F2
P. WISMA KRAFTANGAN/BATIK M'SIA BHD. E2
Q. DAYABUMI COMPLEX F2

BUS-STATIONS

B1. HENTIAN BAS PUTRA (OPPOSITE PWTC) A1
B2. KLANG BUS STAND F2
B3. PUDU RAYA BUS STATION F3
B4. MEDAN MARA BUS STATION C2

● HOTELS

1. CITY HOTEL B2
2. DASHRUN HOTEL C2
3. FURAMA HOTEL F3
4. GRAND CENTRAL HOTEL A2
5. GRAND CONTINENTAL HOTEL C2
6. HOLIDAY INN CITY CENTRE C2
7. K.L. MANDARIN HOTEL F2
8. K.L. STATION HOTEL G1
9. K.L. INTERNATIONAL HOTEL A3
10. MALAYA HOTEL F2
11. OMAR KHAYAM HOTEL C2
12. PAN PACIFIC HOTEL A1
13. PLAZA HOTEL B2
14. PUDU RAYA HOTEL F3
15. SHIRAZ HOTEL C2
16. SOUTH EAST ASIA HOTEL A3
17. YWCA F3

SIGHTSEEING

Sightseeing around Kuala Lumpur is facilitated by the fact that a large number of interesting places are concentrated within the city centre. You can set forth armed with a map, camera, comfortable walking shoes and light clothing, or you may opt for one of the city tours available which introduces you to the varied attractions of the city in air-conditioned comfort.

To assist in your sightseeing, the city's attractions have been grouped here in convenient clusters. Almost a dozen points of interest lie along a roughly circular route in the heart of the city, easily accessible from several major hotels. If you have difficulty in finding your way around, do ask for help — you will find Malaysians, even in this bustling city, friendly and eager to show you the way.

Lake Gardens

Undulating green parkland, within KL's "Green Belt". The Gardens and lake, Tasek Perdana, are among the city's most popular spots for picnics, evening strolls and weekend relaxation. Recreational facilities for boating on the lake are available. Boats may be rented at M$4 per hour. Open School Holidays 10.30am–5.30pm, Sat, Sun and Public Holidays 8am–5.30pm.

National Monument

Located in the Lake Gardens, this is a great sculpture in bronze designed by the creator of the famed Iwo Jima Memorial in Washington. It was constructed in 1966 to commemorate Malaysia's national heroes. The entire structure stands surrounded by a moat of clear water with fountains and ornamental pewter waterlilies.

Parliament House

Stands on elevated grounds in the Lake Gardens commanding an excellent view of the surrounding lawns and gardens. An 18-storey office tower dominates the Complex which includes a low three-storey building containing the House of Representatives, the Senate, various offices, a library, a Banquet Hall and committee rooms. When Parliament is in session visitors may enter Parliament House with prior arrangement with the authorities.

Visitors are required to wear formal national dress of Malaysia or lounge suit; western dress for ladies is acceptable as long as the hemline stays below the knee.

National Museum
A magnificent building based on old Malay style architecture. Two immense murals in Italian glass mosaic, each 35 metres in length and 5 metres high, flank the main entrance, depicting historical episodes and the main cultural activities in the country. Displays within the Museum relate to Malaysian history, arts and crafts, weapons, currency, Malaysian birds and mammals, entomological specimens and Malaysia's major economic activities — rubber industry and tin mining, among others. Open daily 9am–6pm, closed Fridays 12.15pm–2.45pm. Admission is free.

Kuala Lumpur Railway Station
Designed and built at the turn of the 20th Century to replace the original station in existence from 1885. The basic design, beneath the Islamic influenced exterior, resembles the large glass and iron train sheds constructed in England toward the close of the 19th Century. The imposing building opposite the railway station is the Malayan Railway Administration Headquarters.

Masjid Negara (National Mosque)
Malaysia's national mosque is the centre of Islamic activities in the country. The architecture exemplifies a contemporary expression of traditional Muslim decorative art, utilising the traditional abstract, geometric patterns in its grillwork while bands of Koranic verse decorate the Grand Hall. The entire complex occupies a 5.2 hectare site and comprises the Grand Hall, a 73m minaret, a meeting hall, library, offices, ceremonial rooms and a mausoleum. Visitors are required to remove their shoes when entering the Mosque. Ladies must be decently attired. Visiting hours: Sat to Thurs 9am–6pm, Fri 2.45pm–6pm, Muslim visitors 6.30am–10pm.

Sultan Abdul Samad Building
This was formerly known as the State Secretariat and is often portrayed as a distinctive KL landmark. Built in 1894–97, its

curving arches, domes and 41m clocktower make it one of the capital's most frequently photographed buildings. The Judicial Department and High Courts are housed here.

Masjid Jame
Situated at the confluence of the Klang and Gombak rivers, a historic site, and the location where Kuala Lumpur first began as the landing point for boats coming upriver to bring supplies for, and take tin away from, the Ampang mines. The mosque nestles within a grove of coconut palms with its two main minarets rising to the height of the palms. Numerous smaller towers add to the decorative effect, while the prayer hall is surmounted by three domes and opens out on to a walled courtyard known as a "Sahn".

Memorial to Tun Abdul Razak
Located on the fringe of the Lake Gardens, 1.5km from the Railway Station and National Mosque, is Seri Taman, the official residence of the late Tun Abdul Razak, the second Prime Minister of Malaysia who was also popularly known as "The Father of Development". In recognition of his services to the country, Seri Taman has been turned into a memorial, with the aim of preserving materials such as records, documents, speeches, books, audio-visual materials, gifts, awards and memorabilia belonging to or related to him throughout his lifetime. Open Tues-Sun (closed Fri 12 noon–3.00pm). Open Mondays on public holidays and school holidays.

Karyaneka Handicraft Centre
This beautiful building of traditional Malay architecture is located on Jalan Raja Chulan. Inside the items vary widely and among those on display are traditional woven materials and dolls dressed in Malay national dress. Open Tues-Sun 9.30am–6pm, Mon 9.30am–5pm.

National Art Gallery
Housed at the former Hotel Majestic at Jalan Sultan Hishamuddin, it has a permanent collection of fine works by Malayasian artists. Various exhibitions of both local and international artists

are held throughout the year. Open daily 10am–6pm, closed between 12.15pm–2.45pm Fridays. The Gallery is also closed 3 days per year: Hari Raya, Aidil Fitri and Adhar.

Chinatown

Concentrated in one of the city's busiest areas bounded roughly by Jalan Petaling, Jalan Sultan and Jalan Bandar, this is a hive of activity day and night. Wares on sale and display range from textiles, household goods, herbs and ancient remedies, to vegetables, fruits, flowers, cakes, delicacies such as roast duck and birds' nests, and a myriad of other intriguing items. At dusk the mid-section of Jalan Petaling is closed to motor vehicles and the entire area is transformed into an open-air night bazaar (Pasar Malam).

Sri Mahamariamman Temple

This is a Hindu Temple built in 1873. It is one of the largest and most ornate in the country. The elaborate decorative scheme for the temple incorporates gold, precious stones and Spanish and Italian tiles.

International Buddhist Pagoda

This Pagoda reflects the contemporary architectural design of pagodas as portrayed in the Buddhist annals. Buddha images and replicas of pagodas from various countries are enshrined in the octagonal hall at the base of the pagoda. It stands in between a sacred Bodhi tree and a Buddhist Shrine built in 1894 by Sinhala Buddhists. The most impressive antiquity to be seen are the three colossal images on the Buddha.

Chan See Shu Yuen Temple

Built in 1906, this has features typical of a Chinese temple — open courtyards and symmetrically organised pavilions. It serves as the venue for both religious ceremonies and meetings. Paintings and wood carvings provide interior decor while elaborate glazed ceramic sculptures decorate the facade and roof ridges resulting in an extremely ornate over-all effect.

KUALA LUMPUR 93

Merdeka Stadium

Site of one of the most historic events in Malaysia — the Nation's Declaration of Independence in 1957 — hence its name 'Merdeka' meaning independence. Held here are national and international sporting events, as well as the annual National and International Quran Reading Competitions (held during the month of Ramadan). The stadium has a seating capacity of 50,000.

Stadium Negara

An indoor stadium built into a hilly site — an earthen bowl with terraced seats constructed into the sides of the bowl. Its gigantic saucer-shaped roof is one of the largest unsupported roofs in South East Asia. Because of its highly flexible design, the Stadium converts readily from indoor sports stadium to a venue for concerts, exhibitions, conventions and trade fairs.

Istana Negara

The palace, the official residence of His Majesty, The Yang DiPertuan Agong, Malaysia's Supreme Head of State, is surrounded by wide expanses of green lawns. On ceremonial and festive occasions, the fairytale-like palace glitters with lights at night. The Ruler's Conference, various Royal and national ceremonies, investitures and banquets are held here.

Kampung Bharu

Only 10 minutes away from the city centre, Kampung Bharu is noted for its open air night bazaar where an assortment of goods ranging from local handicrafts to a variety of Malaysian food is on sale. The bazaar is also where the variety of Malaysian life can be seen. The bazaar usually comes to life on Saturday evenings, but if you happen to be in KL during weekday evenings, you can still visit the bazaar to shop for souvenirs.

Royal Selangor Golf Club

Located at the junction of Jalan Bukit Bintang and Jalan Tun Razak, about 15 minutes drive from the city centre, the golf club is the oldest club in Malaysia. It is the scene of the annual Malaysian Golf Tournament. An elegent club of international repute, it has three courses, two 18-hole and one 9-hole. Excellent club facilities include pro-shop, tennis courts, squash courts and a swimming pool.

Titiwangsa Lake Gardens
About 18km from the city centre, this recreational park is a popular haunt for relaxation — complete with a man-made lake and children's playground. Here you can jog, picnic, hike or just stroll on green landscaped grounds.

Malaysian Armed Forces Museum
This museum houses pictures, paintings, exhibitions of weapons, uniforms and decorations of all three Services of the Malaysian Armed Forces. Artillery and naval guns, old cannons and vehicles used by the Forces are displayed in and around the Museum building. Open Sat–Thurs, 10am–6pm.

NEGERI SELANGOR DARUL EHSAN

The state of Selangor Darul Ehsan is on the west coast of Peninsular Malaysia and covers 124,450 km^2 (48,037 sq. miles). The capital is Shah Alam. You need a car to move about and see places in Selangor Darul Ehsan. Local buses run from Kuala Lumpur, but can be crowded. The Federal territory of KL is within this state.

Selangor Pewter Factory
Travelling out of Kuala Lumpur along Jalan Pahang you arrive first at the world's biggest pewter factory, still within city limits, which manufactures souvenirs. Malaysian pewter is made of refined tin, antimony and copper. The demonstration showroom is open to visitors from 8.30am to 4.45pm Mon–Sat, 9am–4pm Sun and Public Holidays. You can see how the pewter is worked into beautiful articles and also watch demonstrations of batik making and silverware crafting. Duty-free shopping is available.

Kutang Kraf Batik Factory
Located 15 km (9 miles) off Jalan Damanmsara, in Kampong Sungei Pencala, specialises in exclusive hand-drawn and block-

printed batik. Here skilled craftsmen give a step-by-step demonstration of the batik making process. Lengths of batik are on sale. The factory is open Mon–Fri 9.30am–5pm, Sat 9.30am–4pm. Demonstrations are possible at any time during these hours except during the lunch break, 1–2pm.

National Zoo and Aquarium
Situated 12 km (7 miles) from the city centre, a pleasant 15 minutes' drive. Some 26 ha (64 acres) of shady forestland and a lake provide home to over a thousand different species of Malaysian flora and fauna as well as to a representative collection of species from all over the world — the orang-utan, the gir lion and other rare mammals, birds and reptiles such as the dwarf crocodile. The Aquarium supports 82 species of marine life. Elephant, camel and donkey cart rides as well as boat rides are available. The zoo complex also has a Kentucky Fried Chicken Restaurant. Open daily 9am–5pm. Admission to Zoo and Aquarium: Adults M$3, children M$1, students M$0.50, group concession (on application only and applicable to local Malaysians), camera M$1.

To get there board the Len Chee bus no. 177 or Len Seng bus no. 170 at Jalan Ampang or at any point along this road. Several mini buses also service this area including mini bus no. 17, which can be boarded at Lebuh Ampang.

Mimaland
This 121 ha (298 acres) tourist complex lies 30 minutes' drive (1.8 km — 1 mile) from Kuala Lumpur, on the road leading north-eastwards to Genting Highlands and the state of Pahang. The recreational facilities it offers include swimming, boating and fishing on the lake and jungle trekking. Accommodation in the form of chalets or bagan houses built on stilts on the lake is available. Admission: Adults M$2, children M$1.

Board Len Seng bus no. 174 at Lebuh Ampang. The fare is M$0.10, travel time is 1 hour and buses run every 15 minutes. Or take Mimaland's own direct bus service from ENE Plaza, Jalan Pudu, at regular intervals. The fare is adults M$1, children 50c.

Batu Caves
The northbound road, Jalan Ipoh, takes you to the caves, 13 km (8 miles) from the city centre. They are a massive outcrop of

limestone cliffs, which is mainland Asia's southernmost limestone formation. This is the location of a Hindu shrine, and the destination of an annual pilgrimage by thousands of Hindu devotees during Thaipusam. Access to the caves is by means of 272 steps.

Board Len bus no. 70 at Lebuh Pudu or mini bus no. 11 at the Bangkok Bank. The fare by stage bus is 60c, and buses run every half hour. Travel time is 45 minutes.

Templer Park

Less than 10 km (6 miles) from Batu Caves (22 km from KL) along the same north/south highway lies Templer Park. This is the city dweller's retreat — 1200 ha (2,964 acres) of cool, profusely green parkland with bubbling streams, waterfalls and pools, interlaced with a network of paths which provide access. The Park is home to a large variety of butterflies, flying lizards, several varieties of small animals, birds and insects and monkeys. You can bathe, picnic, explore the interior or just relax.

Board Len bus 66, 78, 83 or 81 at the Puduraya bus terminal. The fare is M$1.20. Travel time is 50 minutes, and the buses run every 15 minutes.

Bukit Takum

Accessible through Templer Park, this massive column of limestone, 350 m (1,145 ft) high, is said to have been formed about 400 million years ago during the Siberian Age. Its botanical wealth includes 204 species of both flowering and non-flowering plants, 17 of them unique to this part of the world, plus several rare orchid species, Just alongside Bukit Takun is Anak Takun, a smaller outcrop riddled with some 366 m (399 yds) of cavernous corridors which are the habitat of several rare cave fauna, and which offer exciting exploration possibilities.

Rubber Plantations

Malaysia is the world's chief producer of natural rubber. In the outskirts of Kuala Lumpur you will frequently see rubber plantations lining the highways. Visits to the plantations to observe the collection and processing of latex can be arranged through local tour operators.

SEREMBAN

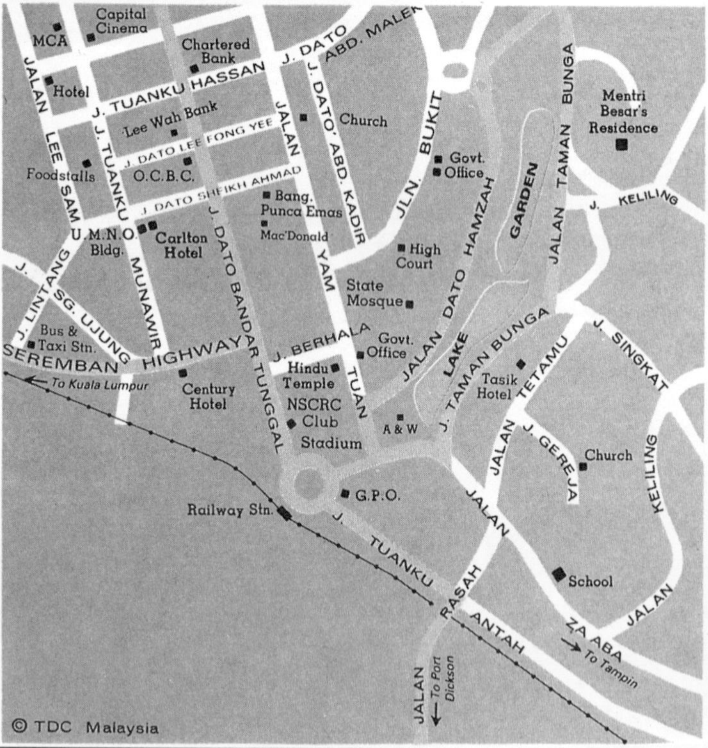

Capital Cinema
MCA
Chartered Bank
J. DATO ABD. MALEK
JALAN LEE SAM
Hotel
J. TUANKU HASSAN
J. TUANKU MUNAWIR
Lee Wah Bank
J. DATO LEE FONG YEE
JALAN YAM TUAN
J. DATO' ABD. KADIR
Church
JLN. BUKIT
Mentri Besar's Residence
Foodstalls
O.C.B.C.
J. DATO SHEIKH AHMAD
Bang. Punca Emas
Mac'Donald
Govt. Office
JALAN DATO HAMZAH
GARDEN
JALAN TAMAN BUNGA
J. KELILING
U.M.N.O. Bldg.
Carlton Hotel
J. DATO BANDAR TUNGGAL
High Court
State Mosque
J. LINTANG
J. SG. UJUNG
Bus & Taxi Stn.
SEREMBAN HIGHWAY
To Kuala Lumpur
J. BERHALA
Govt. Office
LAKE
J. TAMAN BUNGA
J. SINGKAT
Hindu Temple
Century Hotel
NSCRC Club
Stadium
A & W
Tasik Hotel
TETAMU
JALAN J. GEREJA
Church
KELILING
G.P.O.
Railway Stn.
J. TUANKU ANTAH
JALAN RASAH
School
JALAN ZA ABA
To Tampin
JALAN
To Port Dickson
© TDC Malaysia

NEGERI SEMBILAN

Negeri Sembilan in the national language means "nine states" — as the state comprises a loose federation of nine states. With a total area of 6,645 km^2 (2,565 sq. miles) and a 43 km (27 miles) long coastline, this small but pretty state is renowned for its Minangkabau-styled architecture characterised by sweeping buffalo-horn shaped roof peaks, reflecting the influence of the state's first inhabitants who came from Minangkabau in Sumatra. It also boasts of attractive beach resorts, historical sights and recreational areas.

The State is the only one in the country that practises a matrilineal (through the female line) social system (Adat Perpatih).

Negeri Sembilan today is headed by the Yang Di Pertuan Besar who exercises legislative powers on the advice of the Executive Council headed by the Menteri Besar (Chief Minister).

Official business is conducted in Bahasa Malaysia, the national language. English, however, is widely spoken.

SEREMBAN

Seremban, the state capital, is 64 km (40 miles) south of Malaysia's capital city of Kuala Lumpur.

HOW TO GET THERE
The city is accessible by road and rail, and is 1.5 hours from the international airport at Subang (Kuala Lumpur).

TOURIST INFORMATION
State Economic Development Corporation Negeri Sembilan, Jalan Yam Tuan, 70000 Seremban, ph 06-723251.
State Economic Planning Unit, 5th Floor, Block D, State Secretariat Complex, 70503 Seremban, ph 06-722314

ACCOMMODATION
Accommodation is available in the town or by the beaches. The higher-priced rooms usually offer better facilities such as air-

conditioning, hot and cold water, telephone and television. The bigger hotels and resorts also offer bars, restaurants and sea sports facilities. There are enough hotels for you to choose to suit your budget.

Prices we have quoted are in Malaysian Dollars, and apply to a double room. The Telephone Area Code is 06.

International
Ming Court Beach Hotel, 11 Km Jalan Pantai, Port Dickson, ph 405244 — $140; Pantai Dickson Resort, Batu 12, Jalan Pantai, Port Dickson, ph 405473 — $180; Si Rusa Inn Hotel, Batu 7 Jalan Pantai, Port Dickson, ph 405244 — $120.

Good Tourist
Hotel Tasik, Sdn. Bhd., Jalan Tetamu, ph 730 994/5 — $80.

Budget
Carlton Hotel, 47 Jalan Tuan Sheikh, ph 725 336 — $20; International New Hotel, 126 Jalan Veloo, ph 714 957 — $14; Lido Hotel, 8th Mile, Teluk Kemang, ph 405 273 — $22; Milo Hotel, 22–24 Wilkinson St., Port Dickson, ph 723 451; Pantai Motel, 9th Mile, Port Dickson, ph 405 473 — $20; Rest House Bahau, Jalan Taman Bunga, Jempul Bahau, ph 843 322 — $35; Sea View Hotel, 841, Batu 1, Jalan Pantai, ph 471 818 — $25.

LOCAL TRANSPORT

Seremban has a good taxi and bus service to take you around town, as well as to other interesting sightseeing spots within the vicinity. There is also an efficient transport system for inter-state travel from Negeri Sembilan to other states in the country, and inter-district travel from one district to another in Negeri Sembilan.

Taxi
There is a station at Jalan Sungai Ujong for both local and outstation journeys. Taxi fares are as follows:

To Tampin	M$4.00 per person
To Port Dickson	M$2.50
To Kuala Lumpur	M$6.00

NEGERI SEMBILAN 101

To Melaka	M$7.00
To Gemas	M$7.00
To Bahau, Jempol	M$5.00
To Kuala Pilah	M$3.00
To K.Klawang, Jelebu	M$3.00
To Rembau	M$2.00

Bus
The station for local and outstation buses is at Jalan Sungai Ujong. Fares are as follows:

To Tampin/Rembau
Southern Ltd   M$2.35/1.40
                            Every 30 mins service
Mara Express   M$3.00

To Kuala Pilah/Bahau
United Bus   M$2.00/3.00
                            Every 30 mins service

To Port Dickson
Restu Bus Express   M$1.30
                            Every 2 hours service
Bus Utam-Singh   M$1.50
                            Every 30 mins service

To K.Klawang, Jelebu
Lim Omnibus   M$1.80
                            Every 30 mins service

To Petaling Jaya/Klang
Cekap Express   M$2.60
                            Every 20 mins service
Syarikat Bus SKS   M$2.40 (non-aircon)
                            Every 10 mins service
                            M$2.90 (aircon)
                            Every 10 mins service

To Johor Bahru
MARA Express   M$15.20 (aircon)
                           12 noon daily

To Kota Bharu/K.Terengganu
Bumi Express   M$26.00/20.00 (aircon)
                           M$22.00/16.50 (non-aircon)

To Melaka
MARA Labu Sendayan   M$2.85
                           Every 30 mins service

Train
Malayan Railway trains have a stop in the centre of Seremban, Rembau, Tampin, Gemas and Bahau.

Express to Singapore	M$25.00 (aircon)
	M$22.00 (non-aircon)
Concession to Kuala Lumpur	M$4.00 (aircon)

EATING OUT

Negeri Sembilan usually prepares its food heavily chillied and spiced, following the tradition of its early inhabitants from Minangkabau. Of the variety and range, the dishes Masak Lemak Cili Api and Rendang Minang are widely popular. Lemang (glutinous rice cooked in bamboo) is tasty by itself, but more often eaten with "rendang" — a dry curried meat dish.

There are plenty of restaurants in Seremban, and the major hotels serve Western cuisine, Malay Food, Chinese Food and Indian Food to suit a variety of tastes. Here are some examples;

Malay
Flamingo Inn, 1A Jalan Zaaba; Bilal Restaurant, 100 Jalan Dato' Bandar Tunggai; Fatimah Restaurant, 419 Jalan Tuanku Munawir; Jempol Restaurant, Kompleks Negeri; Anira Restaurant, Kompleks Negeri.

Chinese
Sunton Restaurant, 10/11 Jalan Dato' Sheikh Ahmad; Regent Restaurant, 2391–2392 Taman Bukit Labu; Seafood Restaurant,

2017–2018 Blossom Heights, Jalan Tok Ungku; Happy Restaurant, 1 Jalan Dato' Bandar Tunggal.

Indian
Samy Restaurant (bana leaf), 120 Jalan Yam Tuan; Anura Restaurant, 97 Jalan Tuanku Antah.

ENTERTAINMENT
For evening entertainment in Seremban there are a few pubs along Jalan Dato' Bandar Tunggai, Jalan Tuanku Munawir, and a nightclub at Jalan Dato' Abdul Rahman.

SHOPPING
The most popular shopping area is in Jalan Dato' Bandar Tunggal, where you can buy anything from clothes to electrical goods.

SIGHTSEEING

Lake Gardens
Situated in the heart of Seremban there are two lakes surrounded by tropical fauna and flora. A floating stage is the venue for cultural performances held during the weekends. A landscaped garden adds to the attraction.

State Mosque
This modern building, built with nine pillars to symbolise the nine districts of Negeri Sembilan, is situated by the Lake Gardens.

State Executive Council Building
Built in colonial style, it now houses the State Library, and is also quite near the Lake Gardens.

Taman Seni Budaya (Handicraft Complex)
This complex is on a 4ha site at the junction of Jalan Sungai Ujong and the Kuala Lumpur-Seremban expressway, about 1 km from the heart of Seremban. Built in the style of Minangkabau houses of old, local handicraft products of the State are sold here, and visitors also get a chance to see them being made.

Museum
Situated within the Taman Seni Budaya Complex is an actual old Minangkabau wooden house. Old historical artifacts of the State are housed here. Alongside this is another wooden house called Rumah Minang. Part of an old palace, this house was originally built without nails, and has been reassembled similarly here.

OUTLYING ATTRACTIONS

Padas Hot Spring
Located to the south of Seremban on the way to Malacca, the warm waters of the spring are a popular attraction with locals and tourists alike. Refreshment and bathing facilities are available for visitors. Bus service: Southern Omnibus Co. Seremban/Tampin.

Ulu Bendol
This forest reserve about 18 km (11 miles) east of Seremban on the way to Kuala Pilahj, is a great picnic spot. A tropical reserve area, it is surrounded by foliage with a waterfall and lake. Bus service: United Bus Company — Seremban/Kuala Pilah.

Port Dickson
Situated about 32 km (20 miles) west of Seremban, Port Dickson is one of the best known seaside resorts, and probably the favourite playground for Malaysians during holidays and weekends. This scenic resort boasts of superb beaches and crystal-clear water as well as a variety of hotels and holiday bungalows nestled under tall casuarina and banyan trees.

Popular sea sports are windsurfing and water-skiing and necessary gear for these and deep-sea diving is available. Visitors may also become temporary members of the Port Dickson Club, where various tourist amenities are available.

Pengkalan Kempas, Port Dickson
This is a historical site about 35 km (22 miles) from Port Dickson town. An old grave — Keramat Sungai Ujong — marks the last resting place of one of the state's leading historical figures, Ulama Sheikh Ahmad Majnun. Arabic writings found on the megalithic stones behind the grave tell the story of his struggles.

Forest Reserve, 5th km, Jalan Pantai, Lenggeng
About 16 km (10 miles) north of Seremban is a pretty, secluded area where you can picnic by a stream, or trek along the many jungle tracks into the Malaysian forest.

Sri Menanti
It is the state's royal town, and is east of Seremban. The Sri Menanti palace was first built in 1902, and completed 3 years later. Made entirely of wood, the palace's main attractions include beautiful intricate carvings bearing varied local motifs. The palace ceased to be the royal residence in 1931, due to the construction of a new modern palace nearby.

MELAKA (MALACCA)

Melaka is situated on the Western Coast of Peninsular Malaysia facing the Straits of Malacca, about 147 km (91 miles) from Kuala Lumpur and 245 km (152 miles) from Singapore. Melaka is sandwiched between the states of Negeri Sembilan and Johor, and covers an area of 658 km^2 (254 sq. miles). It is divided into three districts — Alor Gajah, Melaka Tengah and Jasin.

HISTORY

581 years ago, a refugee prince called Parameswara sought sanctuary in a fishing village and decreed that a city be built where he stood. He named it Melaka from the Melaka tree. The city became a prosperous and powerful nerve centre of trade between the East and West, and eventually became an empire. It was here that gold, silk, tea, opium, tobacco, perfumes and countless other items from nearby countries and from as far away as Europe and South America changed ships.

Fame of course attracted conquerors who coveted monopoly of the spice trade, and the Portuguese, the Dutch and the English, at different times, took control of the empire until Malaysia obtained her independence in 1957 and Melaka was handed over to its first local Governor.

Each conquering nation left its mark on the city, and today every street tells its own story of conquest and valour, avarice and victory.

HOW TO GET THERE

By Express Bus

Melaka-Kuala Lumpur (ph 06-222503)	— M$ 6.50 Aircon 5.50 non Aircon
Melaka-Seremban (ph 06-220687)	— M$ 3.40 Aircon 2.85 non Aircon
Melaka-Port Dickson-Klang (ph 06-249937)	— M$ 3.20 (PD) 6.00 (Banting) 7.45 (Klang)

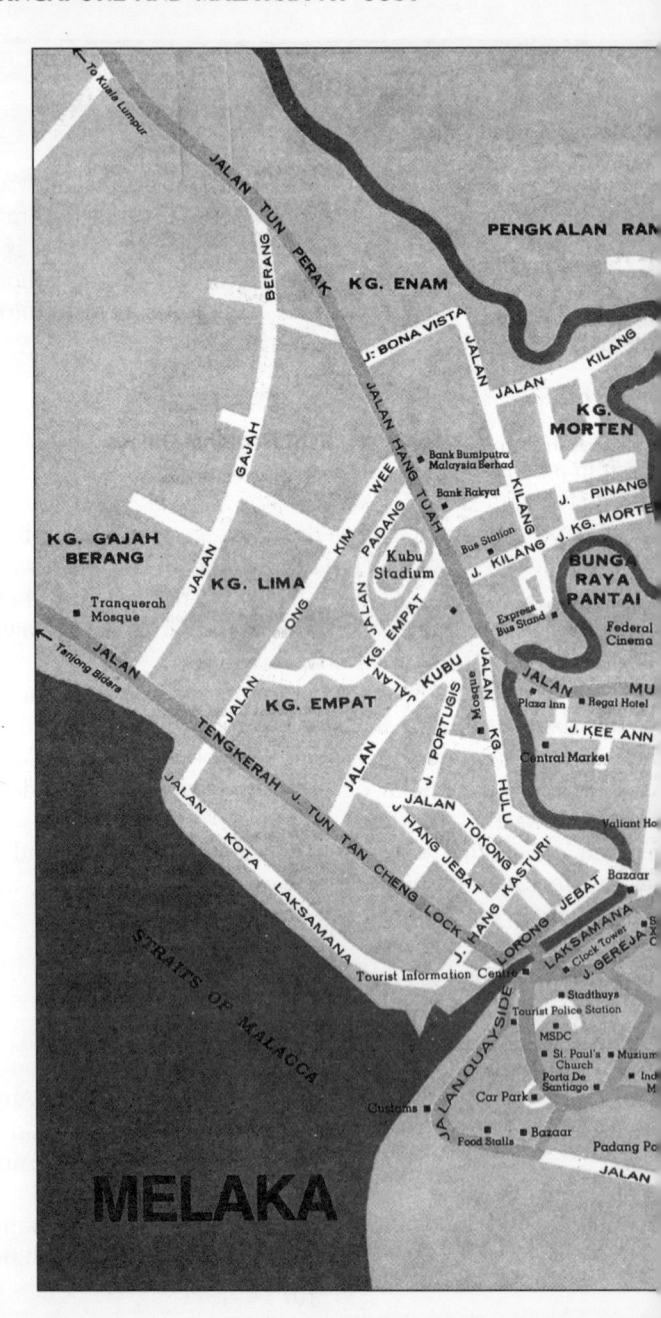

108 SINGAPORE AND MALAYSIA AT COST

MELAKA 109

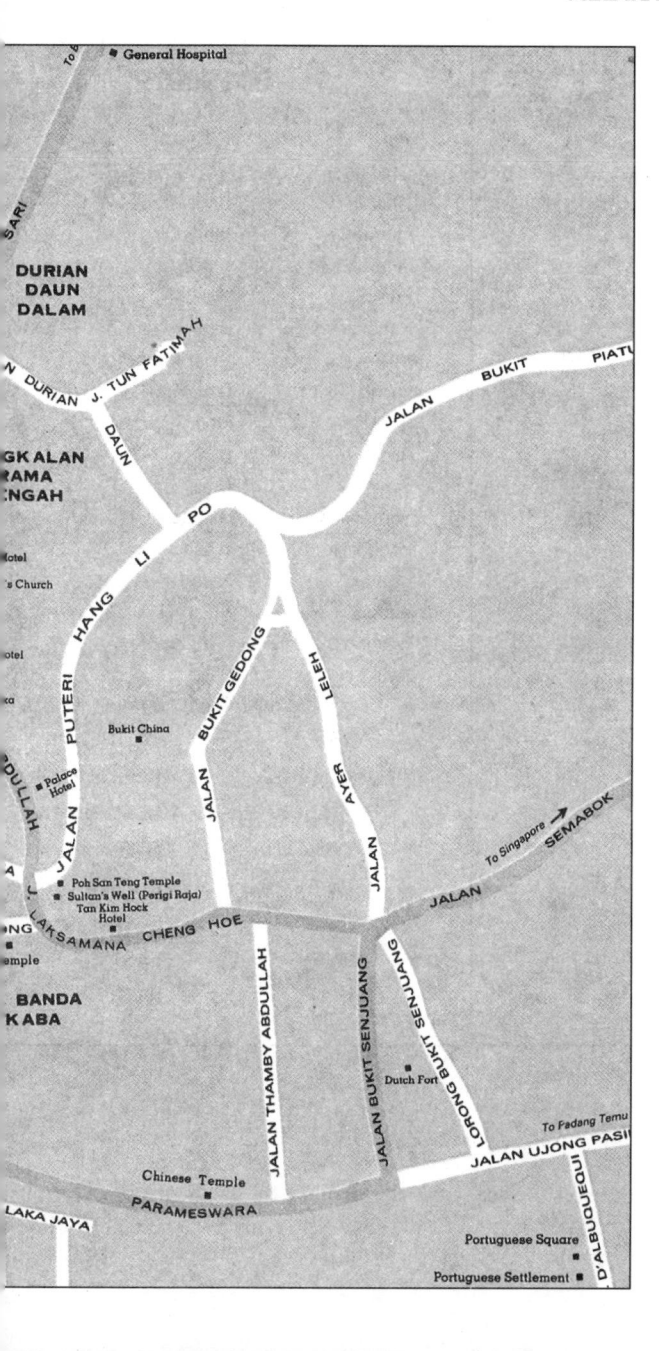

Melaka-Ipoh-Butterworth (ph 06-220687)	— M$13.00 (Ipoh) Air[con]
	17.50 (Taiping)
	21.40 (B/worth)
Melaka-Kuala Terengganu-Kota Bahru (ph 06-248959)	— M$19.00 (KT)
	23.00 Aircon
	— 25.00 (KB)
	29.00 Aircon
Melaka-Ipoh-Lumut (ph 06-249126)	— M$14.50 (Ipoh) Air[con]
	18.50 (Lumut)
Melaka-Kuantan-Temerioh (ph 06-249126)	— M$11.00 (Kuantan)
	5.00 (Segamat)
Tanjong Keramat Express (ph 06-220687)	— M$10.95 (Kuantan)
	13.00 Aircon
	6.50 (Temerioh)
	7.80 Aircon
	3.40 (Bahau)
	4.00 Aircon
Melaka-Johor Bahru-Singapore (ph 06-224470)	— M$ 8.00 (JB)
	10.00 Aircon
	8.50 (Singapore)
	11.00 Aircon
Melaka-Tampin (ph 06-229956)	— M$ 1.60
	2.10 Aircon
Melaka-Muar (ph 06-229956)	— M$ 1.80
	2.30 Aircon
Tampin-Muar (ph 06-229956)	— M$ 3.30
	3.80 Aircon

By Outstation Taxi
From Kuala Lumpur — M$16.00

By Rail
Melaka doesn't have a train station, but the nearest is at Tampin, which is only 38 km (23 miles) north. You are advised to check with the railway offices for schedules and fares — Melaka Rail-

way Office, ph 06-223 091; Tampin Railway Station, ph 06-411 034.

By Ferry
The ferry leaves Dumai, Sumatra on Saturdays at 10am and arrives at Melaka harbour at 2pm. The return journey leaves Melaka on Thursdays at 10am, arriving Dumai at 2pm. Reservations can be made through Madai Shipping Sdn. Bhd., 320 Jalan Kilang, ph 06-240 671.

By Air
Melaka has a small airport which can cater for small aircraft. It is situated at Batu Berendam which is 9.5 km (6 miles) from town. At the present moment there is a weekly flight service every Friday between Melaka and Pekan Baru, Sumatra, Indonesia — Fare M$145 one way, M$290 return. Enquiries should be directed to Malacca Oriental Travel, ph 06-224 877; Atlas Travel, ph 06-220 777; or Pelancongan Kota Melaka, ph 06-247 728.

TOURIST INFORMATION
Melaka Tourist Information Centre, Jalan Kota, ph 06-236 538.
Melaka Tourist Association, 37A Jalan Parameswara, ph 06-221 101.

ACCOMMODATION
Listed below is a sample of the accommodation available. The prices are in Malaysian Dollars, and represent the cost for a double room. The Telephone Area Code is 06.

International
Malacca Village Resort, Ayer Keroh, ph 323 600 — $140; Merlin Inn, Jalan Munshi Abdullah, ph 240 777 — $85; Plaza Inn, Jalan Munshi Abdullah, ph 240 888 — $100; Ramada Renaissance, Jalan Bendahara, ph 248 888 — $95; The City Bayview Hotel, Jalan Bendahara, ph 239 888 — $80.

Good Tourist
Admiral Hotel, Jalan Mata Kucing, ph 226 822 — $50; Hotel Midtown Melaka, 20 Jalan Tun Sri Lanang, ph 240 088 — $68;

Shah's Beach Motel, 6 Mile Tg. Kling, ph 226 202 — $50; Tg. Bidara Beach Resort, Tg. Bidara, ph 531 201 — $70; Tan Kim Hock Hotel, 153 Jalan Laksamana, ph 315 322 — $75.

LOCAL TRANSPORT

Taxis
Taxis are confortable and quick; during the day they will be metered, but between the hours of 12 midnight and 6am an additional 50% of the normal rate will be charged.

Taxis can also be requested by phone (no. 223 630) from the taxi rank, but the fare will be doubled.

A taxi from Melaka will take you to Muar for $3.50 per person ($14 per taxi); to Tampin for $2.80 per person; to Kuala Lumpur for $13 per person ($60 per taxi); to Johor Bahru for $17 per person ($68 per taxi); to Alor Gajah for $2 per person.

Trishaws
Once a common method of transportation, the trishaw — a bicycle with a side car — is now more popular with tourists. These trishaws offer the visitor a novel way to explore parts of the city.

EATING OUT

The Gluttons' Corner, along Jalan Taman, Bandar Hilir, is a favourite eating place for the local people. Here are stalls serving various Chinese, Malay and Indian dishes. Apart from these stalls, there is a wide variety of restaurants, and following is a small selection.

Malay
Restoran Anda, 8B Jln. Hang Tuah, ph 231 984; Melati Lounge, Plaza Inn, ph 227 959; Restoran Kesidang, Ayer Keroh, Country Resort, ph 325 211; Mini Restaurant, Jalan Taman, ph 229 413; Sri Percik, 319 Jln. Kilang.

Nyonya
Ole Sayang Restaurant, 192 Taman Melaka Jaya, ph 231 966; Nyonya Makko Restaurant, 123 Taman Melaka Jaya, ph 240 737.

Chinese
Hiking Restaurant, 112 Taman Melaka Jaya, ph 233 292; Lim Tian Puan Restaurant, 251 Jalan Tun Sri Lanang, ph 222 727; Long Feng Restaurant, Ramada Renaissance, Jalan Bendahara, ph 248 888; Village Court Chinese Restaurant, Melaka Village Resort, Ayer Keroh, ph 323 600.

Portuguese
Restoran De Lisbon, Portuguese Square, Portuguese Settlement, ph 248 067; Restoran De Portugis, Portuguese Square, Portuguese Settlement, ph 243 156; San Pedro Restaurant, Portuguese Settlement.

Western
Kesidang Restaurant, Air Keroh Country Resort, ph 325 211; Summerfield's Ramada Renaissance, Jalan Bendahara, ph 248 888; Trading Post, Melaka Village Resort, Ayer Keroh, ph 323 600; Garden Cafe, Plaza Inn, Jalan Munshi Abdullah, ph 227 959.

Japanese
Karaku, Melaka Village Resort, Ayer Keroh, ph 323 600.

Indian
Banana Leaf Restaurant, Jalan Munshi Abdullah; Sri Lakshmi Villas Restaurant, 2 Jalan Bendahara, ph 224 926; Sri Krishna Bavan Restaurant, 4 Jalan Bendahara, ph 229 206.

SHOPPING

With its ancient history as the main port of South East Asia, it is natural that many fine antiques have come to roost in Melaka.

Its narrow, picturesque streets are full of treasures in the shape of antiques. Visitors should know that an export permit is necessary to take antiques out of the country, and this is available from the office of the Director General of Museums, Malaysia, in Kuala Lumpur.

Jalan Hang Jebat, formerly known as Jonker Street is the place to visit for antiques. Authentic artifacts dating back nearly 300 years can be found in shops here, and can be purchased at reasonable prices.

Prices at shopping complexes are fixed but bargaining is welcomed at smaller retail shops and roadside stalls. The bigger shopping centres can be found in Jalan Munshi Abdullah, Jalan Bunga Raya, Jalan Hang Tuah and Jalan Bendahara.

SIGHTSEEING

The Stadthuys
Situated in the Dutch square are solid testimonies to Dutch masonry and woodwork skills, with heavy, hard wooden doors, thick masonry walls and wrought-iron hinges.

The Stadthuys, believed to have been completed in 1650, once housed the Dutch Governors and their retinue. Only one room still has the original wooden floral ceiling of the 17th century. The Stadthuys now houses the Malacca Historical Museum with the authentic relics of the Portuguese and the Dutch. Also the traditional bridal costumes of the Chinese and Malays are on display.

Christ Church
This is an exquisite piece of Dutch architecture, completed in 1753. It is 82 ft long 40 ft wide and 42 ft high. The ceiling beams were each cut from one single tree and have no joints at all. The handmade pews are the originals dating back over 200 years. Over the altar there is a frieze of the Last Supper in glazed tiles.

The brass bible rest dates back to 1773 and in the centre is inscribed the first verse of St John. On the church floor are tombstones in Armenian Script.

St Francis Xavier's Church
This twin Gothic towered church was built in 1849 by a French priest, Fr Farve, on the site of the former Portuguese Church. It is dedicated to St Francis Xavier known as the Apostle of the East, who spread Catholicism in South East Asia during the 16th century.

St Paul's Church
Built in 1521, this was known as Duarte Coelho, the leading Church for Catholics at that time.

The Dutch renamed the church St Paul's and eventually made the church an extension of the fortress. Evidence of gun embrasures with holes for gun-recoilers in the roof, can still be seen today.

When the Dutch completed the Christ Church in the red-painted Dutch Square in 1753, they made St Paul's Hill into a burial ground for their noble dead. One can see hugh tombstones measuring 8 ft high and 3.5 ft wide; also tombstones with Latin and Portuguese inscriptions.

The open grave inside St. Paul's is where St. Francis Xavier was once buried in 1553, before his body was moved to Goa in India.

A Famosa (Porta De Santiago)
This gateway is the remaining ruin of the once strong fortress built by the Portuguese in 1511 known as A Famosa. During the Dutch attack the fortress was badly damaged and had to be repaired. The Dutch did this in 1670 and renamed this great fortress "Voc" with the crest above the gateway which can be seen till this day. Had it not been for Sir Stamford Raffle's intervention in 1810, the gateway would not exist today.

Malacca Sultanate Palace
This wooden replica of the Sultanate's Palace is situated at the foot of St Paul's Hill. The architectural design of the palace is based on the description of "Malay Annals" or "Sejarah Melayu" and is one of its kind in Malaysia. The palace now houses the Malacca Cultural Museum.

Proclamation of Independence Memorial
Built in 1912 this hall was formerly known as the Malacca Club. Today it houses pictures portraying events leading to the attainment of Malaysia's Independence and the struggles and efforts of leaders like Tunku Abdul Rahman Putra Al-Haj, Malaysia's first Prime Minister.

Visitors can also view a wide range of exhibits which include historical documents, maps, treaties, videos, films, minutes of meetings, news scripts and others all relating to the Independence struggle.

The Baba Nyonya Heritage

This is the first private museum (managed by the Straits-born Chinese known as the "Peranakan") where artifacts of the heritage are on display for the public. The homes which are turned into museums have neo-classical European architecture characterised by Greco-Roman columns. Floral and pictorial motifs grace parts of the front of the house whilst the interior is adorned with intricately carved fittings finished in gold leaf.

Hang Kasturi's Mausoleum

Hang Kasturi is another friend of Hang Tuah who had served the Sultan. However, after the death of Hang Jebat, little is known about him. Today his grave can still be seen at Jalan Hang Jebat, formerly known as Jonker Street.

Kampong Hulu Mosque

This mosque is the oldest in Malaysia. It was built in 1728 by Dato Shamsuddin. The unique architectural style of this mosque can only be found in Malacca.

Cheng Hoon Teng Temple

This temple is the oldest Chinese temple in Malaysia, founded in 1646. It covers an area of 4,600 m^2 (5,474 sq. yds). The eaves of the temple are decorated with figures of mythology, and the wood carvings and lacquer work inside the temple are magnificent.

The main altar houses the "Goddess of Mercy" and on the left altar is the "Queen of Heaven", the special guardian of fishermen and voyagers on the high seas. The railings above the altars depict the life of Buddha. Outside is the courtyard where you can see the "Three Doctrinal Systems" of Buddhism, Confucianism and Taoism, beautifully blended.

All the materials used to build the temple came from China.

Kampong Kling Mosque

One of the oldest mosques with Sumatran architecture, it has a three tiered roof rising like a pyramid, and a carved wooden ceiling. Beside it is an odd minaret structured like a Pagoda. This indicates the architectural mixture of East and West.

MELAKA 117

Sri Poyyatha Vinayagar Moorthi Temple
This Indian temple was built in the early 19th century on land given by the Dutch.

Hang Jebat's Mausoleum
Hang Jebat, along with four of his closest friends, took lessons in the Malay art of self defence, until they had perfected every movement. They saved the life of Bendahara Paduka Raja, Prime Minister of the Sultan Shah. As a reward they were made attendants at court. All of them pledged lifelong service to the ruler. A few years later Hang Jebat was killed by his close friend, Hang Tuah, for betraying the ruler.

Hang Jebat's grave is in Jalan Kampung Kuli, and the grave of the other friend Hang Kasturi is in Jalan Hang Jebat.

Hang Li Poh's Well (Sultan's Well)
This well found at the foot of Bukit China was used by the Princess daily. It is believed that the water has attained purity and whoever drinks from it will return to Malacca at least once more during his lifetime. The well dates back to 1409 and was constructed by the followers of Princess Hang Li Poh.

The well was enclosed with stout walls by the Dutch in 1677 after they conquered Malacca. The well itself in days of old was the main source of water for much of the town, and even during droughts has never dried up. Today the well has been converted into a wishing well and the belief is anyone who throws a coin into the well will return to Malacca.

Sam Po Kong Temple
Dedicated to Admiral Cheng Ho when he visited Malacca in 1409, it is situated beside the Sultan's well. In a tale it is said that on one of his trips from China to Malacca, Admiral Cheng Ho's ship was almost wrecked as there was a hole in the keel. However the ship was saved by a fish known as "Sam Po" hanging itself to the hole.

Bukit China
In 1459 following visits to Malacca by the famous Ming Admiral Cheng Ho, the Emperor of China gave Parameswara, the first

Ruler of Malacca, official Chinese protection. Later, in 1459, the Emperor sent his daughter Princess Hang Li Poh to marry the reigning Sultan Mansor Shah. Her entourage consisted of 500 ladies-in-waiting and the Sultan gave them Bukit China, or Chinese Hill, for their residence. The Portuguese during their occupation built a Franciscan Monastery and also a chapel dedicated to Madre de Deus (Mother of God) on top of this hill. However both the monastery and the chapel were completely destroyed by the Achinese in 1629 when they attacked the Dutch.

Today Bukit China rests in peace as the largest Chinese cemetery outside China (12,000 graves) taking up 25 ha (62 acres), with many of the tombs dating back to Ming times.

St Peter's Church

Built in 1710 by the Portuguese and comprising an architectural mix between the Oriental and Occidental, this church contains the lifesize alabaster statue of The Dead Lord Before The Resurrection. The interior is unique in Iberian design with several corinthian pillars supporting the curved ceiling above the aisle.

St John's Fort

St John's Fort, built on St John's Hill (3 km — 2 miles — from town) was constructed by the Dutch during the latter part of the 18th century, but was once a private Portuguese chapel dedicated to St John the Baptist. It is interesting to note that the gun embrasures of the fort face inland and not towards the seas, as regular attacks came from hinterland and not from the seas as was once the case.

Portuguese Square

Located in the Portuguese Settlement, this is where their descendents live in a close-knit group. The architectural design of the square resembles that of Lisbon. Besides the availability of authentic Portuguese dishes, cultural shows are performed every Saturday night for public viewing.

The Tranquerah Mosque

Architecturally this mosque is unique with a pagoda built in place of minarets, and the mosque itself is somewhat pyramid-shaped instead of dome-shaped as in Moorish type mosques.

Within the grounds of this mosque lies the tomb of Sultan Hussain of Johore who signed the cession of Singapore to Sir Stamford Raffles in 1819.

OUTLYING ATTRACTIONS

Malaysia-in-Miniature

Step into Mini Malaysia and experience the rich Malaysian arts and culture, a heritage moulded by its diverse races, rivalled by few in this part of the world. See the thirteen types of attractively crafted Malaysian traditional state houses, each with a most delightful architecture and design. These houses also contain works of art and culture that are still very much alive. Colourful cultural shows and traditional games staged in the open prove intriguing. Other facilities for visitors include chalets, motels and outdoor games and activities.

Ayer Keroh Recreational Forest

Set admist a splendid green environment about 11 km (7 miles) from town, one can view rich, untouched tropical forests. The trees are all labelled. Away from the hassles of downtown Melaka here you can indulge in refreshing activities like trekking, camping, picnicking or staying in houses on tree-tops. There are barbeque facilities and a children's playground. Huts and cabins are available for rental.

Melaka Zoo

Rated as the best zoo among Southern States for its wild and domestic animals in their natural surroundings and habitats. Recreational facilities are provided for families.

Ayer Keroh Lake

This scenic lake has various water sport facilities such as boating, canoeing, coupled with refreshment kiosks and children's playground.

Ayer Keroh Country Club

Situated about 14 km (9 miles) from the town, the well-known Club has an 18-hole golf course with challenging terrain, bounded by lakes and rain forests.

Durian Tunggai Recreational Lake

This water spot is about 16 km (10 miles) from the town, and facilities include boating, fishing, jogging paths, camping area, windsurfing, merry-go-round, ferry, refreshment kiosk and children's playground.

Hang Tuah's Well

This is a sacred well, believed to be the abode of Hang Tuah's soul which takes the form of a white crocodile; only holy people stand a chance to see the crocodile. Apparently the water has medicinal values and power to give good luck to those who drink it. The well is located about 4 km (2.5 miles) from Melaka town.

Gadek Hot Spring

The Gadek Hot Spring is a popular spot, located along the route to Tampin, about 25 km (15 miles) from Melaka. The sulphur water is believed to possess curative elements for a number of skin diseases. Handicraft shops and beautiful playgrounds make this a perfect outing for a family.

Megalithic Stones

There are over 90 separate sites which are mostly found in Alor Gajah and on the road to Tampin. These components form part of a large cluster which spreads into Negeri Sembilan. They existed centuries ago.

Hang Tuah's Mausoleum

Hang Tuah, the famous Malay warrior during the reign of Sultan Mansor Shah, was buried in this mausoleum in Tg. Kling, which is 15 km (9 miles) from Melaka.

Serkam

Serkam is about 10 km (6 miles) from Melaka, and is well known for its local dishes of fresh grilled fish with an assortment of local dishes. Worth the trip.

Tun Teja's Mausoleum

Situated about 24 km (15 miles) from Melaka in Merlimau, this is the grave of Tun Teja, the daughter of Bendahara Sri Amar Di

Raja Pahang. She was taken to Melaka by Hang Tuah to marry Sultan Mahmud Shah. She died in Merlimau while retreating with the Sultan from a Portuguese attack.

Melaka Traditional House

This colourful intricate wood carving house was built in the 19th century by a Chieftain. It is the only one of its kind in this zone. Situated 5 km (3 miles) from Merlimau Town on your way to Muar.

Dutch Fort

This fort is located at Kuala Linggi, 49 km (30 miles) from Melaka on the way to Port Dickson.

British Graveyard

Located in Alor Gajah town, this graveyard was for British officers killed during the Naning War.

Dol Said's Grave

Dato Dol Said, the brave Chieftain of the Naning War against the British in 1931, was buried here at Taboh Naning about 32 km (20 miles) from Melaka town.

Cape Rachado

This enclave is in Negeri Sembilan and 57 km (35 miles) from Melaka. The headland forest forms an important guideline for migratory birds like sparrows, hawks, honey buzzard, eagles and swifts. In September/October and again March/April large concentrations of hawks and eagles can be seen. There is also a blue lagoon which has interesting marine life and a beautiful beach. The lighthouse towers the cape.

Pulau Besar

Pulau Besar is located in the Straits of Malacca, which is 13 nautical miles off the mainland of Umbai Jetty and 10 nautical miles from Melaka Port. The sandy beaches provide ample opportunities for swimming, fishing, picnicking, camping and snorkelling. The island will be turned into a resort in the near future.

Beaches

There are three beaches, Kelebang Besar, Tanjung Keling and Tanjung Bidara, set against a background of hills and dense green vegetation. In addition, the sea front has a number of popular outdoor eating places.

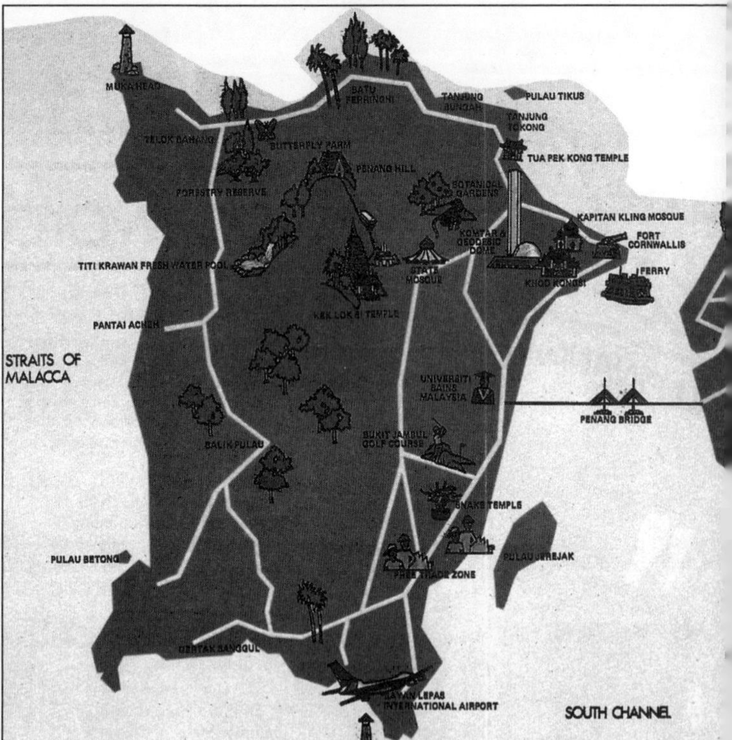
MUKA HEAD
BATU FERRINGHI
TANJUNG BUNGAH
PULAU TIKUS
TANJUNG TOKONG
TELOK BAHANG
BUTTERFLY FARM
PENANG HILL
TUA PEK KONG TEMPLE
FORESTRY RESERVE
BOTANICAL GARDENS
KAPITAN KLING MOSQUE
KOMTAR & GEODESIC DOME
FORT CORNWALLIS
TITI KRAWAN FRESH WATER POOL
STATE MOSQUE
KHOO KONGSI
FERRY
KEK LOK SI TEMPLE
PANTAI ACHEH
STRAITS OF MALACCA
UNIVERSITI SAINS MALAYSIA
PENANG BRIDGE
BUKIT JAMBUL GOLF COURSE
BALIK PULAU
SNAKE TEMPLE
PULAU BETONG
PULAU JEREJAK
FREE TRADE ZONE
GERTAK SANGGUL
BAYAN LEPAS INTERNATIONAL AIRPORT
SOUTH CHANNEL
PULAU RIMAU

PENANG

Penang is situated on the north-western coast of Peninsular Malaysia. It is bounded to the north and east by the State of Kedah, to the south by the State of Perak, and to the west by the Straits of Malacca and Sumatra (Indonesia).

Penang consists of the island of Penang (Pulau Pinang) and a coastal strip on the mainland called Province Wellesley. The island covers an area of 284 km^2 (110 sq. miles), and its shape resembles a swimming turtle. It is approximately 24 km (15 miles) north to south and 14.5 km (9 miles) east to west. The mainland and the island are separated by a channel 3 km (2 miles) wide at the closest point and 13 km (8 miles) at the farthest, and are linked by the Penang Bridge and a 24 hour ferry service.

The capital city of Penang is Georgetown.

HISTORY

In the early 1700s, Penang was viewed as an excellent location for a harbour to repair British ships damaged in monsoons in the Bay of Bengal. In 1786 Captain Francis Light of the British East India Company arrived on the island and formally took possession of it on August 11, following negotiations with the Sultan of Kedah to whom he promised protection. Penang was the first British settlement in the Far East.

August 11 being the birthday of the then Prince of Wales, Light named the island Prince of Wales Island. He named the capital Georgetown after the reigning monarch, George III. Today, Georgetown still retains its name but the island is called Pulau Pinang or Island of the Betel Nut, a palm commonly found in the State.

A strip of land on the mainland was ceded by the Sultan of Kedah in 1800 and named Province Wellesley after the then Governor of India — Richard, Marquis of Wellesley. In 1805, Penang's status was raised to that of Presidency and in 1832 it became part of the Straits Settlements together with Malacca and Singapore.

Penang became a State of Independent Malaya on August 31, 1957. When Malaysia was formed in September 1963, following the merging of Malaya with the former Borneo States of Sabah and Sarawak, Penang became one of its 13 States.

CLIMATE

Penang has an equatorial climate which is warm and humid throughout the year. Average temperature is between 32.2C and 23.3C. Mean annual rainfall of approximately 267 cm (105 in) is evenly distributed, with the wettest months from September to November.

HOW TO GET THERE

By Air
Penang's International Airport at Bayan Lepas is about 16 km (10 miles) from Georgetown. The following airlines have offices in Penang:
Cathay Pacific Airways, AIA Building, 88 Leboh Bishop, ph 04-620 411/4.
Garuda Indonesian Airways, Lot 2.11, Wisma Chocolate Products, 41 Aboo Sittee Lane, ph 04-365 257/375 299.
Malaysia Airline System, Kompleks Tun Abdul Razak, Penang Road, Penang, ph 04-621 403 (reservations ph 620 011, airport ph 830 811).
Northwest Orient Airlines, Northeast Holdings, Southern Bank Building, 21 Leboh Pantai, ph 04-619 487/8.
Singapore Airlines Ltd., Wisma Penang Garden, 42 Jalan Sultan Ahmad Shah, ph 04-363 201.
Thai Airways Co. Ltd., 9 Pengkalan Weld, ph 04-626 622.
Thai Airways International Ltd., Wisma Central, Macalister Road, ph 04-23 484/5.
Bayan Lepas International Airport, ph 04-831 373.

By Rail
Tickets to all Malayan Railway stations in West Malaysia and Bangkok are available at the Railway Booking Station at the Ferry Terminal, Weld Quay (ph 04-610 290), at the Butterworth Railway

Station itself (ph 04-347 962) or from any authorised travel agent in Georgetown.

Bookings of 1st and 2nd class tickets and reservation of sleeping berths can be made 90 days in advance.

To board the train you will have to take the ferry to Butterworth (on the mainland) where the railway station is located. Accommodation is available in 1st, 2nd and 3rd classes. Air-conditioned coaches are also available for 1st class passengers.

By Ferry
A 24-hour service for both passengers and vehicles is provided by the Penang Port Commission. Ferry fares are payable at the terminal at Butterworth on the mainland. The return journey is free.

The fares are as follows:
Adults — 40c
Children over 5 and under 12 years of age — 20c
Car and Driver, 1200cc or under — M$4.00
                1201cc to 1600cc — M$5.00
                Over 1600cc — M$6.00
Lorries, vans and buses (depending on capacity) — M$8.00–M$48.00.

By Road
Driving to Penang is so much easier with the opening of Penang Bridge. A M$7.00 toll is collected from all classes of cars (including passengers) at the Toll Plaza in Prai on the mainland. Those driving from the island to the mainland do not have to pay toll.

TOURIST INFORMATION
Tourist Development Corporation of Malaysia (TDCM), 10 Jalan Tun Syed Sheh Barakbah, 10200 Penang, ph 04–620 066, 619 067.

ACCOMMODATION
There is no shortage of accommodation in Penang, and listed below are a few examples, together with the price ranges. The Telephone Area Code is 04.

International

Bayview Beach Hotel, Batu Ferringhi, 11100 Penang, ph 811 311 — M$80–M$170; Casuarina Beach Hotel, Batu Ferringhi, 11100 Penang — M$140–M$380; The City Bayview Hotel, 25-A Leboh Farguhar, 10200 Penang, ph 363 162 — M$100–M$140; Eastern & Oriental Hotel, 10 Leboh Farguhar, 10200 Penang, ph 375 322 — M$120–M$400; Ferringhi Beach Hotel, 12.5 km Batu Ferringhi Road, 11100 Penang, ph 805 999 — M$170–M$400; Golden Sands Hotel, 87 Batu Ferringhi, 11100 Penang, ph 811 911 — M$165–M$400; Holiday Inn Penang, Batu Feringgi Beach, 11100 Penang, ph 811 601 — M$125–M$320; Palm Beach Hotel, Batu Ferringhi, 11100 Penang, ph 811 621 — M$90–M$140; Hotel Ambassador, 55 Penang Road, 10000 Penang, ph 24 101 — M$65–M$180; Hotel Continental, 5 Penang Road, 10000 Penang, ph 26 381 — M$66–M$180. Rasa Sayang Hotel, Batu Feringgi Beach, ph 811 811 — M$130–M$220; Shangri La Inn, Penang Jln. Magazine 10300 Penang, ph 622 622 — M$115–M$126.

Good Tourist

Hotel Bellevue, Penang Hill, 11300 Penang, ph 892 256 — M$60–M$80; Hotel Central, 404 Penang Road, 10000 Penang, ph 21 432 — M$45–M$60; Hotel Fortuna, 406 Penang Road, 10000 Penang, ph 24 301 — M$40–M$72; Hotel Golden City, 12 Kinta Lanr, 10400 Penang, ph 27 271 — M$55–M$85; Hotel Macalist, 101 Jalan Macalister, 10400 Penang, ph 29 401 — M$40–M$65; Hotel Malaysia, 7 Penang Road, 10000 Penang — ph 363 311 — M$66–$172; Hotel Mingood, 164 Jalan Argyll, 10050 Penang, ph 373 345 — M$35–M$50; Hotel Waterfall, 160 Jalan Utama, 10450 Penang, ph 27 221 — M$69–M$89; Lone Pine Hotel, 97 Batu Feringgi, 11100 Penang, ph 811 511/2 — M$55–M$75; Oriental Hotel, 105 Penang Road, 10000 Penang, ph 24 211 — M$59–M$66.

Budget

Paramount Hotel, 48F Jalan Sultan Ahmad Shah, 10050 Penang, ph 363 649 — M$17–M$38.

LOCAL TRANSPORT

Buses

Sri Negara Buses start from Pengkalan Weld and serve the following areas: Penang Road, Jalan Macalister, Jalan Utama, Jalan

Gottlieb, Bagan Jermal, Mt Erskine and back to Pengkalan Weld.
Green Buses start from Jalan Maxwell and travel to Air Itam.
Blue Buses start from Jalan Maxwell and serve the northern coast of the island, running to Tanjung Tokong, Tanjung Bungah, Batu Ferringhi and Telok Bahang.
Yellow buses start from Jalan Maxwell and serve the southern and western sides of the island going to Bukit Dumbar, Gelugo, Snake Temple, Bayan Lepas, Balik Pulau, Telok Bahang, Batu Maung and Air Itam Village via Relau. You will see that by taking the Blue and Yellow Buses a circuit of the island can be made. The time required for this is about 4 to 5 hours.

MPPP Buses

City transport buses cover the whole of the city, leaving at frequent intervals from the terminal at Leboh Victoria. Fares are from 20c to 55c to any destination. The route number and destination are shown above the windscreen.

Taxis

Airport taxis follow the coupon system with fixed fares. The coupon is for one-way journey from the airport to the destination. The coupon has three sections — one kept by the passenger, the second by the coupon booth at the airport and the third by the taxi driver. The passenger pays for the coupon at the booth, and the driver, after dropping off his passenger, returns to the booth to exchange the coupon for cash.

The various zones with fixed rates are:

Zone 1 (M$5) — Bayan Lepas, Free Trade Zone Area, Snake Temple and Batu Maung.
Zone 2 (M$7.50) — Sungei Nibong, Relau, Batu Uban and Teluk Kumbar.
Zone 3 (M$10.50) — USM, Island Park, Sungei Gelugor, Bukit Gelugor, Brown Garden, Buldt Dumbar and Balik Pulau Kongsi.
Zone 4 (M$13.50) — Jelutong, General Hospital, City, Air Itam and and Balik Pulau.
Zone 5 (M$16.20) — Bagan Jermal, Tanjung Bungah and Penang Swimming Club.
Zone 6 (M$20.20) — Batu Ferringhi.
Zone 7 (M$24.30) — Teluk Bahang until Forest Recreation Park.

The fares for air-conditioned taxis are slightly higher. Taxis not plying the airport route charge by the meter. The rates are 70c for the first mile and 30c each subsequent half mile.

In the city it is advisable to agree on the fare with the taxi driver before boarding. In case of difficulties finding a taxi, contact the following:
Baba & Co, ph 613 653; Bunga Raya Travel & Taxi, ph 365 212; Syarikat Georgetown Taxi & Tour Service, ph 613 853; Island Taxi & Tour, ph 625 127/629 572; Jade Auto Co., pn 23 220.

Car Rentals
Avis Rent-A-Car, ph 373 964/361 685; Bunga Raya Travel & Taxi, ph 365 212/365 778; Hertz Rent-A-Car, ph 375 914; Island Taxi & Tour, ph 625 127/629 572; National Car Rental, ph 372 424/374 152; Kasina Rent-A-Car, ph 811 302/679/988; Sintat Rent-A-Car, ph 811 101/2.

EATING OUT

An abundant supply of fresh seafood comes in every day from the local fishermen, and seafood is available in hotels, restaurants and roadside stalls. Lobsters, crabs, fish, prawns and squids are prepared in a variety of ways — boiled, fried, baked or cooked in sweet-sour sauce.

The fast food stalls on Gurney Drive, Penang Road and Campbell Street in Georgetown are worth trying.

ENTERTAINMENT

There are numerous nightclubs in the city of Georgetown. The bigger hotels have cocktail lounges, coffee shops and restaurants. There are also a number of pubs, and a stroll along the Esplanade or Gurney Drive in the evening can prove to be a refreshing experience.

There are several cinemas featuring the latest films. The titles and times of screening are advertised in the newspapers. Admission: M$2.50 and M$3.00 (Dress Circle).

Concerts and plays are staged regularly at the Dewan Sri Pinang in Lebuh Light amphitheatre at Fort Cornwallis, Geodesic Dome at Komtar, City Stadium in Jalan Perak and Pesta Site in Sungai Nibong.

Cultural presentations and other folk festivals are held occa-

PENANG 131

sionally and during Pesta Pulau Pinang. Leading hotels have their respective cultural floorshows.

SHOPPING

Penang has long maintained its reputation as a shopping centre. It is a warehouse of electronic products, cameras and typewriters from Japan, Germany and other leading manufacturing countries.

Textiles from Japan and the West, silk from India and China, as well as Malay silverware, pewterware, batik, jewellery, glassware and intricately woven rattan furniture are only part of the wide range of products available. The main shopping district in Georgetown is the Penang Road/Burmah Road and Leboh Campbell area. Curios and Handicrafts of Malaysia and neighbouring countries are obtainable from shops in Penang Road and Leboh Bishop. Perfumes are available in many popular imported brands, and there are also locally produced perfumes like Regence Parfums. Most shops are open from 10am–10pm.

Off the main shopping areas, along Rope Walk, there are several junk shops worth a visit.

TOURS

Most travel agents offer the following types of tours — the Hill and Temple Tour, the Round-Island Tours, the City and Shopping Tour and the Mainland Tour.

Hill and Temple Tour
This tour includes the Pagoda of Ten Thousand Buddhas (Kek Lok Si), the only one in South East Asia; a tortoise sanctuary with 100 year old reptiles; the legendary Four Gates of Heaven; the Black Water Village; a funicular train up Penang Hill to the Hill Mosque and Hindu Temple, with a great view over Georgetown; the Botanic Gardens.

Round Island Tour
A 70 km (45 mile) journey along scenic beaches, through unspoiled countryside and onto Georgetown. Drive along Batu Ferringhi Beach, then visit the Craft Batik factory; rubber plantations; the Snake Temple; early Chinese settlements and Fort Cornwallis.

City and Shopping Tour
Shop for souvenirs and bargains at Penang's wayside stalls, emporiums and department stores. Then tour the waterfront, visit the State Museum and see the Khoo Clan House in Cannon Square.

Mainland Tour
Cross by ferry to the mainland at Butterworth, then drive into the state of Perak, passing padi fields, Malay Kampong style villages and oil palm plantations. Taiping is a small town with beautiful lake gardens and the oldest museum in Malaysia. Continue to the royal town of Kuala Kangsar for lunch at a local rest house, then visit the Royal Mosque overlooking the Perak river. Continue on to the Sultan's palace and ceremonial guest house, former residence of the royal family. The return journey is by the 13.5 km (8.5 mile) Penang Bridge.

Penang Grand Tour
This tour includes the most important sights of the Island, and includes visits to Malay Kampong style villages, rubber estates, the Snake Temple, Penang Hill by funicular railway, Khoo Kongsi Clan house, Fort Cornwallis in Georgetown, and a drive along the waterfront before returning to the E & O Hotel.

SIGHTSEEING

GEORGETOWN
Acheen Street Mosque
One of the oldest mosques in Penang, built by Syed Sheriff Tengku Syed Hussain Aidid, who came to the island in 1792 from Acheh, Sumatra. In a will made in 1820, Syed Hussain left a piece of land for the mosque, which was built next to his tomb. This mosque is reminiscent of Egyptian architecture, and halfway up the minaret is a round window which, according to popular belief, was originally a hole made by a cannon ball fired during fighting between two secret societies during the Penang riots in 1867.

Khoo Kongsi

Kongsis or clan houses are associations which originated in China centuries ago for people of the same surname. Today, they look after the affairs of members and also safe-guard the principles of ancestral worship. The idea of a temple was first mooted in 1835 and was completed 8 years later. The Leong San Tong (Dragon Mountain Hall) of the Khoo Kongsi in Cannon Square is definitely worth a visit.

Kapital Kling Mosque

Built about 1800 by an Indian Muslim merchant, Cauder Johudeen, who was the Kling Kapital (Indian Muslim headman) at that time. Situated in Lebuh Pitt, the domeshaped and well placed minaret reflect Islamic architecture of Indian influence.

Sri Mariamman Temple

Built in 1883, and situated in Lewbuh Queen, this temple contains the statue of Lord Subramaniam, decorated in gold, diamonds and other precious stones. The statue is led in a chariot procession during the Thaipusam festival.

Kuan Yin Temple

Popularly known as the Temple of the Goddess of Mercy, it was built in 1800 through the joint efforts of the first Chinese settlers, the Hokkien and Cantonese communities.

Situated in Lebuh Pitt, this temple is one of the busiest in Penang especially during the Goddess' birthday celebrations in March and October when puppet shows are staged in the vicinity.

St George's Church

Built by convict labour in 1818, its foundation stone was laid in 1817. It is the first Anglican Church to be built in Singapore and Malaya.

St George's Church is more than a Christian edifice, it is one of the oldest landmarks in Malaysia. Apart from the original flat roof, which was altered to its gable shape, the church still looks as it did in the old days. The first marriage to be conducted in this church was on June 20, 1818, between the Governor of the

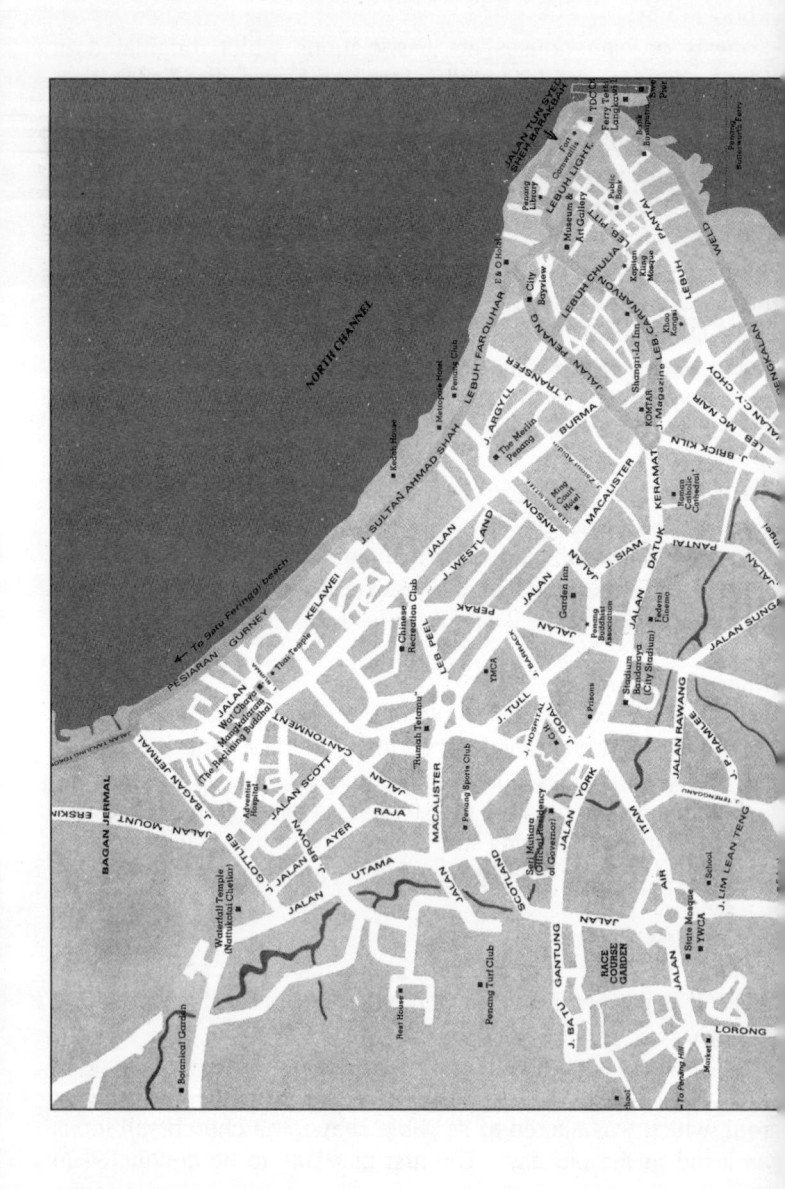

134 SINGAPORE AND MALAYSIA AT COST

PENANG 135

PENANG
(George Town)

East India Company, W.E. Phillips, and Janet, daughter of Colonel Bannerman. It is symbolical of Penang's early history, for in its grounds stands a monument to the memory of Captain Francis Light, founder of Penang. The church is situated in Lebuh Farquhar.

Penang Museum & Art Gallery

Formerly the Penang Free School, it was built in 1816 in Lebuh Farquhar. When the Free School moved to its present premises in Green Lane in 1928, the building was taken over by the Hutchings School.

During the outbreak of the Pacific War (1941–45), the building was badly damaged, leaving only the main block, which currently houses the Penang Museum and Art Gallery. During the war, the school was occupied by the Japanese Navy while the playground was used by the Japanese for planting tapioca and vegetables.

Cathedral of the Assumption

One of the oldest Roman Catholic churches in Malaysia. Devoid of any pretensions, the atmosphere in the church is sanctified simplicity. The church is located in Lebuh Farquhar.

Logan Memorial and High Court

This marble statue which stands in the compound of the High Court in Lebuh Farquhar, is dedicated to James Richardson Logan, a prominent lawyer and one-time editor of the Penang Gazette. Logan devoted his life to serving the public, and advocating the freedom of speech, law and order till his death in 1869. The Memorial and High Court are in front of the Penang Museum & Art Gallery.

Cheong Fatt Tze Mansion

This Chinese mansion of 18th and 19th century Chinese architecture is believed to be one of the only three such buildings remaining outside China. The others are in Manila and Jakarta.

The Mansion, in Lebuh Leith, was built by Thio Thian Siat, a Kwang tung businessman and son of the Grand Taifung, a scholar.

Clock Tower

The clock tower was presented to the town in 1897 by Mr Cheah Chen Eok, a Penang millionaire, in conjunction with Queen Victoria's Diamond Jubilee. It is 60 ft high — a foot for each of the 60 years of the Queen's reign, and cost about M$35,000 to build. The tower is situated in Jalan Tun Syed Sheh Barakbah.

Fort Cornwallis

A 200-year-old landmark where Captain Francis Light landed in 1786. Built between 1808 and 1810, it was originally a wooden structure but was later replaced and rebuilt by convict labour. Its walls are moss covered, and protruding from the ramparts are several age-old cannons retrieved by the British from pirates who had captured them from the Johore Sultanate, then a Dutch protectorate.

The main cannon "Seri Rambai" is said to date back to 1618, and if you happen to see flowers and joss-sticks near the main cannon, do not be surprised for according to local belief childless women can conceive by placing flowers in its barrel and offering special prayers. Location — Esplanade.

Municipal Council Building

Construction of this imposing building, which is located at the Esplanade, started in 1900 and was completed in 1903. The building was the seat of the local government until recently, the Municipal Council offices are now located at Komtar.

Dewan Sri Pinang

This is a multi-purpose hall for conferences, concerts and exhibitions. It has an auditorium which can seat 1,300 delegates with three other smaller meeting rooms. The Penang Public Library is also situated on the first floor of the building in Jalan Tun Syed Sheh Barakbah.

BEYOND GEORGETOWN

Air Itam Dam

It can be reached from the road leading to the Kek Lok Si Temple. The dam, at 233 m (762 ft) above sea level offers a panoramic view of Air Itam.

Butterfly Farm

Opened in March 1986, it's the world's largest butterfly farm with 3,000 living specimens of over 50 species. The farm itself occupies 0.8 ha (2 acres), with a garden enclosure, breeding area, laboratory, exhibition area, souvenir shop and information centre. Other interesting features include a lily pond, artificial waterfalls, a rock garden, tunnel and bubbling mud pool.

There are many educational exhibits and facilities for observing the life cycle of butterflies. Located at Telus Bahang, beside the Forest Recreation Park, it is open 9am–5pm.

Botanic Gardens

Occupying 30 ha (75 acres) the gardens have a fine collection of the flora and fauna of Malaysia and other parts of the tropics. They are well-known for their friendly Rhesus monkeys. Located off Jalan Waterfall in Botanical Gardens Road.

Natukkotai Chettiar Temple

This is the largest Hindu temple in Penang, dedicated to the deity Lord Bala Subramaniam. Before the shrine is a peacock given to Subramaniam by his mother, Parvathi, as his attendant 'vakanan' (vehicle). Located at the Jalan Waterfall, the temple is one of the important centres of rites and ceremonies during the Thaipusam festival.

Forest Recreation Park

The Park, situated 22 km (14 miles) from Georgetown, covers more than 100 ha (247 acres) and it surrounded by virgin jungle. Opened in 1974, it is designated as a recreation area and also as a centre of research for botany and zoology. A forestry museum houses exhibits of tropical timbers and their products, and preserved exhibits of insect species which commonly attack timbers. There are also freshwater pools, footpaths, rest huts, and a children's playground. Located at Teluk Bahang, it is open 8am–6pm daily, and admission is gratis.

Kek Lok Si

The largest Buddhist Temple complex in Malaysia is situated at Air Itam. Work on the Kek Lok Si started in 1890 and took more than two decades to complete. The temple is dominated by the seven-tier Ban Po Thar pagoda, which rises 30 m high. The pagoda combines Chinese, Thai and Burmese architecture and craftmanship. The octagonal base is typically Chinese, the middle tiers Thai, and the spiral dome Burmese.

Penang Hill
A popular spot for locals and visitors, Penang Hill is 830 m (2,714 ft) above sea level, and consequently 3C cooler than the lowlands. A 30 minute funicular train ride takes you to the summit, which affords a magnificent panoramic view of Georgetown and the coastal areas of the mainland, and has a children's playground, tea kiosk and a hotel. The timetable for the train follows:

Departures from Lower Station
6.30am–7am   — every 15 minutes
7.30am–1pm   — every 30 minutes
1.15pm–2pm   — every 15 minutes
2.30pm–9.30pm — every 30 minutes
Up to 12 midnight on Wednesday and Saturday.
Departures from Upper Station
6.30am–7.15pm — every 15 minutes
7.45am–9.45pm — every 30 minutes
Up to 11.45pm on Wednesday and Saturday.

Fares: Return ticket M$3.00 — Adult
                M$1.50 — Child.
More information on Penang Hill is obtained in the section on Hill Resorts.

Snake Temple
Built in 1850, it is dedicated to the deity Chor Soo Kong and is a sanctuary for pit vipers which can be seen coiled round vases, beams and potted plants. Although poisonous, they are not known to bite. Devotees refer to these snakes as "officers" of the deity and regard them as "holy and harmless".

Tourists who feel they must experience everything offered may pose for photographs with a pit viper coiled round their neck, but this is not necessarily recommended. The Temple is located at Bayan Lepas.

State Mosque

Completed in 1980, it stands on a 4.5 ha (11 acres) site at the Jalan Air Itam/Jalan Mesjid Negeri junction. The mosque, which took more than four years to build, can accommodate 5,000 worshippers.

Always remember when visiting a mosque or temple to dress accordingly, and to remove your shoes.

Wat Chayamangkalaram

This Buddhist Temple of Thai architecture in Lorong Burmah houses the world's third largest reclining Buddha, measuring 33 m (108 ft). Behind the statue are niches where urns containing the ashes of the dead are stored.

Photography is not allowed inside the Temple.

Youth Park

This is one of the very few such parks in Malaysia. Centre piece of the park is the roller-skating rink. The complex is ideal for picnicking, hiking, camping, archery and aero modelling. It is situated on Quarry Drive, a short distance from the Botanical Gardens.

MAINLAND ATTRACTIONS

Bird Park (Seberang Jaya)

The country's first bird park, it offers a fine collection of approximately 800 birds from over 100 species, mostly imported from all over the world.

Sacred Heart Church (Pagar Teras, Bukit Mertajam)

Built by the French Mission in 1882, the church used to be the focal point for Roman Catholics in the area until it was abandoned during the Emergency when the residents of Pagar Teras were resettled. A long flight of stairs leads to the ruins of the Church, designed after the famous Notre Dame Cathedral of Paris.

Cherok To'kun Relic (Bukit Mertajam)
A large, smooth block of granite bearing inscriptions in Chinese, Jawi, Tamil, English and classical Indian writing (probably Pali), believed to have been written in the 4th and 5th centuries.

Mengkuang Dam (Bukit Mertajam)
The state's largest dam with a volume capacity of about 24 million cubic metres. Scenic surroundings make the site a favourite place to relax.

SPORT AND RECREATION

Horse Racing
Races are held on selected weekends at the Penang Turf Club in Batu Gantung. It is an extremely popular event with on-course and off-course betting. Live telecasts are provided for off-course betting.

Tennis and Squash.
Courts are available at most of the leading hotels. Hourly rates are inclusive of the use of racquets and balls.

Bowling
Penang's bowling alley offers excellent facilities with automatic lanes for both young and old ten-pin bowlers. Several major tournaments are held annually.

Swimming
Most hotels have swimming pools. In addition, the Chinese Swimming Club and Universiti Sains Malaysia each offer an olympic-size pool. Swimming in the sea is safe throughout the year.

Watersports
The beaches along the north coast are suitable for most watersports. Facilities for para-sailing, water skiing, wind surfing, sailing, etc. are available at most beach hotels, or from private operators.

Penang Grand Prix

The exciting grand prix makes an annual comeback at the Esplanade street circuit in August. The circuit weaves its way around the historical parts of Georgetown, including the clock tower, Fort Cornwallis and the pier.

Golf

Penang has two 18-hole golf courses, one at Batu Gantung, and the other at Bukit Jambul near the airport.

Bukit Jambul Country Club
Weekdays — M$50 per person per day.
Weekends/public holidays — M$100.
Caddy fee — M$10 for 18 holes.
Contact — Secretary, Island Golf Properties, c/- Penang Development Corporation, ph 832 111, or Club Supervisor, ph 838 552.

Penang Turf Club
Weekdays — M$30 per person per day.
Weekends/public holidays — M$50.
Caddy fee — M$9 for 18 holes.
Contact — Hon. Secretary, Golf Section, Penang Turf Club, ph 27 270/21 518.

Dragon Boat Race

The race which originated from China, attracts teams from all over the world to compete in June each year. Over 50,000 spectators gather to watch and cheer. Each boat bears a dragon's head and has a 27 man crew, comprising 24 oarsmen, a cox swain, gong beater and a cheerleader.

PERLIS

Perlis, the northern-most state, lies close to the border with Thailand, 56 km (35 miles) north-west of Alor Setar in Kedah. It is an important rice-growing state and its capital, Kangar, is a small bustling town with another picturesque mosque.

HOW TO GET THERE

By Bus
Bus Services run from Butterworth and Alor Setar to Kangar.

By Train
The International Express train stops at Arau and Padang Besar.

By Car
Kangar is 56 km (35 miles) north-west of Alor Setar in Kedah, on the main road north to Thailand.

By Taxi
Taxis will take passengers from Butterworth or Alor Setar to Kangar.

TOURIST INFORMATION
Perlis Tourist Association, c/- Perlis Inn, Kangar, ph 04-752 266/7.

ACCOMMODATION
There is not a wide choice of accommodation in Kangar. Perlis is mostly a border state for people travelling between Malaysia and Thailand. Here we have mentioned a few hotels, with prices for a double room in Malaysian Dollars.

Federal Hotel, 104A&B Jalan Kangar, ph 04-751 288 — $50; Hotel Ban Cheong, 76A Main Road, ph 04-761 184 — $21; Hotel Malaysia, 67 Jalan Jubli Perak, ph 04-761 366 — $33; Sri Perlis Inn, Jalan Kangar, ph 04-763 266 — $90.

SIGHTSEEING

Arau
The royal town of Perlis has a fine Istana (Royal Palace).

Padang Besar
Pedang Besar is the border town straddling the Malaysian-Thai border. It is very popular with locals and visitors alike with a two-way flow across the border. There is an Immigration and Customs post here for entry and exit formalities.

Kuala Perlis
A small market town at the mouth of the Sungei Perlis, 14 km (9 miles) from Kangar and the jump-off point for the islands of Langkawi.

Kaki Bukit
This is a tin mining town. Tin is taken from underground caves and crevices in the limestone cliffs.

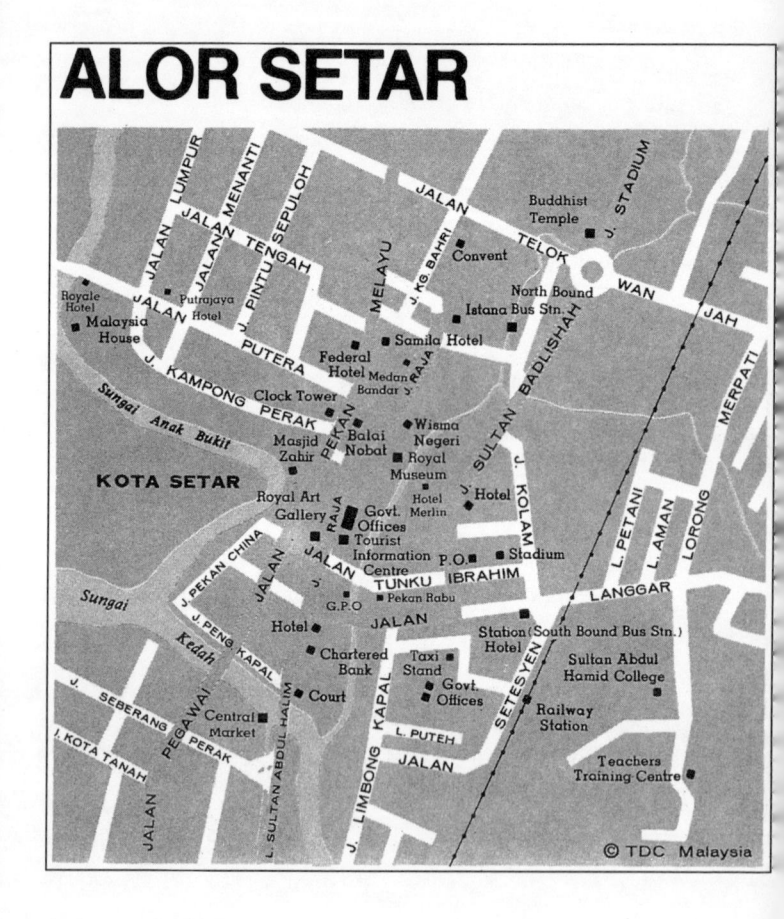

ALOR SETAR

KEDAH

Kedah, a northern State with a population of 1.4 million, covers an area of 9,414 km^2 (948,778 ha). It is north-west of Perak, south-east of Perlis, and south of Thailand.

Known as the "Rice Bowl of Malaysia", Kedah produces approximately 44% of Malaysia's rice needs. Interesting and beautiful sights abound in the state, whether you visit the mountains, the beaches, an island, a Malay village or one of Kedah's small rural towns.

Alor Setar, the state capital, is 96 km (60 miles) from Butterworth.

HOW TO GET THERE

By Air
From Kuala Lumpur, MAS flies into Alor Setar. If you are travelling from Penang, MAS fly into Langkawi as well as Alor Setar.

By Train
There are services from Kuala Lumpur, Bangkok and Haadyai, Thailand, to Kedah.

By Bus
Buses also travel from Kuala Lumpur, Bangkok and Haadyai, and if you are travelling from Thailand you enter Kedah through Bukit Kayu Hitam, a town which has a duty free shopping complex.

By Boat
The Gadis Langkasuka Ferry departs from Penang and Phuket, Thailand, for Kedah via the island of Langkawi.

TOURIST INFORMATION
Kedah Tourist Information Centre, c/- Kedah Tourist Association, Tunjang Express, 5–7 Bulatan Wan Jah, 05200 Alor Setar, ph 04-724 357/728 980.

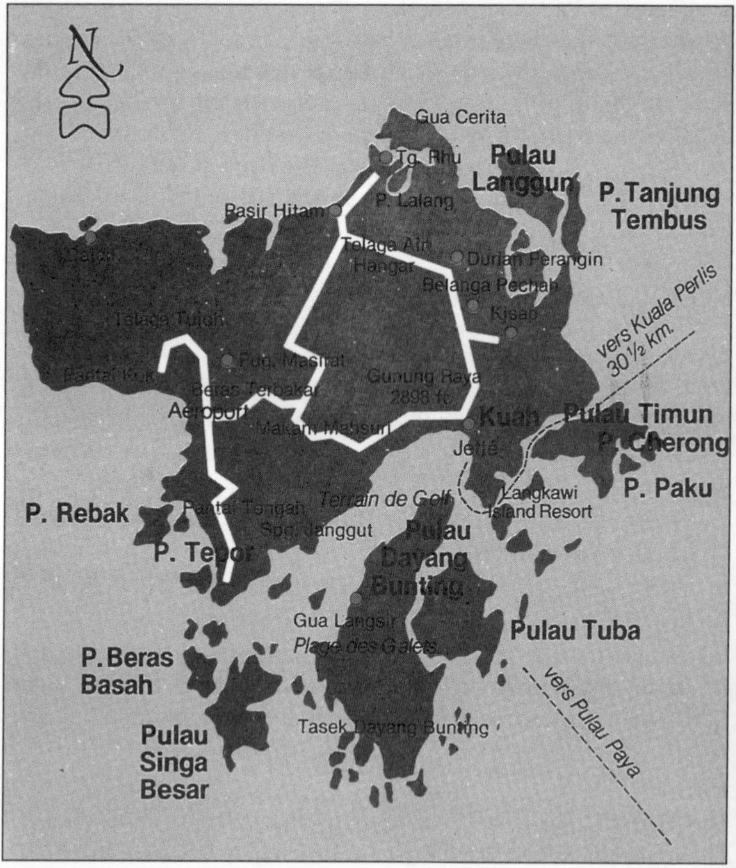
N
Gua Cerita
Tg. Rhu
Pulau Langgun
P. Tanjung Tembus
Pasir Hitam
P. Lalang
Telaga Air Hangat
Durian Perangin
Belanga Pechah
Kisap
vers Kuala Perlis 30 ½ km.
Pdg. Masirat
Gunung Raya 2898 ft.
Beras Terbakar
Aeroport
Makam Mahsuri
Kuah
Jetté
Pulau Timun
P. Cherong
P. Paku
Langkawi Island Resort
Terrain de Golf
P. Rebak
Pantai Tengah
Spg. Janggut
Pulau Dayang Bunting
P. Tepor
Gua Langsir
Plage des Galets
Pulau Tuba
P. Beras Basah
vers Pulau Paya
Tasek Dayang Bunting
Pulau Singa Besar

ACCOMMODATION

Here are a few examples of the accommodation available in Alor Setar. The Telephone Area Code is 04, and prices are in Malaysian Dollars for a double room.

Kedah Merlin Inn, Lot 134 Jalan Sultan Badlishah, ph 735 917 — $360; Hotel Samila, 27 Jalan Kanchut, ph 722 344 — $82; Mahawangsa Hotel, 449 Jalan Raja, ph 721 835 — $70; Royale Hotel, Jalan Putra, ph 730 922 — $50; Hotel Putra Jaya, 250B Jalan Putera, ph 730 344 — $40; Hotel Regent, 1536 Jalan Sultan Badlishah, ph 721 291 — $40; Station Hotel, 74 Jalan Langgar, ph 723 855 — $20.

SHOPPING

Pekan Rabu (Wednesday Market)
Opposite the Government Offices building in Alor Setar, is a market which used to be held weekly on Wednesdays, hence its name. Now it is open all week from morning until midnight with stalls selling local handicrafts as well as food.

SIGHTSEEING

Masjid Zahir
The largest mosque in Kedah is a stately and serene building, used by the Ruler of the State and the people of Alor Setar. An annual Koran reading competition takes place here.

Balai Besar
Facing Masjid Zahir, though with a large space in between, is Balai Besar, the audience hall. This hall, built in 1898, embodies some aspects of Thai architecture. The Sultan holds audience in this building on his birthday and on other festive occasions.

Gunung Jerai (Kedah Peak)
At 1,206 m (3,944 ft), Bunung Jerai is the highest spot in northern Peninsular Malaysia. Myths and legends abound around this peak. According to the annals, a king who had fangs and lived on blood, used to live in the Bujang Valley on the foothills of this mountain.

Bujang Valley

Based on archaeological evidence, this valley is believed to have been an important trade centre in the region between the 5th and 8th Centuries. So far more than 40 temple sites have been discovered and a number of temple bases have been restored. A museum at Bukit Batu Pahat houses artifacts, books and documents of the valley. It is an ideal place for nature lovers and could qualify as one of the country's historical parks.

Kuala Kedah

Located on the mouth of the Kedah River about 10 km (6 miles) from Alor Setar, Kuala Kedah is a fishing village, and the boats returning to the harbour with their catch at sunset are worth seeing. There are several small restaurants here that serve fresh seafood.

LANGKAWI

Part of the State of Kedah, Langkawi is a group of 99 islands, most of them uninhabited, 27 km (17 miles) off the coast of Kuala Perlis and 112 km (70 miles) north of Penang, at the point where the Indian Ocean melts into the Straits of Malacca.

The islands were once a haven for pirates, but now they are the ideal place for people who do not want crowds, and who want to get away from it all. The main industry is still fishing, and tourism is just in its infancy.

The main island, Pulau Langkawi, from which the group takes its name, was once the subject of a seven-generation curse by a Malay Princess, Mahsuri, unjustly accused of adultery and executed, but the curse has now expired.

The island "capital" is Kuah, which has a population of over 2,000. The main road in Langkawi passes through Kuah, and goes to the various points of interest scattered throughout the northern, western and southern reaches of the island.

HOW TO GET THERE

By Air

MAS flies daily from Kuala Lumpur to Langkawi via Penang. The one-way fares are as follows:

Kuala Lumpur-Langkawi — M$112.00
Penang-Langkawi — M$42.00

By Ferry
The ferry 'Gadis Langkasuka' leaves Penang on alternate Fridays at 11pm and returns the following Sunday at 9am. The fares are M$35 one-way and M$65 return. For enquiries contact Sanred Delta Marine, ph 04-379 325, or Asian Overland, ph 03-292 5622. From Kuala Perlis, six ferry boats and a hovercraft provide scheduled crossings to Langkawi. The fares vary from M$4.50 to M$10 depending on the speed of the service. The slowest ferry takes one hour forty-five minutes, while the hovercraft takes approximately 35 minutes.

ACCOMMODATION
On the main island you can choose from a range of accommodation to suit your taste. However, the most impressive is The Langkawi Island Resort, managed by the Tourist Development Corporation of Malaysia, which provides all the amenities expected from any international hotel. It has 219 air conditioned rooms, and the prices range from M$95 to M$800.

Other suggestions are:
Government Rest House, Kuah, ph 04-788 127 — M$8 to M$22; Hotel Asia, ph 04-788 216 — M$21 to M$48.30; Hotel Langkawi, ph 04-788 248 — M$12–M$40; Mutiara Beach Hotel, ph 04-788 488 — M$70–M$120.

LOCAL TRANSPORT
Taxis operate on the island, and the fare from the ferry landing point to Kuah is M$1 per head on a shared basis.

ENTERTAINMENT
The entertainment offered here is the island itself. This is not the place for jet set living, but rather more for the relaxed beachcombing type of holiday. Of course, the hotels and beach resorts offer exotic seafood, cooked as only the locals know how, but you won't find streets of restaurants offering dishes from different Asian countries as in other areas.

If you go to Langkawi looking for a place to relax, soak in

the sun and turn a lovely golden-brown, you will not be disappointed. There are enough beaches here (at Pulau Beras Basah and Pulau Singa for instance) to provide you with your own private niche with nothing except the imprints of your own feet in the sand for miles around. The islanders of course have their own favourite beaches, but don't limit yourself to just one or two.

Pantai Rhu (Casuarina Beach) is lined by tall swaying casuarina trees, and is one of the best on the island. At low tide you can walk across the sandy stretch that joins Pantai Rhu to a neighbouring island. However, when the tide swells, the sandy strip is covered. Pantai Rhu is 22.5 km (14 miles) by land from Kuah.

At the southern tip of the island is a beautiful kilometre-long beach, Pantai Tengah (Central Beach). This is accessible by road from Kuah and is situated in a sheltered bay, with calm water suitable for water-skiing.

Other popular beaches include the Beach of Black Sand where the ground is literally covered with black sand, and Pebble Beach on Pulau Dayang Bunting, which is strewn with pebbles. Then there is Burau Beach on the west coast which has a white sandy shoreline and clear blue water.

The seas around the Langkawi group are clear in many spots, and excellent for snorkelling. One such spot, Pulau Paya, is a cluster of little islands whose seabeds are interlaced with beautiful corals.

SIGHTSEEING

The Langkawi Island Resort will organise tours of the island, or you can rent a car, bicycle or motorcycle to reach many of the attractions on the Island.

Kuah

This is a one-street town along the water front, and the bay is full of sunken fishing boats. Its main attraction is a picturesque mosque with Moorish arches, minarets and a golden dome, surrounded by palm trees.

Durian Perangin

This pretty waterfall is at the 9th milestone from Kuah, along a road, lined with rubber plantations, which turns off the main road. It is well sign-posted.

Mahsuri's Tomb

In a little village 12 km (7 miles) from Kuah, this spot is recommended for lovers of folklore. It was here that the Malay princess, Mahsuri, was executed, and the story says that she proved her innocence when white blood streamed from her body. The blood seeped into the earth, accounting for the unusually snow-white nature of Langkawi's shores.

Padang Masirat (Field of Burnt Rice)

During an invasion after Mahsuri's death, the islanders scorched their rice fields rather than abandon them to the invaders. Today, 19 km (12 miles) from Kuah, the charred remains can still be seen at Padang Masirat. Occasionally traces of burnt rice are brought to the surface by heavy rains.

Telaga Tujuh (The Seven Wells)

A fresh water stream cascades 91 m (298 ft) down through a series of seven pools. While it can be great fun sliding from one pool to another, the rock surfaces tend to be slippery, and it is not advisable to attempt sliding from the top-most pools. The lower pools are not hazardous, but still children should not be allowed to play without adult supervision.

Telaga Air Panas (Hot Springs)

The legend that surrounds this hot spring is that there was a bitter quarrel between two of the island's leading families because of a rejected offer of marriage. The boy's family raided the girl's village and a violent battle ensued. All the pots, pans, plates and saucers in the village were shattered. A pot was flung at a place thereafter called "Belanga Pecah" (Broken Pot). Gravy was spilt at Kuah (gravy) and seeped into the soil at a place called Kisap (seep). Finally a jugful of hot water was spilt at the present site of Telaga Air Panas (Hot Spring).

Tasek Dayang Bunting (The Lake of the Pregnant Maiden)

This is a fresh water lake on the isle of the same name. According to local folklore, a married couple, childless for 19 years, drank from the lake and subsequently the wife gave birth to a baby girl. The lake has become a popular destination for childless couples from all over Malaysia.

Gua Langsir (Cave of the Banshee)
Near the Lake of the Pregnant Maiden, this cave is over 91 m (298 ft) high and is home to thousands of bats, which perhaps explains its reputation of being haunted.

RECREATION
Apart from the beaches already mentioned Langkawi has several lagoons which are excellent for water-skiing, or you can rent a boat and tour around the entire 99 islands.

If golf is your forte, on the main island about 6.4 km (4 miles) from Kuah, there is a 9-hole golf course managed by the District Office. The green fee is M$10.

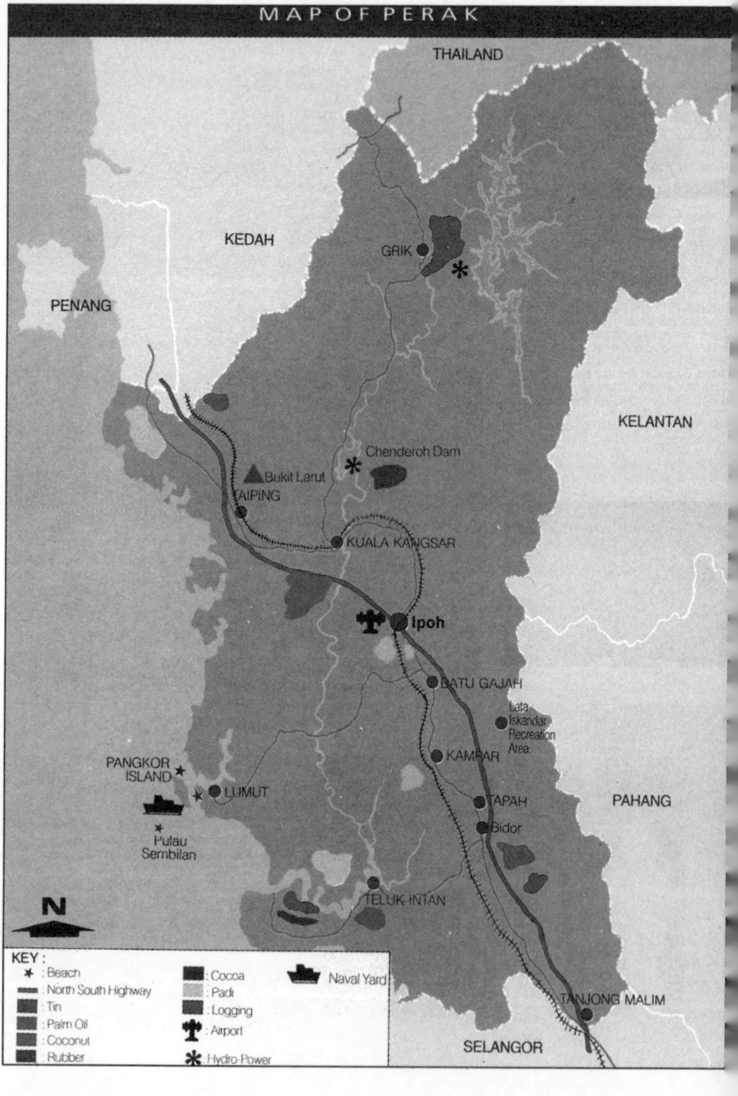
MAP OF PERAK
THAILAND
KEDAH
PENANG
GRIK
KELANTAN
Chenderoh Dam
Bukit Larut
TAIPING
KUALA KANGSAR
Ipoh
BATU GAJAH
Lata Iskandar Recreation Area.
KAMPAR
PANGKOR ISLAND
LUMUT
TAPAH
PAHANG
Bidor
Pulau Sembilan
TELUK INTAN
N
TANJONG MALIM
SELANGOR
KEY :
: Beach
: North South Highway
: Tin
: Palm Oil
: Coconut
: Rubber
: Cocoa
: Padi
: Logging
: Airport
: Hydro-Power
Naval Yard

PERAK

Perak has the world's richest tin deposits in its Kinta Valley. Covering an area of 21,000 km² (8,106 sq. milles), it has a population of almost 2 million people.

Perak is divided into nine districts and its major towns include Ipoh, Kuala Kangsar, Taiping, Teluk Intah and Lumut. Kuala Kangsar is the royal town of Perak, while Ipoh is the state capital and the administration centre of the state.

HISTORY

The state of Perak Darul Ridzuan, the "Land of Grace" has been in existence since prehistoric times. Remnants of the Stone Age period have been found in Kota Tampan in Lenggong.

In the early days the Malay Peninsula was well-known for its rich mineral resources, especially tin and gold. It is for this reason that the Peninsula was named "The Golden Chersonese" by the Greeks. One of the minerals, tin, was found in abundance in Perak. It is popularly believed that this state was called 'Perak" because of the silver colour ("perak" in the Malay language) of the tin ore.

This mineral wealth played an important role in determining the historical and economic growth of Perak. Perak's tin resources attracted such foreign powers as the Portuguese, Achinese, Bugis, Siamese, Dutch and finally the British.

Perak is governed by a constitutional monarch or sultan. Under the sultan is the State Council comprising the state assemblymen and headed by the Mentri Besar who is the Chief Executive of state. The state's sultanate system is unique and rich in tradition. It does not practise the common hereditary system where the eldest son automatically becomes the ruler once the father dies. Traditionally six people have the right to succeed to the throne in sequence when the sultan dies. They are the Raja Muda, Raja di Hilir, Raja Kecil Besar, Raja Kecil Sulung, Raja Kecil Tengah and Raja Kecil Bongsu.

The men who fill all the above positions are descendants of Sultan Ahmaddin Shah, the 18th Sultan of Perak.

The present and 34th Sultan of Perak is Sultan Azlan Muhibbuddin Ghafarullahu-Lahu Shah.

HOW TO GET THERE

By Air
MAS has daily flights to Ipoh from Kuala Lumpur, Penang and Kota Bharu.

By Train
The mail train service from Kuala Lumpur to Butterworth stops at Tanjung Malin, Tapah, Kampar, Batu Gajah, Ipoh, Kuala Kangsar and Taiping in the state of Perak. It leaves Kuala Lumpur at 8.30am and arrives at Butterworth at 6.10pm.

The Ekspres Rakyat and Ekspres Sinaran Pagi/Petang also have daily services leaving Kuala Lumpur at 2pm and 3pm respectively, arriving at Butterworth at 8.40pm and 9.30pm. The Ekspres Rakyat stops at Tapah, Kampar, Ipoh, Kuala Kangsar and Taiping, and the Ekspres Sinaran Pagi/Petang at Ipoh, Kuala Kangsar and Taiping.

The one-way fares, in Malaysian Dollars from Kuala Lumpur at time of printing are:

To	AFC	ASC	SC	TC
Tapah	26.00	15.00	12.00	9.00
Kampar	28.00	16.00	13.00	9.00
Ipoh	32.00	18.00	15.00	11.00
Kuala Kangsar	39.00	21.00	18.00	13.00
Taiping	43.00	23.00	20.00	14.00

AFC = First class air-conditioned.
ASC = Second class air-conditioned.
SC = Ordinary second class.
TC = Third class ordinary (only on Ekspres Rakyat)

By Bus
Air-conditioned express buses from Kuala Lumpur charge M$8.60 to Ipoh, while those from Butterworth charge M$12.00.

By Taxi
Out-station taxis to Ipoh are available from most major towns.

TOURIST INFORMATION
Perak Tourist and Bumiputra Service Center, State Economic Planning Unit, Jalan Dewan, 30000 Ipoh, ph 05-532 800.

ACCOMMODATION
There is a wide variety of accommodation in the principal towns of Perak. We have listed a few here with prices in Malaysian Dollars for a double room. The Telephone Area Code is 05.

Ipoh
Excelsior Hotel, Clarke Street, ph 536 666 — $118; Royal Casuarina Hotel, 24 Jln Gopeng, ph 505 555 — $150; Station Hotel, Club Road, ph 512 588 — $70–300; Eastern Hotel, 118 Jln Sultan Idris Shah, ph 543 936 — $95; Lotte Hotel, 97 Jln Raja Ikram, ph 542 215/7 — $75; Mikado Hotel, 86–88 Jln Yang Kalsom, ph 515 855 — $75–85; French Hotel, 60–62 Jln Raja Ikram, ph 513 455 – $79–85.

Caspian Hotel, 6–10 Jln Jublee, ph 542 324/6 — $40; City Hotel, 79 Jln Chamberlain, ph 512 911 — $32–34; Diamond Hotel, 3–9 Jln Ali Pitchay, ph 513 644 — $35; Fairmont Hotel, 10 Kampar Road, ph 511 100 — $48–52; Golden Inn Hotel, 17 Jln Che Tak, ph 530 866/8 — $40; Hollywood Hotel, 72–76 Chamberlain Road, ph 515 322 — $35; Merlin Hotel, 92–98 Jln Clare, ph 541 531 — $41–50; New Perak Hotel, 20–26 Jln Ali Pitchay, ph 515 011 — $36–40; Winner Hotel, 32–38 Jln Ali Pitchay, ph 515 177 — $30–69.

Kuala Kangsar
Double Lion Hotel, 74 Jln Kangsar, ph 851 010 — $16–50; Tin Heong Hotel, 34 Jln Raja Chulan — $20

Lumut
Lumut Country Resort, 331 Jln Titi Panjang, ph 935 009 — $80; Phin Lum Hooi Hotel, 93 Jln Titi Panjang, ph 935 641 — $10–12.

160 SINGAPORE AND MALAYSIA AT COST

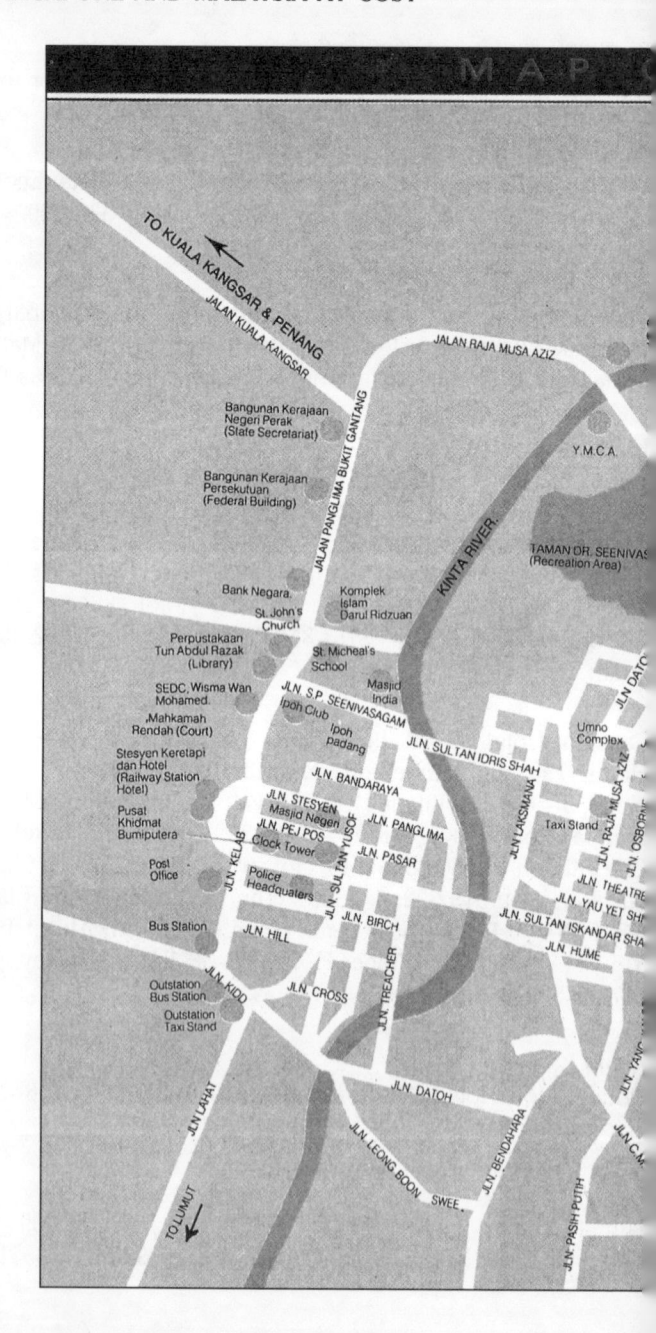

PERAK 161

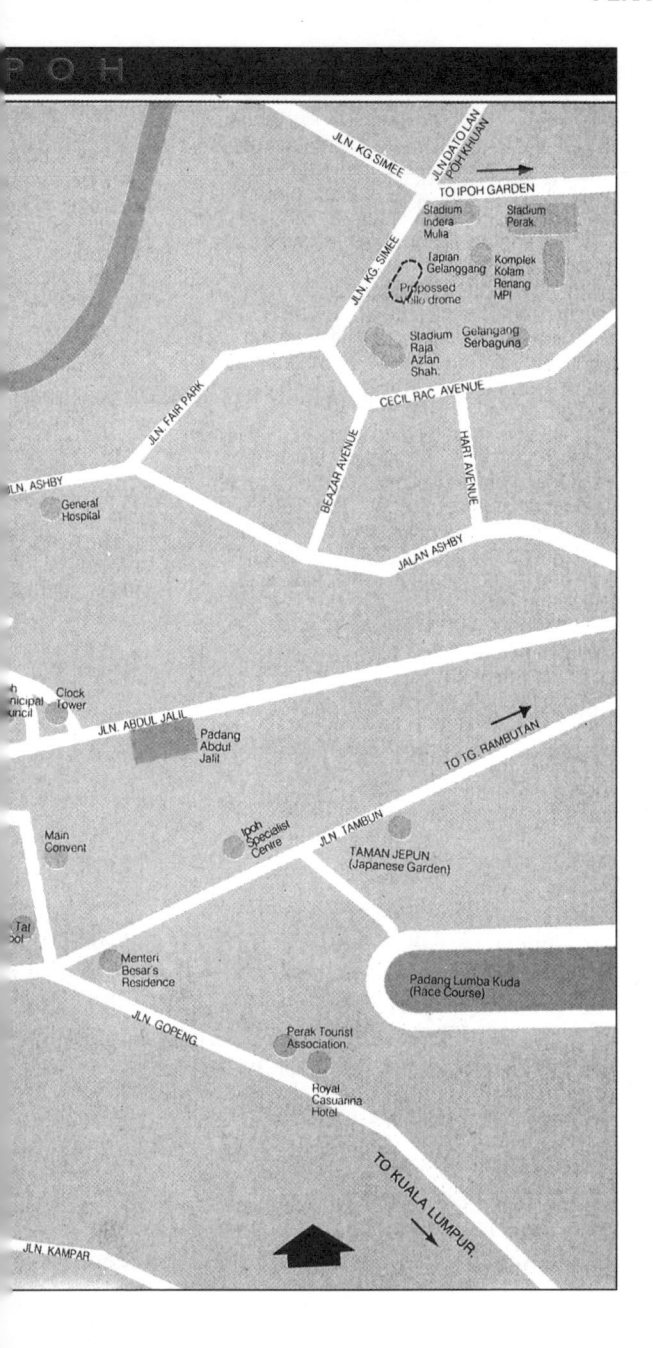

Pulau Pangkor

Pan Pacific Resort Pangkor, Teluk Belanga, ph 939 091 — $150 (garden view), $170 (ocean view); Pangkor Bay Village, Teluk Belanga, ph 557 627 — $80; Sea View Hotel, Pasir Bogak, ph 939 056/7 — $65–75; Beach Huts Hotel, Jln Pasir Bogah, ph 939 159 — $50–80; Min Nin Hotel, 1-A Jln Besar, ph 939 294 — $24–32.

Taiping

Panorama Hotel, 61–79 Jln Kota, ph 834 192 — $58–88; Meridien Hotel, 2 Simpang Road, ph 831 133 — $58–75.

Hong Kong Hotel, 79 Barrack Road, ph 823 824 — $26; Lake View Hotel, 1A Circular Road, ph 824 941 — $24–30; Latin Quarter Hotel, 17 Harisson Street, ph 823 733 — $23; Mikado Hotel, 14 Boo Bee Street, ph 821 366 — $30; Mirama Hotel, 30 Jln Peng Loong, ph 821 077 — $24–28; Oriental Hotel, 14 Barrack Hotel, ph 825 433 — $24–36; Peking Hotel, 2 Jln Idris, ph 822 975 — $16–22; Swiss Hotel, 37 Jln Panggong Wayang, ph 824 899 — $18–25; Town Hotel, 220 Jln Kota, ph 821 166 — $33; Yeh Lai Shang Hotel, 36–38 Tupai Road, ph 824 244/5 — $18–22.

Tanjong Malim

Mee Chew Hotel, 1 Jln Loke Yew, ph 346 496 — $20; Tanjong Hotel, 1 Jln Chong Ah Peng, ph 346 159 — $11; Yik Mun Hotel, Lot 6043 Jln Slim Lama, ph 346 546 — $20.

Teluk Intan

Angsoka Hotel, 24 Jln Changkat Jong, ph 623 755 — $36–55; Anson Hotel, Jalan Sekolah, ph 626 166/7/8 — $33–66; Asia Hotel, 12 Jln Raja, ph 621 172 — $11; Kok Min Hotel, 1065A Jln Anderson, ph 621 529 — $12; Kok Thye Hotel, 120-A Jln Pasar, ph 621 947 — $9–22; Merlin Hotel, 30F Jln Changkat Jong, ph 621 355 — $20; Metro Hotel, 68 Jln Pasar, ph 621 522 — $17–24.

EATING OUT

Perak has an astonishing variety of eating places, ranging from expensive restaurants to open-air food stalls which serve Eastern and Western dishes, including Malay, Chinese, Indian, Japanese, Thai, Korean and Continental. Some establishments organise live music and floor shows. Certain restaurants in the cities hold Malaysian Cultural Shows, which make dining interesting.

Whether it is early morning, lunchtime, snack time, evening or supper time, little roadside stalls with portable tables and chairs appear everywhere to quench the thirst and appease the appetite. Here dining is value for money with no service charge or tipping.

In Ipoh, typical open-air food stalls can be found along Osborne Road, at Ipoh Garden and opposite the old post office building.

ENTERTAINMENT

When the sun goes down, Ipoh becomes alive with its variety of entertainment as the nightclubs, discos and pubs open for business. There is an abundance of places of entertainment to suit diverse tastes and the different age groups. Among the famous discotheques in Ipoh are the Excelsior Club, the Blue Diamond and El-Amigo.

There are also cinema theatres and bowling alleys, and horse racing is a favourite local sport.

SHOPPING

Shopping in Perak is a unique experience. Ipoh, the capital city, offers many shopping areas filled with a wide variety of goods, ranging from huge department stores to colourful bazaars with bargains.

Super Kinta, the biggest shopping complex in Malaysia in terms of size, is in Ipoh, as are the Yik Foong Complex and Perak Emporium. Other major shopping areas in Ipoh are along the Sultan Idris and Laksamana Roads. These complexes are open from 10am to 10pm.

Tekat Benang Emas (Gold Embroidery)

This is a decorative embroidery that uses gold thread to satin-stitch elaborate swirls and abstract designs on a velvet base. The intricacy of the design depends on the person's creativity and skill. It is popularly used for bed-spreads, pillows and cushions that are a part of a traditional Malay bridal bedroom set, and also the bride's handbag.

Tekad Benang Emas is available at Kampung Padang Changkat, Kuala Kangsar and at any of Perak's handicraft centres.

Bamboo Works of Art

Creating products from bamboo is a fascinating art. The long and rigid bamboo is first made pliable and then carved by skilled and patient craftsmen.

The heart of the industry is at Kampung Berala, Kati, where an exclusive bamboo-making centre is situated about 15 km (9 miles) from Kuala Kangsar town. Examples of crafted bamboo products are coin-boxes, penholders and picture-frames.

Sea-shell Designs

A wide range of handicrafts and antiques is typical to the state of Perak. Among the prized art forms are the sea-shell and sea-coral creations.

Lumut is popular for its corals and sea-shells, which make attractive decorative pieces. The corals and shells are shaped into flowers, ships, birds and other forms. These sea-shell and coral designs are favourite tourist items. They are available in all of Perak's handicraft centres.

Traditional Handicraft

This is a prominent cottage industry in Perak. It is predominantly found in Kuala Kangsar and Taiping. There are a number of handicraft centres which sell local goods. These are to be found at Enggor in Kuala Kangsar, the Ipoh Railway Station and the Tourism and Bumiputera Service Centre in Ipoh.

Labu Sayong (Earthenware)

Labu Sayong is a type of earthenware popular among the Malays in the kampung (village). It is a water pitcher, shaped like a pumpkin, to keep water cool. Water stored in these pitchers is also locally believed to have medicinal value.

The Labu Sayong is primarily produced at Kampung Kepala Bendang in Sayong, located about 15 km from Kuala Kangsar town. For those interested, there is a centre in Enggor, close to Kuala Kangsar, which besides offering a course in pottery, also sells finished wares.

SIGHTSEEING
IPOH

Geology Museum
This museum (Musium Batu Batan) was established under the Geological Survey Department in Ipoh, in 1957. The main feature of the museum is its collection of more than 600 kinds of minerals, classified according to chemical contents and structures. Open 8am–4.15pm Mon–Fri, 8am–12.45pm Sat. Admission is free, but visitors must first get entry permission from the information counter.

Kellie's Castle, Batu Gajah
This is an interesting site to visit. It is located near Batu Gajah, about 30 minutes by car from Ipoh. The castle belonged to William Kellie Smith, an Englishman, who was a rubber plantation owner. It is full of mystery. It is believed that the castle has more rooms than apparent, and a secret tunnel, which no-one can find.

The construction of the castle was abruptly stopped after Kellie Smith left for England. He was reported missing and later found dead at Lisbon in 1926.

Tambun's Pre-Historic Painting Cave
Visitors interested in archaeology will certainly like to visit this cave (in Malay Gua Lukisan Pra-Sejarah Tambun). It is located about 6 km (4 miles) from Ipoh, in one of the limestone hills at Gunung Churam. There is a gallery of ancient paintings which were done about two thousand years ago, and which are similar to the cave paintings found in Australia.

Limestone Caves (Sam Poh Tong and Perak Tong)
Located only 5 km (3 miles) from the southern part of Ipoh town, the Sam Poh Tong cave temple is accessible by car. Opened by a Buddhist monk 20 years ago, it is the largest temple in this area. There is a definite aura to the cave with the natural stalactite and stalagmite formations beside the various replicas of the Buddha.

Nearby there is a tunnel which leads to a tortoise pond. According to Chinese mythology, the tortoise symbolises long life. There is also a wishing well, but remember you are only allowed one wish per coin. The temple is open at all times.

Another impressive cave temple is the Perak Tong at Kuala Kangsar Road, Ipoh. Opened in 1926 by a Buddhist priest from China, this temple has 40 Buddha statues, with a 12.8 m (42 ft) Buddha in a sitting position presiding. Beyond the main altar a path leads into the cave's interior. After a steep climb of 385 steps, the cave opens again to reveal a good view of the surrounding countryside.

Meh Prasit Temple

Also known as the Wat Thai, this temple houses the largest statue of Lord Buddha in Malaysia — 24.38 m long, (80 ft) 6.4 m (20 ft) high and 4.5 m (15 ft) wide. Inside the huge head of the reclining statue is a glass case containing a tiny fragment of a bone of Lord Buddha. Glued to the body of the statue are thousands of gold leaves specially imported from Thailand.

Tambun Hot Springs

A 15 minute drive from Ipoh town, at the foot of a limestone hill, this recreation park provides facilities such as a sauna bath, restaurants, lounge and bathrooms. It is open daily from 3pm–12 midnight, and the entrance fee is M$4.50.

Other hot springs found in Perak are at Kampung Ulu Slim in Slim River, Kampung Air Panas in Grik Sungkai, Pengkalan Hulu and Manong in Kuala Kangsar.

Japanese Garden

Located close to the Perak Turf Club in Ipoh, this park illustrates Japanese culture. Among the many features are the red bridge across the stream, goldfish pond, a small house of traditional design, a man-made waterfall and a large floral clock. Admission is free.

DR Seenivasagam Park

This park is right in the town of Ipoh, and is a popular place for relaxing. There is also a roller skating rink and a mini-locomotive track.

KUALA KANGSAR

Masjid Ubudiah
This is one of the most beautiful mosques in Malaysia. Built during the reign of Sultan Idris Murshidul'adzam Shah I, the 28th Sultan of Perak, it stands beside the Royal Mausoleum at Bukit Chandan, Kuala Kangsar, 51 km (32 miles) from Ipoh. Construction began in 1913 but was interrupted several times. Finally in 1917, the $200,000 mosque was opened by Sultan Abdul Jalil Karamtullah Shah. This imposing landmark, designed by a European engineer, has become a symbol of pride for Muslims in Perak.

Malay College
Opened in 1905 this was initially known as the Malay Residential School. At that time admission to the college was a privilege only enjoyed by families of Royalty and Malay dignitaries. The name Malay College or Maktab Mellayu was adopted in 1909, and it is now the aspiration of every Malay boy to study at this college.

Istana Iskandariah
This palace, the official residence of the Sultan of Perak, is situated at Bukit Chandan, formerly called Changkat Negara. It was built in 1930 to replace the old palace, and is designed to have a few domes resembling a mosque. The front of the palace facing the sun gives the impression that the sun always shines upon Perak Darul Ridzuan, the "Land of Grace".

Istana Kenangan
Istana Kenangan, also known as Istana Lembah or Istana Tepas, has been converted into the Perak Royal Museum. The most interesting fact about the building, formerly a palace, is that it was built without any architectural plan, and without using a single nail.

Located near Istana Iskandariah, the Sultan of Perak's official palace at Kuala Kangsar, it was given the name Istana Kenangan in 1960 when it was restored through the initiative of Tunku Abdul Rahman, the first Prime Minister of Malaysia. Among the items displayed are Royal Regalia, photographs of the royal family, traditional regalia and illustrations of the history of monarchy in Perak.

KUALA KANGSAR

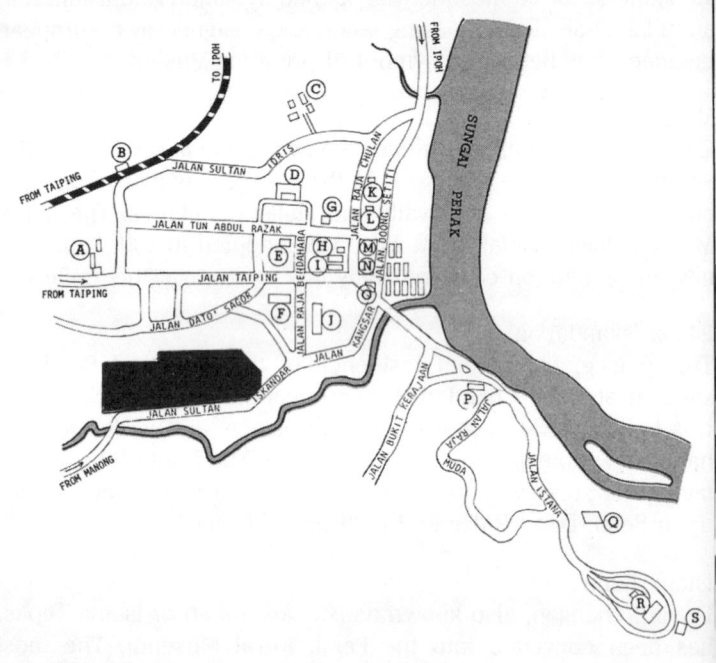

A. DISTRICT HOSPITAL
B. RAILWAY STATION
C. LADIES HOSPITAL
D. MALAY COLLEGE
E. MERDEKA HALL
F. CLIFFORD SCHOOL
G. MASJID RIDZWANIAH
H. DISTRICT OFFICE
I. DISTRICT PUBLIC HEADQUARTERS
J. BUS STATION
K. TELECOMS
L. SUPERMARKETS
M. IDRIS CLUB
N. COURT
O. POST OFFICE
P. REST HOUSE
Q. MASJID UBUDIAH
R. ISTANA ISKANDARIAH
S. ISTANA KENANGAN

Royal Mausoleum

The Royal Mausoleum is located about .8 km (.5 mile) south of Kuala Kangsar, adjacent to Masjid Ubudiah. There are a total of 7 mausoleums of the sultans of Perak, three of which are found inside the main mausoleum, while the rest are outside.

Besides the Royal Mausoleum there are other well-known mausoleums such as the Daeng Sedili and Tok Janggut at Kota Lama Kiri, Kuala Kangsar. The tomb of J.W.W. Birch, the first British Resident of Perak, who was killed in Pasir Salak, is located at Pulau Besar, as is the mausoleum of his assassin, Si Puntum.

The First Rubber Tree

The planting of nine rubber trees in 1877 by the then British Resident, Sir Hugh Low, marked the beginning of the Malaysian rubber industry. Today only one out of the original nine stands in the grounds of the District Office in this royal town.

Tugu Keris

Tugu Keris, literally translated as Dagger Monument, is located at the Government Hill near the Rest House in Kuala Kangsar. It was built in 1963 to commemorate the installation of the late Sultan Idris Shah, the 33rd Sultan of Perak. The 'Taming Sari' designed dagger, with its eyes pointing to the sky, is a symbol of power. Hang Tuah, the great Malay warrior, was the owner of the original Taming Sari.

TAIPING

Perak Museum

This museum, the oldest in the country, was built in 1883 and houses an interesting collection of ancient weapons, ornaments, aboriginal implements and archaeological specimens from pre-historic times until the British era. Open daily from 9.30am–5pm.

Railway Museum

Located near the Taiping Railway Station, it is the only one of its kind in Malaysia. It was here that the first railway line was built between Port Weld (now known as Kuala Sepetang) and Taiping in 1885. Admission is free.

170 SINGAPORE AND MALAYSIA AT COST

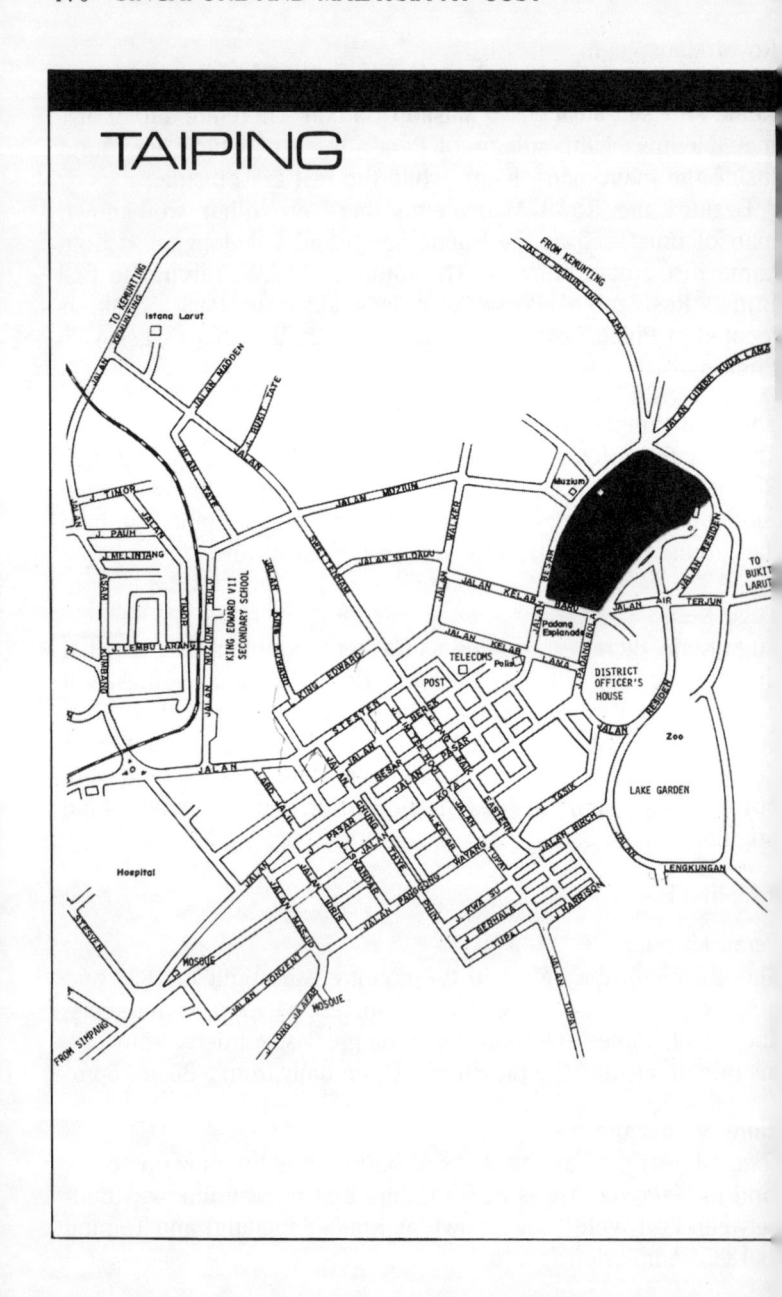

TAIPING

Taiping Lake Gardens
This 62 ha (153 acre) park includes a beautiful lake, in which one can fish or aquabike ride. It has lush green lawns and a profusion of flowers. There is a also a golf course in the middle.

Taiping Zoo
One of the oldest in the country, this zoo is situated in the Lake Gardens and houses a variety of animals. One interesting feature is the presence of monkeys roaming about freely in the grounds. Also known as Taman Mergustua Idris Shah, the entrance fee is 50 cents.

TELUK INTAN

The Leaning Tower
84 km (52 miles) from Ipoh this tower is the main feature in the centre of the town of Teluk Intan, and is known as the Leaning Tower of Malaysia. The tower slants to the left, reminiscent of the Pisa Tower in Italy, and is situated in the centre of town.

The pagoda-like structure was built in 1885 by a Chinese contractor, Leong Choon Choong. The dominating 25.5 m (83 ft) tower appears to be made up of eight storeys instead of three. Initially the tower was used as a water storage tank for the town of Teluk Intan. This use was stopped in 1919 when the town commenced obtaining its water from Changkat Jong.

War Memorial Monument
This memorial was constructed to commemorate Malaysian soldiers who died in the cause of peace and freedom.

BEACH RESORTS

LUMUT
The town of Lumut is 84 km (52 miles) south of Ipoh and can be reached by bus or taxi from Butterworth, Kuala Lumpur and other major towns. Lumut Country Resort is the place to stay if you are looking for a hotel of international repute, but there are also government resthouses and other smaller hotels in the town.

The Sea Festival in Lumut held in August about every two years has not failed to attract tourists.

Teluk Batik

Beautiful golden beaches, white sandy shores, cool refreshing sea air await tourists at Teluk Batik, situated 6.4 km (4 miles) from Lumut. Apart from camping, you can stay in comfortable chalets by the beach. For reservations contact the Manager, Teluk Batik Chalets, ph 935 544.

PULAU PANGKOR

This beautiful island, still relatively unspoiled and underdeveloped, may be reached by ferry boat from Lumut in half an hour.

Pantai Puteri Dewi (Golden Sands)

This is beautiful stretch of golden sandy beach on the north-west coast of Pangkor. There's a legend behind the origin of the name of Pantai Puteri Dewi. A Sumatran princess came to this island in search of her warrior lover. Broken-hearted after learning of his death, she took her own life.

The ferry to this beach, and the Pan Pacific Resort, leaves Lumut from 8am to 4pm daily and the journey takes about 45 minutes.

Pasir Bogak

They say the best parts of Pasir Bogak are the water and outdoor activities — scuba-diving, fishing, camping, etc. The shallow crystal-clear water allows more than a glimpse of the vast coral reef that surrounds the island.

Accessible by ferry from Lumut, the journey takes only 30 minutes, and the ferry runs from 7am till 7pm. It is also possible to get there by taxi from the jetty at Pangkor. Accommodation ranges from hotels, government rest houses to budget "Atap Huts" at Mini Camps. The "Atap Hut" is triangular in shape and very quaint.

Pulau Pangkor Laut

Popularly known as "Fantasy Island" this is every tourist's dream. Pretty maidens welcome you with garlands and warm smiles to brighten up your holiday.

Pulau Pangkor Laut is an island resort of international standard, offering excellent facilties, including 72 wooden atap chalets, swimming pools, fishing, sports hall, disco, restaurants, etc. It is situated to the west of the southern tip of Pulau Pangkor, and the ferry trip from Lumut takes 45 minutes.

Emerald Bay, is a popular beach on this island, with translucent, emerald-green water and snow-white sandy shores.

There are other beach resorts that might stir interest and adventure...Pantai Rubiah in Lumut and Teluk Nipah in Pangkor. You can also hire boats to discover the islands on the outskirts of Pulau Pangkor, such as Pulau Sembilan and Pulau Mentagor. A whole array of outdoor sights and activities are offered.

HILL RESORT

BUKIT LARUT

Bukit Larut, formerly known as Maxwell Hill, is Malayasia's oldest hill resort. For further information see the section on Hill Resorts.

EAST COAST — KELANTAN

Long famous for the gentle nature of its people, the East Coast States of Malaysia, comprising the states of Kelantan, Terengganu and Pahang, is a comparatively undisturbed area with traditional skills such as fishing, boat-making and village handicrafts being maintained until the present day. It is much quieter than the west coast and to many people this is the reason for its charm.

KELANTAN

Kelantan, which means "Land of Lightning", is situated in the north-eastern corner of Peninsular Malaysia, and its rustic setting amidst padi fields and picturesque villages, will give you insights into a way of life that has endured the passing of time. Unspoilt beaches stretch along its 96 km (60 miles) coast. It has an area of 13,931 km^2 (5,377 sq. miles) and the capital is Kota Bharu.

HOW TO GET THERE

By Air

MAS flies from Kuala Lumpur, Penang and Alor Setar into Kota Bharu daily. The flight from KL takes 45 minutes.

By Bus

From Kuala Lumpur the express bus fare is M$25, from Kuantan, M$15, and from Kuala Terengganu, M$5.70. Through the North-East Highway, buses go direct to Butterworth, charging fares of M$18. They also operate direct runs to Johor Bahru and Malacca. The fare is M$28 for Johor Bahur and M$25 for Malacca.

The bus stations in Kota Bharu are at Jalan Hamzah and Jalan Pendek.

By Taxi

From Kuala Lumpur the taxi fare is M$40 per head, from Kuantan, M$25 and from Kuala Terengganu M$10. Some taxis also ply directly between Kota Bharu and Johor Bahru. The fare is M$46.

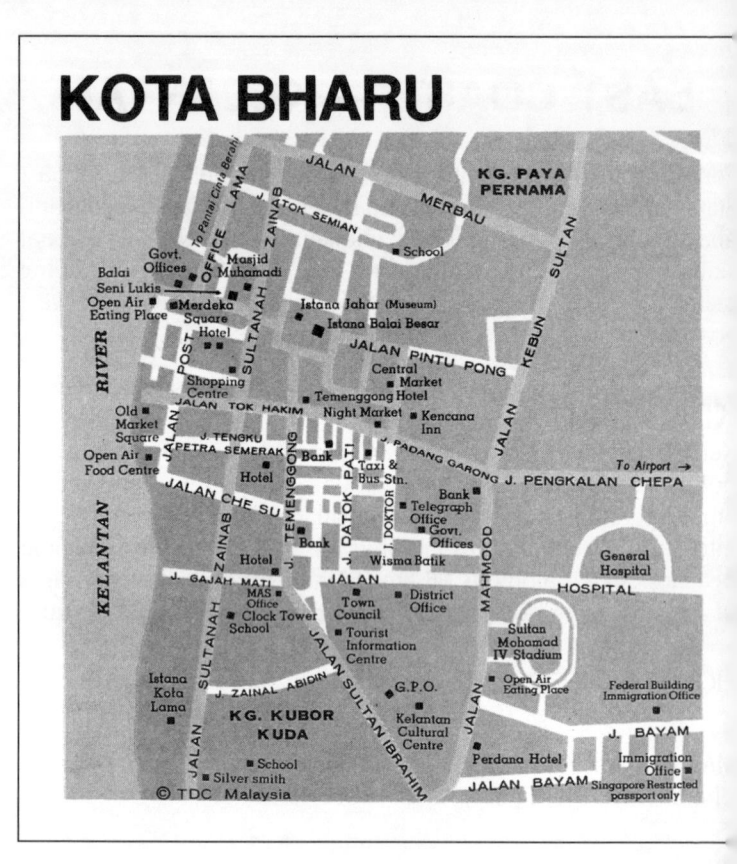

KOTA BHARU

TOURIST INFORMATION
Tourist Information Centre, Jalan Sultan Ibrahim, Kota Bharu, Kelantan, ph 09-785 534/783 543.

ACCOMMODATION
Hotels in Kota Bharu are numerous, ranging from luxury class to the very modest no-frills establishments. Here we have listed a few, and the prices quoted are for a double room, in Malaysian Dollars. The Telephone Area Code is 09.

Perdana Hotel, Jalan Mahmud, ph 785 000 — $75; Kobaru Hotel, Wisma Suara Muda, Jalan Doktor, ph 749 397 — $60; Kencaca Inn, Lot 177–181, Jalan Padang Garong, ph 747 944 — $58; Pantai Cinta Berahi Resort, Pantai Cinta Berahi, ph 781 307 — $55; Temenggong Hotel, Jalan Tok Hakim ph 783 130 — $55; Murni Hotel, Jalan Dato Pati, ph 782 399 — $52; Indah Hotel, 236A Jln Tengku Besar, ph 785 081 — $48.

Irama Baru Hotel, 3180A Jalan Sultan Ibrahim, ph 782 722 — $35; Suria Hotel, Jalan Padang Garong, ph 746 477 — $30; Long House Beach Motel, Pantai Cinta Berahi, ph 740 090 — $20; Milton Hotel, 5471A Jalan Pengkalan Chepa, ph 782 744 — $20.

LOCAL TRANSPORT

Many points of interest in Kota Bharu are within walking distance of each other, while outlying attractions can be quite easily reached by bus, car or trishaw. In order to get the most out of your tour, we suggest that you use local tourist guides.

Bus
The Syarikat Kenderaan Melayu Kelantan (SKMK) bus service takes you around town as well as to the outskirts and well-known tourist desinations. Visitors may board the bus at the Jalan Pendek Bus Station (for travel within Kota Bharu) or the Langgar Bus Station, Jalan Pasir Puteh and Jalan Hamzan Bus Station (for travel out of Kota Bharu).

Bus Services (External)
1. Kota Bharu-K. Terengganu
ETD 8am, 9.30am, 11.30am, 1pm, 3pm, 4.30pm and Thurs & Fri only 6.30pm — Kota Bharu Station.
2. Kota Bharu-Dungun
ETD 8.30am, 2pm — Kota Bharu Station.
3. Kota Bharu-Kuantan
ETD 12 midnight, 11pm, 8.30am, 10am, 3pm, 11pm — Kota Bharu Station.
4. Kota Bharu-Rompin
ETD 9am, 8pm — Kota Bharu Station.

5. Kota Bharu-Segamat-Johor Bharu
ETD 9am, 8pm — Kota Bharu Station.
6. Kota Bharu-Singapore
ETD 9am, 8pm — Kota Bharu Station — 8pm Langgar Bus Station.
7. Kota Bharu-Kuala Lumpur
ETD 8pm — Langgar Bas Station.
8. Kota Bharu-Penang
ETD 9pm — Kota Bharu Station.
9. Kota Bharu-Temerioh
ETD 9am, 9pm — Kota Bharu Station.
10. Rantau Panjang-Kuantan
ETD 11am — Rantau Panjang Station.
11. Rantau Panjang-Johor Bahru
ETD 7.30pm — Rantau Panjang Station.

Taxis
Kota Bharu has a good taxi service which enables visitors to get around town. Taxis may either be hired at the taxi stand at Jalan Pendek, or hailed from the roadside. Generally, however, taxis in Kota Bharu are utilised for long-distance travel. For sightseeing there are some taxis which may be hired at M$10 per hour or M$60 per day.

For more information regarding taxis, enquire from the Malay Drivers' Association, Jalan Dato Pati, ph 09-785 624.

Trishaws
Trishaws abound in Kota Bharu. These three-wheeled carriages with their quaint foldable oilskin roofs are a popular mode of transport. For the visitor it is ideal, since you may get a running commentary from the trishaw pedlar as you pass all the places of interest, and if you like, you may stop the trishaw to take photos. Trishaws do not have meters so it is advisable to determine the price of the ride before stepping into one. You may most certainly bargain, but the normal fare for a 10 minute trip should not exceed M$3.

EATING OUT
Kota Bharu offers a variety of food for all tastes and temperament. While food stalls are scattered all around the town and

many of the major hotels have their own restaurants, you may want to try the Central Market. Among the various delicacies, you will find an array of Kelantan cakes. Peculiar to this part of the country, these cakes have such exotic names as Cik Mek Molek, Buah Tanjong, Nasi Kaya, Jala Mas, Tepung Pelita and Akok. Not to forget the eating plaza near Merdeka Square; here food stalls open from sundown to late in the evening. Besides satay or Malaysian shish kebab, you may enjoy Kelantanese gourmet delights like ayam percik, nasi dagang and laksa.

ENTERTAINMENT

Night owls in Kota Bharu can visit the Layang Lounge in Hotel Perdana, especially if you are looking for non-stop entertainment.

For a slower pace, the Wayang Lounge in the same hotel has a resident singer and organist.

SHOPPING

Central Market
Already mentioned for its food stalls, you can also shop here for batik, bamboo articles and aluminium ware.

Jalan Temenggong
Along this street you will find shops selling batik of all designs and material: voille, cotton, rayon and even silk.

Wisma Batik
This shop is located on Jalan Maju. Handicrafts on sale here include songket, silverware and of course, batik.

Kampung Penambang
About 3.2 km (2 miles) away from Kota Bharu, the village specialises in such fabrics as batik and songket. You can also see the articles being produced.

Semasa Batik
Also a major production centre for batik, Semasa Batik is 3 km (2 miles) from Kota Bharu.

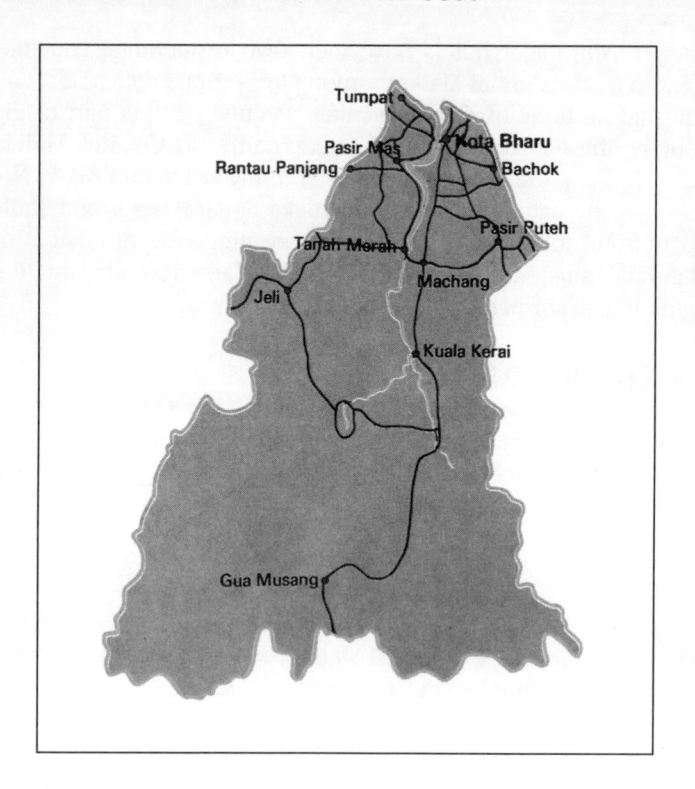

Local Handicraft Centre
Located at Kampung Badang, 9.7 km (6 miles) from town, the centre has on sale handicraft such as batik, songket and silverware.

Jalan Sultanah Zainab
Also known as Jampung Sirih, the shops in this area stock batik and silverware. At Kelantan Handicraft you will find a wide range of colourful kites.

Tourist Information Centre
Here on display is a wide variety of handicraft such as bamboo articles, kites, tops and shadow puppets — all of which make excellent souvenirs and gifts.

EAST COAST 181

SIGHTSEEING

KOTA BHARU

Gelanggang Seni

The town's cultural centre, Gelanggang Seni is a must for the visitor. Every Wednesday and Saturday you can watch interesting performances of "gasing", or top-spinning, kite-flying, "wayang kulit", or shadow puppet theatre, "silar", or the Malay art of self-defence, and traditional art forms like the Berdikir Barat, Rebana etc. For details contact the local Tourist Information Centre.

Wau

Kite-flying has come a long way in Kelantan. The Malay Annals mentions it as being in existence as early as 1500, during the early days of the Malacca Sultanate.

Wau, or kites, come in all shapes and colours, but the most popular is the Wau Bulan or Moon Kite. It is so named because its tail piece resembles the crescent. It is the Wau Bulan that Malaysian Airlines has chosen as its logo, symbolising controlled flight.

Kite competitions are held every Saturday afternoon at the Gelanggang Seni, except during the Fasting Month.

The State Mosque

Only a few paces away from the Istana Jahar is the State Mosque. Completed in 1926 during the reign of Sultan Ismail, the Mosque took ten years to build. Adjacent to the State Mosque is the State Religious Council Building. Completed in 1914 during the reign of Sultan Muhamad, it contains records of the development and spread of Islam in the region.

Wayang Kulit

This is a very unique form of theatre employing the principle of light and shadow. The puppets are crafted from buffalo hide and mounted on bamboo sticks. When held up behind a piece of white cloth, with an oil lamp as the light source, shadows are cast on the screen.

The plays are invariably based on romantic tales, and the Tok Dalang is the genius behind the entire performance. It is he who sits behind the screen and narrates the story. With a traditional orchestra in the background, the Tok Dalang modulates his voice to create suspense thus heightening the drama.

Wayang Kulit performances are staged at the Gelanggang Seni every Wednesday night; at Kampung Gerong about 6 km (4 miles) from Kota Bharu; at Kedai Lalat, 15 km (9 miles) away; or at Kampung Tawang, 26 km (16 miles) away.

Merdeka Square
Right in the centre of town is Merdeka Square. Built to commemorate the Malay warriors and patriots who died during the First World War, it is also the place where the Malay nationalist, Tok Janggut, was hanged for opposing the British.

Raft Houses
These bamboo structures are on the banks of the Kelantan River, and have been occupied for many years.

Istana Balai Besar
In the northern part of town is a palace of old-world charm, the Istana Balai Besar. Built in 1844, this historic building replaced the Istana Kota Lama as the state's seat of administration. The Istana Balai Besar or "The Palace with the Large Audience Hall" actually houses the Throne Room, the Hall of Audience and the State Legislative Assembly Hall. It has a beautifully carved interior and still serves as a venue for important occasions such as royal wedding ceremonies.

Istana Jahar (Museum)
Situated just beside the Istana Balai Besar, it was built during the reign of Sultan Muhamad IV and completed in 1889. An imposing piece of architecture with intricately carved beams and wooden panels, the Istana Jahar is a historical landmark, now converted into the State Museum. Open 10.30am–6pm, closed Wednesdays.

EAST COAST 183

BEYOND KOTA BHARU

Beach of Passionate Love
Situated about 10 km (6 miles) north of Kota Bharu, Pantai Cinta Berahi, or the Beach of Passionate Love, is surely one of the more famous of Malaysian beaches.

Other Beaches
Pantai Dasat Sabak is another picturesque beach about 10 km (6 miles) from the town. Fishermen come ashore here with their daily catch. The fishing villages along this beach also provide vivid glimpses of rural life.

About 58 km (36 miles) from Kota Bharu at Dalam Rhu, is Pantai Bisikan Bayu, or the Beach of Whispering Breeze. Here you will find the crystal clear waters ideal for snorkelling, scuba-diving, swimming and fishing.

Pantai Irama or Beach of Melody is about 25 km (15.5 miles) south of Kota Bharu, in the district of Bachok. It has long stretches of clean, white sand and tall, swaying casuarinas.

Pantai Kuda is another popular spot, situated about 25 km (15.5 miles) north-west of Kota Bharu.

Wat Photivihan
The district of Tumpat on the Thai border offers scenic views of the countryside with traditional wooden houses built on stilts, buffaloes roaming free in the mud, and farmers toiling in green padi fields. To get there you cross the Sultan Yahya Bridge, the longest bridge in the East Coast.

In the vicinity there are several Buddhist temples or wats, the most famous of which is the Wat Phothivihan, with its reclining Buddha. It is located at Kampung Jambu, about 12 km (7 miles) north of Kota Bharu. To get there take the no. 29 bus to Kampong Jambu from Kota Bharu bus station. On arrival at Kampong Jambu, a sign-posted turning indicates the way to the temple.

Not far from the Sultan Yahya Bridge is the town of Pasir Mas, and 15 km (9 miles) further along is Lake Toban, a freshwater lake popular with picnickers and fishing enthusiasts.

Jeram Pasu Waterfall
This scenic waterfall is in the district of Pasir Puteh, about 39 km (24 miles) south of Kota Bharu, off the trunk road to Kuala Terengganu.

Kuala Besar
15 km (9 miles) from Kota Bharu, this fishing village has been called the soul of Malaysia's East Coast.

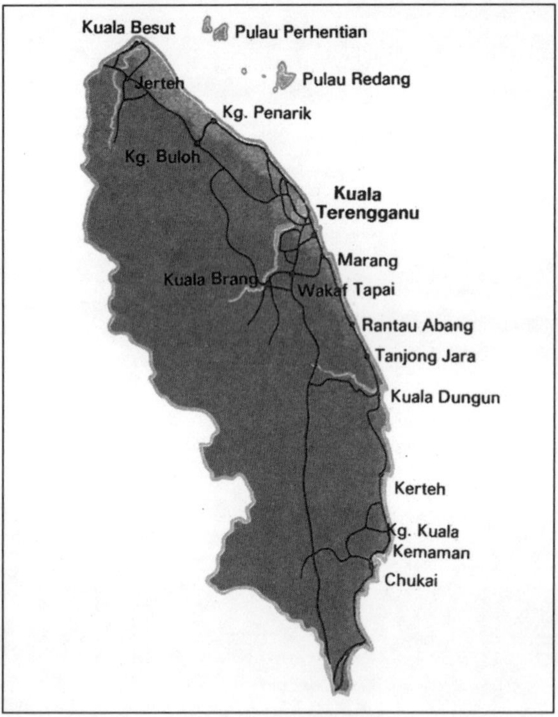
Kuala Besut
Pulau Perhentian
Pulau Redang
Jerteh
Kg. Penarik
Kg. Buloh
Kuala
Terengganu
Marang
Kuala Brang
Wakaf Tapai
Rantau Abang
Tanjong Jara
Kuala Dungun
Kerteh
Kg. Kuala
Kemaman
Chukai

TERENGGANU

The State of Terengganu, with a land area of 12,995 km² (5,016 sq. miles) is between the States of Kelantan and Pahang. From the northern border with Kelantan, the coastline of Terengganu stretches down 225 km (140 miles) to the border with Pahang. Within this stretch are found blue waters, sparkling white sand and picturesque lagoons with fishing villages, which rival any beach scene anywhere in the world.

Terengganu played a significant role in Malay history. The earliest evidence of Islamic presence in the Peninsula was found in Kuala Brang in the form of an inscribed stone (batu bersurat) dated circa 1303, which may be seen in the National Museum.

The average temperature throughout the year lies in the region of 26C (80F), with perennial sunshine save for the monsoon season from around November–January.

KUALA TERENGGANU

The capital of Terengganu, Kuala Terengganu, is on the coast halfway between Kota Bharu and Kuantan. It is basically a fishing town, but is now becoming a busy petroleum centre. The town stands on the Terengganu River and has two main streets, an excellent market and a small esplanade.

HOW TO GET THERE

By Air
MAS has flights from Kuala Lumpur, Penang and Johor Bahru to the Sultan Mahmud Airport, which is 18 km (11 miles) from Kuala Terengganu — Airport Information Counter, ph 09-664 500.

Johor Bahru to Kuala Terengganu
First Class — M$233 single, M$466 return.
Economy — M$163 single, M$326 return.

Kuala Lumpur to Kuala Terengganu (Direct)
First Class — M$123 single, M$246 return.
Economy — M$86 single, M$172 return.

KUALA TERENGGANU

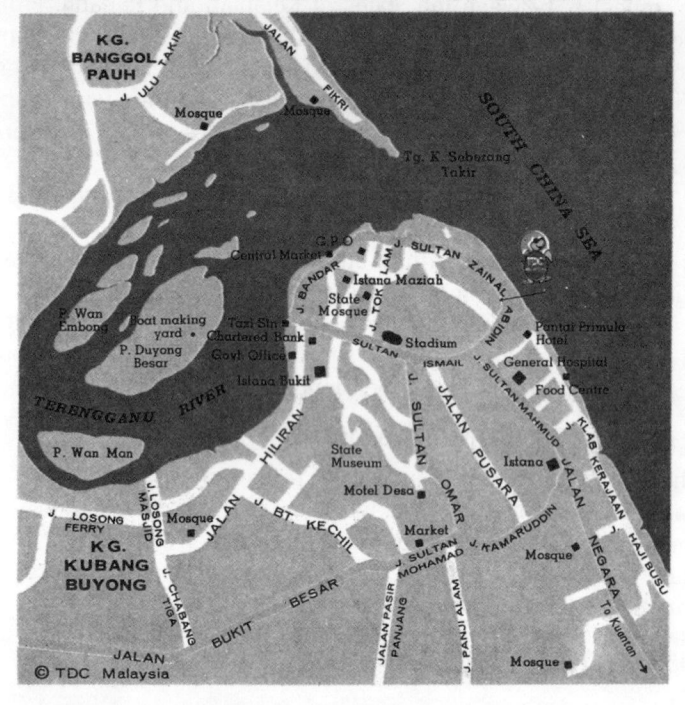

Penang to Kuala Terengganu (Direct)
Economy — M$80 single, M$160 return

Kuala Lumpur to Kerteh (Direct)
Economy — M$80 single, M$160 return.

Kuala Terengganu to Kerteh (Direct)
Economy — M$40 single, M$80 return.

By Taxi
Taxis from Kota Bharu charge M$12 per person, from Kuantan, M$17 per person.

By Bus
Kuala Lumpur to Kuala Terengganu — M$20 (aircon), M$17 (non-aircon).
Butterworth (Penang) to Kuala Terengganu — M$23 (aircon), M$21 (non-aircon).
Johor Bahru to Kuala Terengganu — M$22 (aircon), M$18 (non-aircon).
Singapore to Kuala Terengganu — M$23 (aircon).
Kuantan to Kuala Terengganu — M$8 (aircon), M$7 non-aircon).
Kota Bharu to Kuala Terengganu — M$7 (aircon), M$6 (non-aircon).
All express buses operate in and out of Kuala Terengganu from the Central Bus Station at Jalan Masjid Abidin.

TOURIST INFORMATION

Tourist Development Corporation Malaysia, East Coast Region Office, 2243 Tingkat Bawah, Wisma MCIS, Jalan Sultan Zainal Abidin, 20000 Kuala Terengganu, ph 09-621 433/893.

Economic Planning Unit, Terengganu State Secretariat, Wisma Badul Iman, Jalan Sultan Ismail, 20503 Kuala Terengganu, ph 09-631 957.

ACCOMMODATION

A range of accommodation facilities are available in town or by the beaches. International standard hotels provide first-class amenities and those by the beaches usually have tour programmes for visits to surrounding attractions. Prices shown below are for a double room, and are in Malaysian Dollars. The Telephone Area Code is 09.

International
Motel Desa, Bukit Pak Apil, Kuala Terengganu, ph 623 438 — $100; Motel Sri Marang, Kg. Pulau Kerengga, Kuala Terengganu, ph 632 566 — $140; Muni Hotel, K 312, Jalan Che Teh, Kemaman, ph 592 366 — $120; Pantai Primula Hotel, Jalan Persinggahan, Kuala Terengganu, ph 622 100 — $300; Rantau Abang

Visitor Centre, 13th Mile, Jalan Dungun, Dungun, ph 841 533 — $90; Tanjong Jara Beach Hotel, 8th Mile off Jalan Dungun, Dungun, ph 841 801 — $350.

Good Tourist
Merantau Inn, Kuala Abang, Dungun, ph 841 131 — $66; Seri Hoover Hotel, 49 Jalan Sultan Ismail, Kuala Terengganu, ph 624 655 — $62; Warisan Hotel, 65 Jalan Paya Bunga, Kuala Terengganu, ph 622 688 — $58.

Budget
Bunga Raya Hotel, 105-11 Jalan Banggol, Kuala Terengganu, ph 621 166 — $30; City Hotel, 97-99 Jalan Banggol, Kuala Terengganu, ph 621 481 — $30; Duin Hotel, K 355, Jalan Kg. Tengah, Kemaman, ph 591 801 — $29; Meriah Hotel, 67 Jalan Paya Bunga, Kuala Terengganu, ph 622 655 — $32; Pulau Kapas Resort, 21600 Marang, ph 681 044 — $28; Sri Dungun Hotel, K-135, Jalan Tambun, Dungun, ph 841 881 — $38; Sri Terengganu, 120 A-B, Jalan Sultan Ismail, Kuala Terengganu, ph 634 622 — $48; Terengganu Hotel, 12 Jalan Paya Bunga, Kuala Terengganu, ph 622 900 — $30.

LOCAL TRANSPORT

Taxis
The taxi station is located close to the jetty at the end of Jln. Sultan Ismail/Jln. Hiliran (ph 621 581). Taxis, apart from airport and hotel transfers (M$12-M$15) are also for sightseeing around Kuala Terengganu (about M$5) and other places of interest, such as the Sekayu Waterfalls (M$20/trip) and the nearby towns of Rusila and Kuala Ibai.

Boats
Passenger boats are the main means of transport for residents and visitors to Pulau Duyong at the mouth of the Terengganu River. A short ride there costs 30 sen per person. A return boat ride may be chartered at M$7. Licensed passenger boats are available for hire out to the islands from the main jetties in and around Kuala Terengganu. PLEASE DO NOT USE FISHING BOATS as they are not licensed or equipped to ferry passengers.

Trishaws
An economical and convenient way to get around the town of Kuala Terengganu, but remember to agree on the fare before the ride.

EATING OUT
There are many good restaurants in Juala Terengganu, serving Malay, Chinese, Indian and Siamese dishes. Western cuisine can be found at the hotels along with a local menu. Make sure you try Taman Selera in Kuala Terengganu, which serves a variety of local food from 7pm to midnight nightly. Other recommended restaurants are:

Malay
Buyong Restoran, Jalan Kota Lama; Zainuddin Restoran, Jalan Tok Lam; Nara Restoran, Jalan Banggol; Istiqial Restoran, Jalan Banggol; Mali Restoran, Jalan Banggol; Rumah Cik Wan, Jalan Sultan Zainal Abidin; Rhusila Coffee House, Pantai Primula Hotel, Jalan Persinggahan (also Chinese and Western).

Chinese
Restoran Good Luck, Jalan Engku Sar; Restoran Kui Ping, Jalan Engku Sar; Restoran Lee Kee, Jalan Engku Sar.

Indian
Taufik Restoran, Jalan Masjid; Dewi Restoran, Jalan Kampung Dalam.

Western
McDota Fried Chicken Restaurant, Jalan Kota Lama.

ENTERTAINMENT
Nightly activities need not end with the fabulous sunsets of Terengganu. There are places to go to and things to do well into the small hours of the morning.

Not to be missed, particularly till the end of September is turtle-watching at the 18 km stretch of sand at Rantau Abang. For further information, see the Sightseeing section.

For an evening of more active involvement, try the Disco Club at the Pantai Primula Hotel in Kuala Terengganu, perched on top of the building with magnificent view.

In the same hotel, but more subdued and elegant, is the Bayu Lounge, a favourite spot for a night on the town.

SHOPPING

There is a one-stop shopping centre at Jalan Sultan Ismail where apart from traditional handicrafts, fashion wear in contemporary hand-printed designs can be obtained.

Local handicrafts can be found in market squares, bazaars and little shops in Kuala Terengganu. The central market in the capital offers great scope for souvenir hunting, where wares such as batik, brocade, songket, brassware, mats and baskets are displayed alongside fresh produce.

Other shops include —
Noor Atikah Songket, Bangunan MARA, Jalan Masjid Abidin.
Syarikat Usaha Desa Terengganu, Sdn. Bhd., 73 Jalan Sultan Ismail, ph 621 539.
Suterasemai Centre, Tapak Perindustrian Chendering, Chendering, ph 671 355.
Karyaneka Handicraft Centre — In Kg Rusila, this centre has a variety of all the local handicrafts of Malaysia, such as hats, bats, food covers, floor mats and decorative wall pieces made from mengkuang (local screwpine) in bright colours as well as in its natural shade. Creative batik products, songket, intricate silverware, traditional wood-carving and sculptures are also available, with prices ranging from M$1 for a small souvenir to a few hundred dollars for a piece of hand-woven songket in gold or silver.

At the back of the showroom is the first demonstration and training centre of Kraftangan, a government agency set up for the promotion of cottage industries throughout the country.

For batiks, we suggest you try Wan Ismail Wan Omar, Depar Sekotah Ugama Ladang, Jalan Sultan Zainal Abidin, ph 623 311 Wan Mohammad Batek, Jalan Ladang Sekolah; Noor Arfa Batek 796 Jalan Sultan Mahmud, ph 627 173.

A relatively new industry in Malaysia is the production of silk and silken goods. The silk weaving centre is at Kuala Ibai, 6 km (4 miles) from Kuala Terengganu, and silk materials, batik shirts, clothes and scarves are on sale there. The brand name is Suteramas, and it is sold into Japan and the US.

SIGHTSEEING

The Waterfront
This is a very interesting part of Kuala Terengganu. From this bustling district you can hire a boat for a small sum to ferry you to some of the idyllic islands, or take the passenger boat to Seberang Takir, well-known for its panoramic view of the South China Sea, and its dried fish and fish cracker industry.

Kampung Dalam Kota
A quaint little Malay village near the central market, which has a cluster of wooden pavilions with hand-carved high roofs, and ornately carved homes.

Masjid Abidin
This stately mosque is located at Jalan Masjid, and was formerly known as Masjid Besar (Big Mosque) or Masjid Putih (White Mosque). An historical place of worship, it was originally constructed of wood by the late Sultan Zainal Abidin II but it was later rebuilt using bricks and concrete and further improved during the reign of Sultan Zainal Abidin III.

Marang Fishing Village
Only 15 km (9 miles) from Kuala Terengganu, this fishing village is noted for its salted fish, fish and prawn crackers and other delicacies. Several handicraft houses also make and sell traditional woven crafts from the pandanus or "mengkuang" leaf.

State Museum
Located at Jalan Cherong Lanjut, this museum has many interesting exhibits from Terengganu's history, and also includes an old bicycle used by the Japanese soldiers during their attack on the Malay Peninsula during World War II.

Istana Maziah (Maziah Palace)

Situated near Bukit Puteri in Kuala Terengganu, the palace is the venue for royal birthdays and weddings, conferments of titles and welcoming of dignitaries. It was built to replace the Istana Hijau (Green Palace) that was destroyed by fire. The splendid architecture makes the palace one of Malaysia's cultural attractions.

Sekayu Waterfalls

A favourite with both locals and visitors alike, this seven layered waterfall is tucked away in the rain forest and is a great picnic spot. Just 56 km (35 miles) or 45 minute's drive from Kuala Terengganu, two resthouses and three chalets offer comfortable accommodation. Rates per night for resthouse and chalet respectively are M$30 and M$36. Bookings and enquiries can be made from Jabatan Perhutanan Daerah, Kuala Berang, Hulu Terengganu, ph 09–811 259.

Pulau Kapas

From Marang Jetty, south of Kuala Terengganu, take a boat and head out about 6 km to this island renowned for its clear emerald waters and beautiful coral. From the Second World War until late last year, Pulau Kapas was uninhabited. Construction of ten chalets, a small restaurant and three A-frame huts began in 1987, and at time of printing six of the chalets are open and ready for business. This unspoiled paradise is litter-free, and the three young Malaysians who live on the island are vehement that visitors "take nothing but photographs, and leave nothing but footprints".

The return boat fare to the island is M$15, and reservations for the chalets or huts can be made through the Manager, Ali, at the Pulau Kapas Resort Office, ph 632 989.

Rantau Abang (Turtle Watching)

60 km (37 miles) south of Kuala Terengganu is Rantau Abang where annually between May and September female Leatherback turtles make their lonely way from the high seas to lay their eggs in the unusually large brown-grained sand found here. The turtle inches her way ashore to lay the eggs in a large crater-like depression which she laboriously digs with her flippers.

The Leatherback turtle is extremely sensitive to noise or light, so if too many tourists gather, or if they make too much noise, the turtle will return to the sea without laying her eggs.

The area is one of only six in the world visited by these turtles. A total of 10 Malay-style chalets with restaurant and bar facilities provide accommodation. A Turtle Information Centre in the vicinity gives further information on this rare species.

Other beaches on the East Coast where turtles may be seen are Kuala Abang, Ketapong Kubur and Jambu Bongkor.

Bukit Keluang/Dendong Beach Park
This beach park in Besut, about 140 km (87 miles) north of Kuala Terengganu, is accessible by road right up to the sea front. Three hillocks ("bukit") with their contained beaches and the convergence of the Sungei Keluang Besar, the nearby Pulau Ru and the sea into this area have created one of the most scenic sites in Malaysia. There are toilets and change rooms, food and drink vendors, and a boardwalk along the seaward bluff of Bukit Keluang which provides access to numerous small coves and beaches at low tide.

Pulau Perhentian
Off the north coast of Terengganu is the island of Pulau Perhentian. It is approximately 59 km (37 miles) from Kota Bharu in Kelantan, but the best way to get there is by boat from Kuala Besut. The boat trip takes 3.5 hours and the return fare is M$180. The island is a must for scubadiving, snorkelling, coral hunting and swimming enthusiasts.

Accommodation is available in the form of bungalows (M$40 per night) and chalets (M$20 per night), but guests are required to bring their own cooking utensils and food. For bookings and further information phone the District Office, Besut — 976 328.

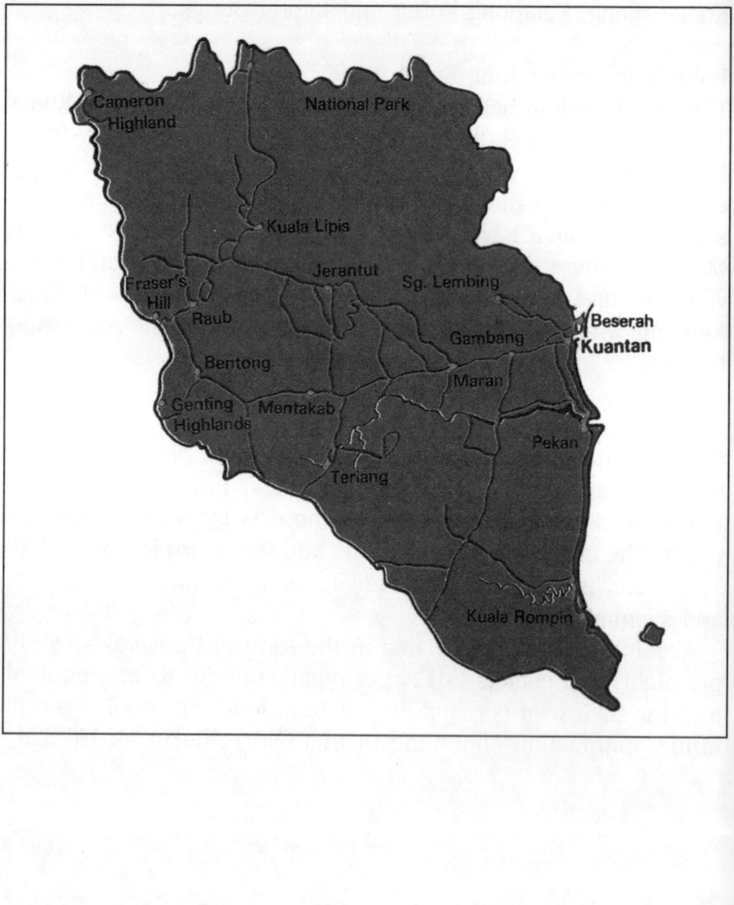
Cameron Highland
National Park
Kuala Lipis
Jerantut
Sg. Lembing
Fraser's Hill
Raub
Beserah
Gambang
Kuantan
Bentong
Maran
Genting Highlands
Mentakab
Pekan
Teriang
Kuala Rompin

NEGERI PAHANG DARUL MAKMUR

Pahang is the largest State in Peninsular Malaysia. With an area of 35,960 km^2 (13,880 sq. miles), it has vast tracts of rainforests and part of these form the National Park. Kuala Tembeling, the gateway to the National Park, is in Pahang Darul Makmur.

On the coast the scenery as well as the mode of life is similar to those in Kelantan and Terengganu. Fishing and village handicraft are maintained, and Pahang's speciality is songket, the distinctive Malaysian brocade, the skill of making it having been passed on from generation to generation.

The capital of Pahang is Kuantan.

KUANTAN

This is a colourful, bustling coastal town mid-way between Singapore and Kota Bharu. Kuantan has excellent hotels and restaurants and a very colourful fish market with fresh catches of fishes, prawns, squids and other varieties from the South China Sea.

HOW TO GET THERE

By Air
MAS flies to Kuantin from Kuala Lumpur, Johor Bahru and Singapore. The return fare Kuala Lumpur-Kuantin is M$122.

By Bus
From Kota Bharu the express bus fare is M$15, from Kuala Terengganu M$7 and from Kuala Lumpur M$11.

By Taxi
The taxi fare from Kuala Terengganu is N$17, from Kota Bharu N$25 and from Kuala Lumpur M$23 per person.

TOURIST INFORMATION

Industrial and Tourism Division, State Economic Development Corporation, 14th Floor, Teruntum Complex, Jalan Mahkota, 25000 Kuantan, ph 522 346.

State Development Corporation, Pahang Darul Makmur, 13/16 Tingkat, Komplek Teruntum, Jalan Mahkoa, 25000 Kuantan, ph 505 566.

ACCOMMODATION

There is a wide variety of accommodation in Kuantan itself, and of course north of the town is Cherating Beach, and the famous Club Mediterranee, and the Cherating Holiday Villa, which combine activities with glamour and large doses of sophistication. Club Mediterranee has 300 rooms and the prices range from M$165 to M$220 per night, which includes all holiday activities and sporting facilities, in fact everything except bar and boutique purchases. They also arrange package tours including airfares from various countries, and full details of these should be obtained from your local travel agent.

The Cherating Holiday Villa, Lot 1303 Mukim Sungei Karang, Cherating, ph 03-243 4693, has 54 rooms and the prices range from M$65–M$120.

Listed below are some examples of accommodation in Kuantan. The prices are for a double room in Malaysian Dollars. The Telephone Area Code is 09.

International
Chendor Motel, Batu 29, Jalan Kemaman, ph 591 369 — $120; Champagne Emas Hotel, 3002, Jalan Haji Ahmad, ph 528 820 — $120; Hyatt Kuantan, Telok Cempedak, ph 525 211 — $200; Merlin Inn Resort, Teolk Campedak, ph 522 388 — $170; Ramada Beach Resort, Kuantan, ph 587 544 — $350; Samudra Hotel, Main Road, Kuantan, ph 522 688 — $125.

Good Tourist
Beserah Hotel, 2 Jalan Beserah, ph 526 144 — $65; Simgifa Hotel, 9th Mile, Kuantan Port, ph 587 254 — $50; Suraya Hotel, Jalan Haji Abdul Aziz, ph 524 266 — $78.

Budget
Baru Raya Hotel, 134 Jalan Besar, ph 522 344 — $34; Embassy Hotel, 60 Jalan Teluk Sisek, ph 524 844 — $26; Pahang Hotel, 7 Main Road, ph 521 614 — $34.

EATING OUT
Of course, if you are staying at one of the resorts, meals are provided, and the large hotels have international standard restaurants, but here are a few you might like to try —

Bilal Restaurant, 30 Jalan Tun Ismail, ph 523 217; Honeycomb Coffee House, 2610-A Jalan Alor Akar, ph 523 434; Hooner Restaurant, 80-A Jalan Teluk Sisek, ph 523 412; Kuantan Bowl, Kompleks Terunturn, ph 527 565; Restaurant Champagne Emos, 3002 Jalan Haji Ahmad, ph 528 820; Restoron Tiki, 9 Jalan Haji Abdul Aziz, ph 522 272; Tawakkal Restaurant, 13 Jalan Haji Abdul Aziz, ph 522 637.

ENTERTAINMENT
Visitors to Pahang need not despair, Kuantan has nightclubs and discos like Lips, in Jalan Besar, near the Samudra Riverview Hotel. The latter's Muara Lounge overlooking the swimming pool and spa baths provides nightly music.

Slightly out of Kuantan, but only just, is the Gloria Maris Resort at the beach at Batu Hitam, which offers value entertainment. Barely 1 km away is the Keluarga Restaurant also at the beach which provides food and entertainment till 3am.

SIGHTSEEING

Tanjong Lumpur
A fishing village situated by the mouth of the Kuantan River, it is easily reached by a short boat-ride from the river jetty. Colourful trawlers and fishermen unloading their catch add rustic charm to the scene.

Beserah
This small fishing village 10 km (6 miles) north of Kuantan is a centre for local handicrafts such as batik and carvings. Shell

200 SINGAPORE AND MALAYSIA AT COST

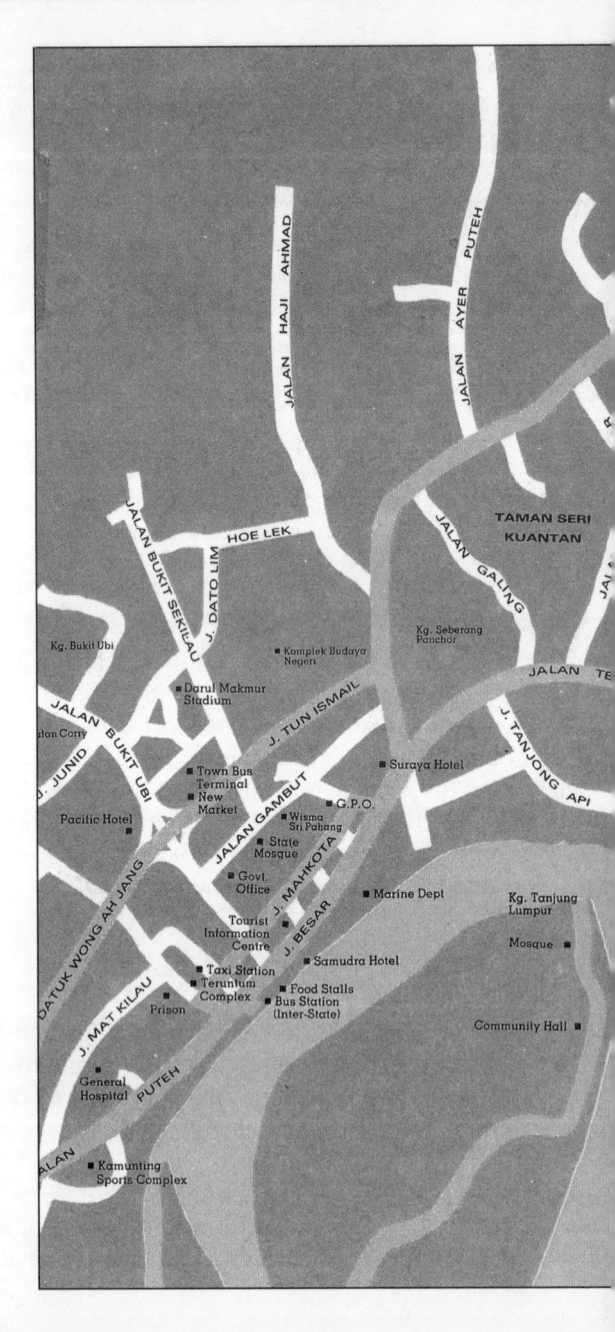

NEGERI PAHANG DARUL MAKMUR 201

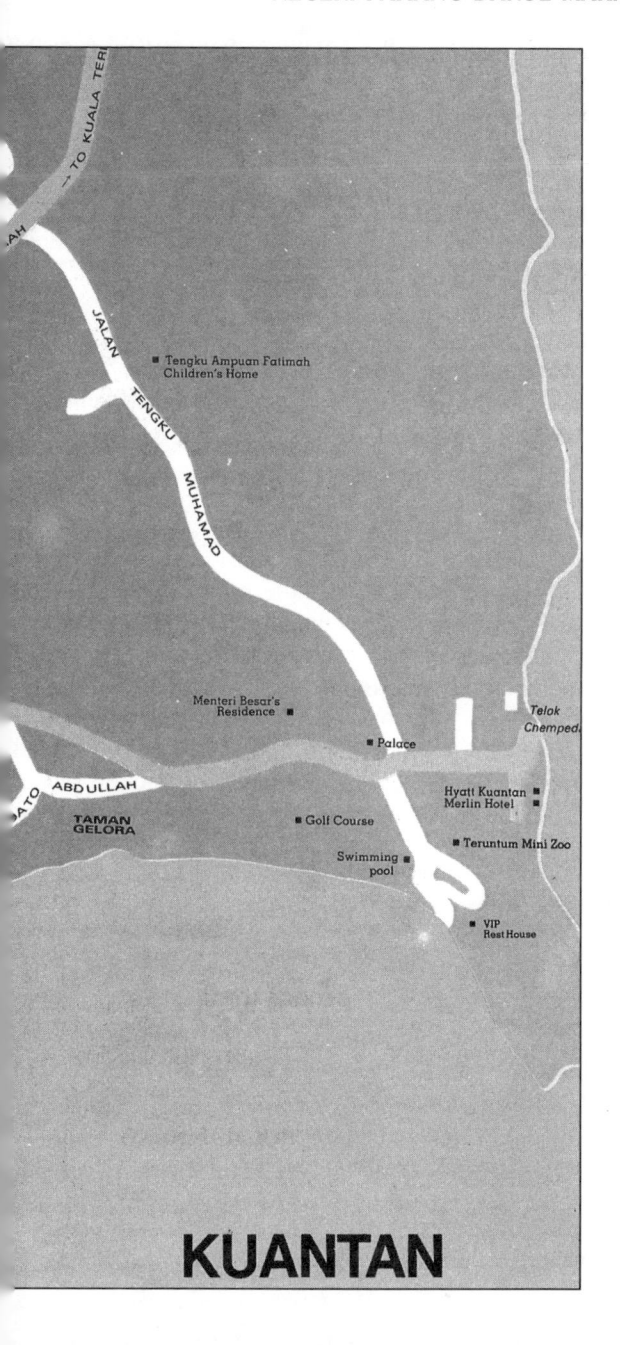

KUANTAN

items can be obtained from the village of Sungai Karang, a bit further north. Kite-flying, top spinning contests and monkeys gathering ripe coconuts may also be seen here.

Panching Cave

Visit the Panching Cave, where a 9 m (30 ft) reclining statue of Buddha is flooded with sunlight at 11.59am daily from an aperture in the cave's roof.

Telok Chempedak

This is a fabulous stretch of beach, and nearby is the Karyaneka Handicraft Centre. From the delicate "Dara Jade" jewellery to hand-painted pottery, the centre has some great gift and souvenir ideas.

Tioman Island

This well-known island is 39 km (24 miles) long and 19 km (12 miles) wide. It may be reached in three hours by launch from Mersing. Normally one trip a day is operated at around noon, and the fares are M$30 adults, M$15 children under 12 years of age. Covered with jungle and quite mountainous, Tioman is still idyllic with waters so clear that you see coral when you swim there. The reefs make it ideal for snorkelling and watching tropical fish in their natural habitat. Waterfalls complete the picture of perfection. It is possible to stay on Tioman in a modern hotel, and sometimes this is necessary because launch departure time is uncertain.

MAS flies daily to the island from Kuala Lumpur.

Kenong Rimba Park

This jungle park is situated along a wet and wild valley of a small river called Sungai Kenong. Kampong Kuala Kenong, which is the entry point to the park, is just one hour thirty minutes by boat from Kuala Lipis, which was once the capital of Pahang State.

Further in the park there is another solitary village, Kampong Dusun, where birds come down to feed, then the track leads into deep jungle.

Trekking along the jungle trails within the park is an unforgettable experience as there are always fresh signs of elephants

A Hotel in Penang (Golden Sands)

Trishaw Tour in Arab Street, Singapore

Shopping in Chinatown, Singapore

Central Business District, Kuala Lumpur

rhinoceros and tigers. There are several caves to be explored, as well as an aboriginal race called Batik (nothing to do with Batik painting).

There are several camp-sites in the park, and for more information contact The Tuah Travel Agency in Kuala Lipis, who arrange organised tours.

Taman Negara
For information on this Park see the Chapter on National Parks.

JOHOR

Johor Darul Takzim is the southernmost state in Peninsular Malaysia. Because of its location, it was known as Hujung Tanah (Land's End) in the old days. Its present name is said to come from an Arabic word "Jauhar" (Precious Stones), given by Arab merchants who first traded in this State.

Johor is the only state on Peninsular Malaysia to have both an east coast and a west coast. Consequently it has both the economic development associated with the West Coast, and beautiful beaches and off-shore islands characteristic of the East Coast.

Covering an area of about 18,985 km^2 (7,328 sq. miles), Johor is bounded by Pahang (north), Negeri Sembilan and Melaka (west), South China Sea (east) and the Straits of Johor (south). It is linked to Singapore by the approx. 1 km long Johor Bahru Causeway. The population of approximately 2 million people comprise 54.8% Malay, 38.4% Chinese, 6.3% Indian and others.

The capital is Johor Bahru.

JOHOR BAHRU

The Gateway to Malaysia from the south, Johor Bahur, or JB as it is referred to, is one of the fastest developing capitals in the country. Having been declared a municipality since April 1, 1980, the town has a population of more than 750,000 people. Way back in 1855, it was named Tanjung Putri before Sultan Abu Bakar decided to rename it in 1866.

HOW TO GET THERE

By Air

MAS has daily flights from Kuala Lumpur and Kota Kinabalu, and scheduled flights from Kuala Terengganu, Kuching and Kuantan to Johor Bahru.

The Senai International Airport is less than 25 km (15.5 miles) from JB, and air-conditioned coaches ply to and from the airport to the town for M$4 per person, and to Orchard Road, Singapore for M$10 per person.

206 SINGAPORE AND MALAYSIA AT COST

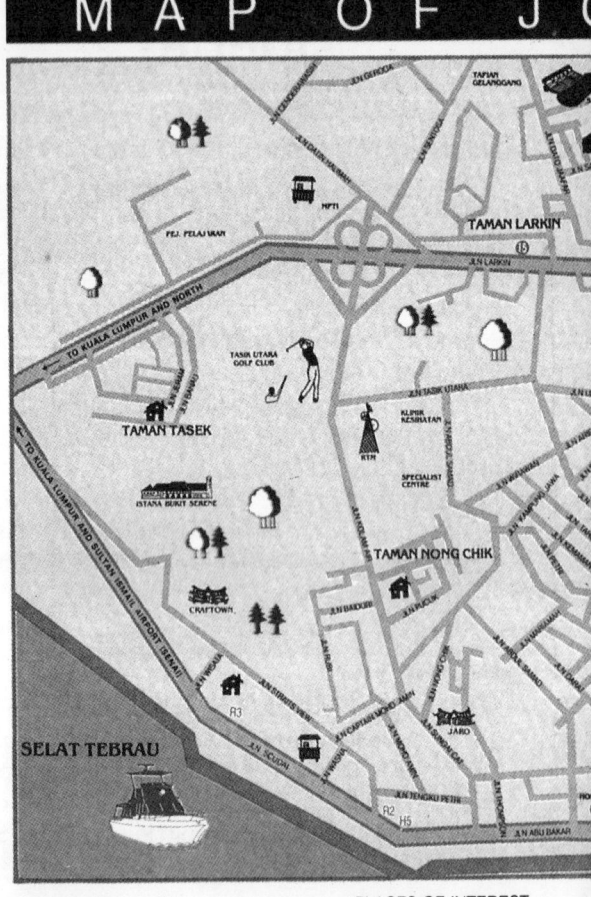

MAP OF JO

HOTELS

- H1 Holiday Inn
- H2 Merlin Inn
- H3 Merlin Tower
- H4 Rasa Sayang
- H5 Straits View Hotel
- H6 Tropical Inn

RESTAURANTS

- R1 Blue Star Restaurant
- R2 Jaws 5 Seafood Restaurant
- R3 JB Restaurant

PLACES OF INTEREST

Istana Besar

Kompleks Islam

Zoo

The Royal Mansoleum

Johore Area Rehabilitation

Organisation (JARO)

Istana Bukit Serene

Johor Craftown

Handicraft Centre

JOHOR 207

JOHOR BAHRU

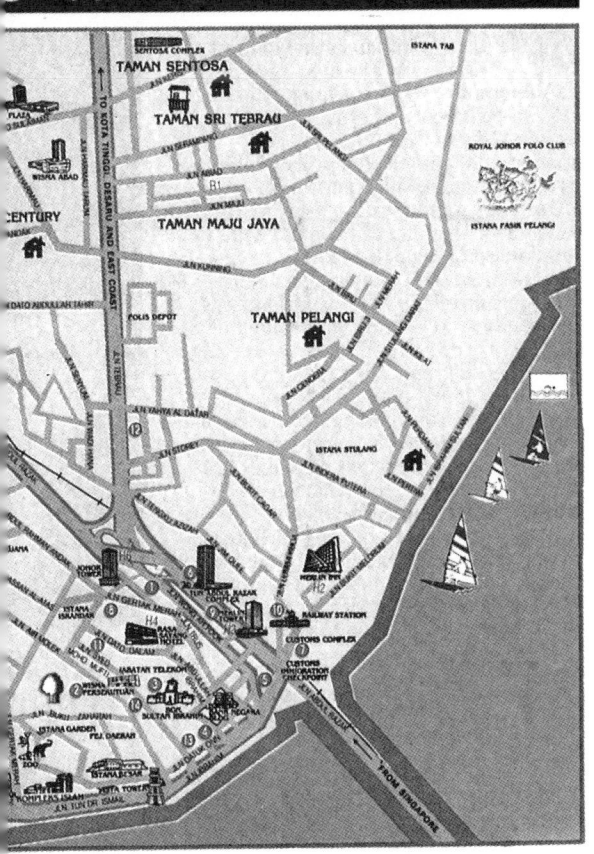

PUBLIC FACILITIES

1. Tourist Development Corporation of Malaysia Malaysia Airline System
2. Federal Government Office Complex (Wisma Persekutuan)
3. State Government Office Complex (Sultan Ibrahim Building)
4. General Post Office
5. Tourist Police Station
6. Tun Abdul Razak Complex
7. Customs Complex
8. Bus Terminal
9. Taxi Station
10. Railway Station
11. Telecoms Department
12. Police Traffic Station
13. Johor Bahru Town Council (Majlis Perbandaran JB)
14. Dewan Jubli Intan
15. Fire Bridge Station
16. Holiday Plaza

For further information contact Malaysian Airline System, Orchid Plaza, off Jalan Wong Ah Fook, Johor Bahru, ph 07-220 888 (Reservations), 07-226 032 (Administration), 07-241 985 (Airport).

By Bus
All express buses arrive and depart from Bangunan Mara, JB. Bus routes are from Kuala Lumpur (M$15), Alor Setar (M$34), Butterworth (M$29), Kota Bahru (M$29), Kuala Terengganu (M$22), Ipoh (M$23) and Melaka (M$10).

There are also two buses that carry passengers daily from Singapore to Johor Bahru. For further information contact National Express Kuala Lumpur, 03-238 6990, or Johor Bahru, 07-227 220.

By Rail
Malayan Railway operates both day and night services to Johor Bahru. The second class air-conditioned coach fare from Kuala Lumpur to JB is M$27, while that from Singapore is M$8. Railway Station, ph 07-224 727

By Taxi
Outstation taxis run trips from Kuala Lumpur, Malacca, Kuantan and even from Kota Bharu to Johor Bahru. Taxi Station, ph 07-234 944.

TOURIST INFORMATION

Johor Tourist Development Corporation, ph 07-223 590/91; Johor Tourist Police, ph 07-232 222; Johor Tourist Association, ph 07-241 122; Johor Economic Planning Unit, ph 07-237 344/45.

ACCOMMODATION

One can choose to stay at the Holiday Inn, an international standard hotel in the heart of JB itself, or at any of the 3- or 4-star hotels scattered around the town. Merlin Inn has a magnificent view of the Straits of Johor, while the 104 room Merlin Tower along Jalan Meldrum has a panoramic view of the town. The smaller hotels are popular among travellers on a budget. The

Straits View Hotel, built in the 1930s, maintains an old world charm of the colonial period.

Following is a list of some of the choices, with prices in Malaysian Dollars for a double room. The Telephone Area Code is 07.

International
Holiday Inn Johor Bahru, Jalan Dato Sulaiman, ph 323 800 — from $110 to $850; Merlin Tower Hotel, Jalan Meldrum, ph 225 811 — $180; Merlin Inn, Lot 5435 Jalan Bukit Meldrum, ph 228 581 — $180; Regent Elite Hotel, 1 Jalan Siew Nam, ph 223 811 — $95; Tropical Inn, 15 Jalan Gereja, ph 221 888 — from $110.00 to $450.

Good Tourist
Straits View Hotel, 1D Jalan Skudai, ph 224 133 — $83; First Hotel, Jalan Station, ph 222 888 — $80; Rasa Sayang Baru Hotel, 10 Jalan Dato Dalam, ph 224 744 — $60; Singrena Hotel, 176-180 Jalan Sri Pelangi, ph 326 433 — $50; Top Hotel, 12 Jalan Meldrum, ph 224 755 — $56.

Budget
Hawaii Hotel, 21 Jalan Meldrum, ph 226 332/3 — $33; Hotel Le Tian 2 Jalan Siew, ph 228 151 — $36; JB Hotel, 80A Jalan Ah Fook, ph 224 989 — $32; Johor Hotel, 69 Jalan Sultan Ibrahim, ph 224 395 — $28; Leo Court Hotel, 90 AB Jalan Serampang, ph 339 245 — $44; Malaya Hotel, 20 Jalan Bukit Meldrum, ph 221 691 — $27; Mareera Hotel, 42A Taman Maju Jaya, ph 332 492 — $33; Moi Li Hua Hotel, 2J ABIAD Taman Tebrau Jaya, ph 323 277 — $38; Wato Inn, 15, R. Jalan Bukit Meldrum, ph 221 328 — $47.

LOCAL TRANSPORT
Taxis are the main form of transport in Johor Bahru, and for sightseeing to other places of interest such as Kota Tinggi and Desaru. Decide on the fare before the ride as most taxis do not have meters. Taxi Station, ph 07-234 494.

Trishaws are also available in KB.

EATING OUT AND ENTERTAINMENT

Johor Bahru has a busy nightlife from 7pm onwards. The hawkers' centre near Kompleks Tun Razak is usually packed during dinner time. The "laksa Johor" is a must for every first-timer down south. A variety of herbs and spices are used to make the gravy which is brownish in colour and spicy to taste. "Santan" (coconut milk), "kerisik" (fried coconut), onions, cucumber, "daun selasih" and other ingredients add to the taste, not forgetting the dash of chilli and half-lime for that truly Malaysian flavour. All these for a surprising M$1.50 only. The dish is also available at the hawkers' centre opposite the railway station during the day.

Along the road one can also see stalls selling "ayam percik". This is barbequed chicken served with a special satay sauce. Johor is also famous for its "longtong" which is glutinous rice made into compact cubes and served in curry. Other scrumptious food are "satay", "mee goreng", "rojak", "nasi tomato", "mee bandung", etc.

The Taman Sri Tebrau hawker centre offers mainly Chinese food, and there are quite a few stalls selling claypot rice and barbequed seafood, wrapped in banana leaves.

Jaw's 5 Seafood Restaurant, situated along Jalan Scudai, is very popular with the locals, Singaporeans and international tourists. There are attap-roofed huts designed in ancient Malay style, as well as a modern air-conditioned building to dine in comfort. The menu incorporates the best of Sze Chuan, Cantonese, Hainanese and Shanghai cuisines, and the prices are reasonable.

JB Seafood Restaurant,' 10, 2 1/2 miles, Jalan Scudai, is a spacious restaurant which also overlooks the Straits of Johor.

At Kukup, a little Chinese fishing village on the southernmost west coast of Johor, there are lots of restaurants built on stilts, which specialise in seafood. From here you get a good view of the Straits of Malacca and the Indonesian shores.

Kong Kong fishing village on the east side of Johor is also renowned for its seafood.

SHOPPING

Clay Industries Sdn Bhd, is one of the oldest and largest manufacturers of ceramic products and has a large range of tableware and decorative sculptures. It started as a small cottage industry dealing in clay sub-soil pipes and latex cups. Today the company has expanded throughout Malaysia and sells its wares under the brandname Claytan.

For those interested to see how the ceramic items are produced, enquiries may be made through the administration office in Air Hitam, Johor, ph 07-784 201, to arrange for a tour of the factory.

JB Crafttown Handicrafts Centre, 36, 3 1/5 M/S, Jalan Scudai, ph 07-367 346, is one handicraft shop you can't afford to miss. There is a wide variety of hand-drawn batik materials and paintings, Malaysian oil and water-colour paintings, straw mats, songket and hand-drawn T-shirts to choose from, not to mention the many souvenirs and trinkets. The centre is open daily from 8.30am to 5.30pm, and they will also arrange free tours of JB town and the centre itself to promote tourism in Johor.

SIGHTSEEING

JOHOR BAHRU

Istana Besar
This palace, in Jalan Scudai, was built by Sultan Abu Bakar in 1866, and is the venue for royal ceremonies, investitures, state banquets and receptions. Part of it is being converted into a museum.

Istana Serene
Also in Jalan Scudai, this is the residence of His Highness the Sultan of Johor. The Royal Mausoleum is close by, and it has been the burial place for the Johor royal family since the change of the capital from Johor Lama. The mausoleum is not open to the public, but some fine examples of Muslim tombs can be found in the grounds.

Abu Bakar Mosque
Set on a hill, this is considered to be one of the finest mosques in Malaysia. The intricate architecture was designed by Tuan Haji Mohammad Arif, and it took eights years to build. It was finished in 1900 at a cost of M$400,000.

Sultan Ibrahim Building

Situated on Bukit Timbalan, this building houses the State Council Chamber, the State Secretariat and Government offices. The Saracenic character of the Grand Hall certainly interests the visitor.

JOHOR

Air Hitam

A favourite stopover for travellers, this busy little town, 88 km (55 miles) north of JB, is well-known for its pottery and clay products. There are also many coffee shops and roadside stalls, which are open 24 hours, and provide really good food. Air Hitam has been aptly nicknamed "the town which never sleeps".

Johor Lama

Of considerable historical interest, Johor Lama is a small village on the Johor River, 30 km (19 miles) from Johor Bahru. Archaeological excavations have uncovered interesting relics and the fort has been restored.

Until 1587, Johor Lama was the royal seat of the Johor Kingdom and a thriving trading port. In that year however, the three-year quarrel between Johor Kingdom and the Portuguese culminated in a Portuguese raid on Johor Lama. With 3 galleons, a number of smaller ships and 500 men, the Portuguese attacked the Johor fort from July 20 to August 15, 1587. When the fort fell, the city was sacked and a large booty of precious metals and other treasures was carried away by the Portuguese. The city never recovered after that.

Today, Johor Lama is easier reached by launch than by road.

Gunung Ledang

Johor's highest peak soars to 1,395 m (4,562 ft) above sea level and is also known as Mount Ophir. Thick jungles, exotic plants and a promise of adventure greets the daring and adventurous. Gunung Ledang is also surrounded with a host of fascinating legends. The rulers of the ancient Majapahit empire described the mountain as "meledang-ledangkan diri" meaning "shimmering by itself" as it was believed to be rich in mineral deposits. That was how the mountain got its name.

Mersing

Mersing, 136 km (84 miles) from Johor Bahru, the take-off point to many islands off its shore, has its own appeal. In the town there is a wide bay with a rocky beach and a mangrove forest in front of the resthouse. At low tide one can walk across to an opposite islet. In past years a rumour of sunken treasure being found off the Mersing coast near Pulau Batu Gajah turned Mersing from a quiet town into a tourist mecca.

The Merlin Inn located on Endau Road offers comfortable accommodation from M$50.

Desaru

A resort approximately 98 km (61 miles) north-east of Johor Bahru, Desaru has more than 25 km (15 miles) of unspoilt beaches. All kinds of sports, from snorkelling, swimming and canoeing to jungle-trekking can be enjoyed here. For those who enjoy golf, there is an 18-hole course.

Three top-class hotels are already established at Desaru offering impressive resort facilities, with emphasis on sea sports.

ISLANDS

Pulau Rawa

Rawa, about 16 km (10 miles) from Mersing, is one of the many splendid islands of Johor. The lovely beaches are formed of white coral sand and virtually covered with tall palms. There are coves to explore, and an off-shore coral reef teeming with marine life.

The island resort is run by the family of the late Tunku Mohammed Archibald of Malay royalty. Boats can be hired around the islands for snorkelling and fishing, and there is an aqua shop with equipment for hire and an array of T-shirts for sale. Rawa Island Resort also has a restaurant which serves a wide variety of local, Western and Chinese food.

Rawa Safaris in Mersing operate return boat trips for groups of 12 and below for a round fare of M$100. The trip lasts 1.25 hours each way. Bookings should be made at least one week in advance.

Rawa Safaris also have accommodation with large chalets

(four double rooms with verandah, shower and toilet attached), and small chalets for two persons. Enquiries ph 07-791 204/5.

Pulau Sibu

This is another of Malaysia's picturesque islands. There is accommodation in the form of Sibu Island Cabanas, which offer rooms and deluxe bungalows, and return ferry transfer can be arranged at M$22 adult and M$16 children, ph 07-317 216.

There is also a fishing village within walking distance from the resort, and indeed fishing and snorkelling seem to be the only activities. An ideal place to get away from it all.

SABAH AND SARAWAK

Sabah and Sarawak, the two States on the island of Borneo, are for the adventure-minded. Both states have large hinterlands of green forests, long road and river journeys and colourful native culture and handicrafts. There are enough natural attractions to satisfy the most ardent adventurer.

Visit passes to Malaysia do not automatically entitle entry to Sabah and/or Sarawak. Additional permission from the immigration departments of the respective states is required.

SABAH

There is 1,440 km (893 miles) of coastline in the State of Sabah, with the South China Sea on the west and the Sulu and Celebes seas on the east. Known as "The Land below the Wind" because it lies below the typhoon belt, Sabah is mountainous with lush tropical rain forests. Kota Kinabalu, the capital, is the eastern gateway to Malaysia with direct air links to Brunei, Hong Kong, the Philippines, Singapore, South Korea, Indonesia and Taiwan.

KOTA KINABALU

Kota Kinabalu is a relatively new town, as evidenced by the many high-rise buildings. The original town was razed during the Second World War and so a new carefully planned town was built. With a population of more than 41,000, the city takes particular pride in its gold-domed State Mosque which is centrally positioned and overlooks most of the town.

HOW TO GET THERE

By Air

MAS has flights to Kota Kinabalu from Kuala Lumpur, Johor Bahru, Kuching, Singapore, Hong Kong, Manila, Brunei, Jakarta, Seoul and Taipei.

Singapore Airlines has direct flights from Singapore to Kota Kinabalu.

216 SINGAPORE AND MALAYSIA AT COST

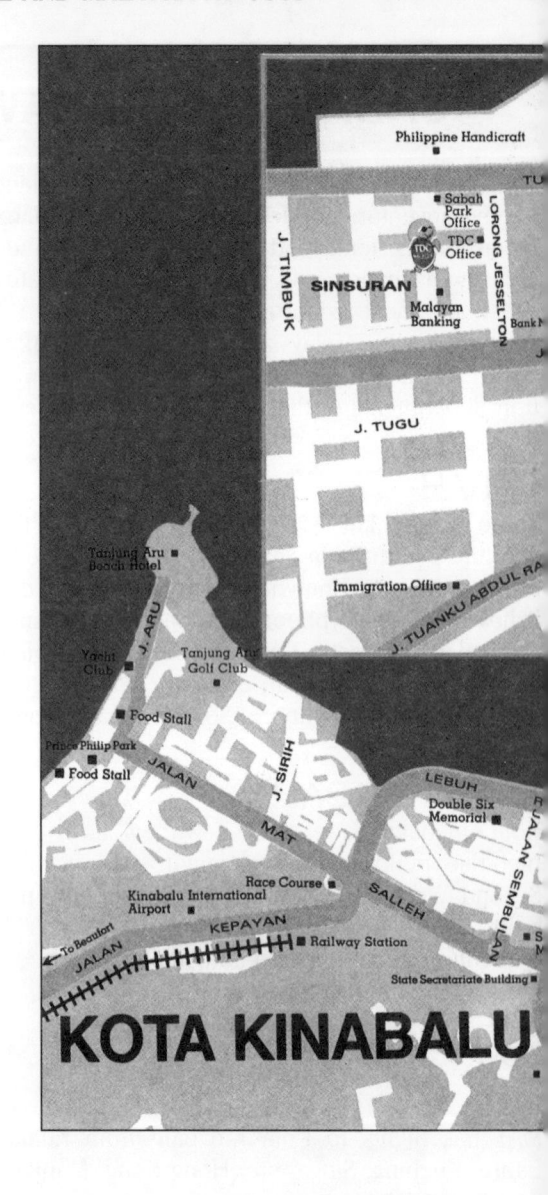

KOTA KINABALU

SABAH AND SARAWAK 217

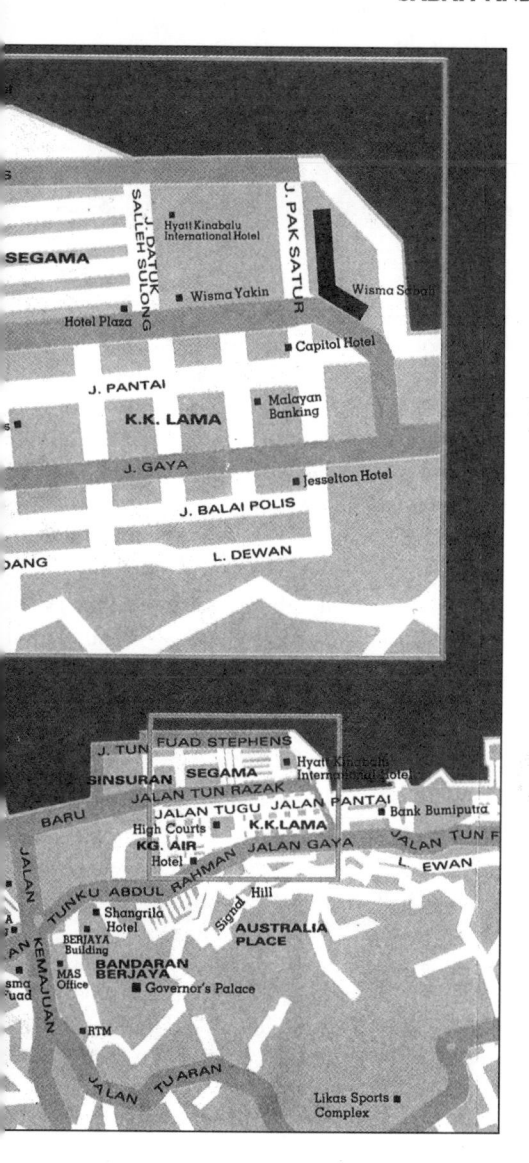

Top map (inset):

- J. DATUK SALLEH SULONG
- J. PAK SATU(R)
- SEGAMA
- Hyatt Kinabalu International Hotel
- Wisma Yakin
- Wisma Sabah
- Hotel Plaza
- Capitol Hotel
- J. PANTAI
- K.K. LAMA
- Malayan Banking
- J. GAYA
- Jesselton Hotel
- J. BALAI POLIS
- L. DEWAN

Bottom map:

- J. TUN FUAD STEPHENS
- SINSURAN
- SEGAMA
- Hyatt Kinabalu International Hotel
- JALAN TUN RAZAK
- BARU
- JALAN TUGU
- JALAN PANTAI
- Bank Bumiputra
- High Courts
- K.K. LAMA
- KG. AIR Hotel
- JALAN GAYA
- JALAN TUN F
- L. EWAN
- TUNKU ABDUL RAHMAN
- Signal Hill
- Shangrila Hotel
- AUSTRALIA PLACE
- BERJAYA Building
- BANDARAN BERJAYA
- MAS Office
- Governor's Palace
- RTM
- JALAN KEMAJUAN
- JALAN TUARAN
- Likas Sports Complex

TOURIST INFORMATION
Tourist Development Corporation Malaysia, Sabah Region Office, Block L, Lot 4 Bangunan STPB, Bandaran Sinsuran, ph 088-211 698/732.
Sabah Tourist Association, Sabah Tourism Promotion Corp., Airport Counter, Kota Kinabalu International Airport, ph 088-224 911 ext. 335.

ACCOMMODATION
There is a wide choice of accommodation in Kota Kinabalu, ranging from the Hyatt Kinabalu International Hotel in Jalan Datuk Salleh, ph 219 888, whose rates range from M$185 to M$1,250 per night, to the smaller budget hotels. Here we have listed some, with their rates in Malaysian Dollars for a double room. The Telephone Area Code is 088.

International
Hotel Capital, 23 Jalan Haji Saman, ph 53 433 — $250; Hotel Kinabalu, 59–60 Bandaran Berjaya, ph 53 233 — $150; Hotel Shangrila, Bandaran Berjaya, ph 56 100 — $155; Sabah Inn, 25 Jalan Pantai, ph 53 322 — $108; Winner Hotel, 9 & 10 Jln. Haji Saman — $140; Ang's Hotle, 28 Jalan Bakau, ph 55 433 — $96.

Good Tourist
Asia Hotel, 68 Bandaran Berjaya, ph 53 533 — $50; Diamond Inn, P.O. Box 11809, ph 225 222/5 — $60; Eden Hotel, 1–2 Jalan Sentosa, ph 53 577/8 — $80; Hotel New Sabah, 9–11 Jalan Padas, Segama Complex, ph 56 200 — $69; Hotel Rakyat, Block 1, Sinsuran Complex, ph 211 100/3 — $50; May Plaza, P.O. Box 1011 — ph 215 416 — $70; Nan Xing Hotel, 32–34 Jalan Haji Saman, ph 51 433 — $70; Pine Basy Hotel, 19 Jalan Sentosa, ph 59 450 — $55; Sea View Hotel, 31 Jalan Haji Saman, ph 54 422 — $66.

Budget
Central Hotel, 5–7 Jalan Tugu, ph 51 544/5 — $44; Federal Hotel, 16 Jalan Haji Yaacub, ph 51 191 — $40; Kin Fah Hotel, 7 Jalan Haji Yaacub, ph 53 833 — $40; New Capital, 7 Jalan Laiman Diki,

Bajau, Sabah

Toy Stall, Kuala Lumpur

Rungus Boys, Sabah

ph 53 011 — $36; Putra Hotel, 1 Jalan Haji Yaacub, ph 53 933 — $44.

LOCAL TRANSPORT

Shared taxis, mini-buses, ordinary buses, boats and a rail line that stretches from Beaufort and Tenom in the south, are the forms of transport available.
MAS operates daily flights to Labuan, Sandakan, Lahad Datu and Tawau.

SHOPPING

The Novitan Gift Centre in the Tanjung Aru Beach Hotel has a wide range of Borneo handicrafts, batik dresses/shirts, Sabah pearls, pottery, Sabah hats/baskets, T-shirts, silver accessories, antiques, spices and pewter.
There is a night market in the centre of the town where you can get bargain priced goods, and authentic food.

SIGHTSEEING

Kota Belud

This small town 77 km (48 miles) from Kota Kinabalu is galvanised into life every Sunday when the 'Tamu' or open market takes place. Not only are goods exchanged here, but news and gossip as well.

The Bajau horsemen, who wear jewelled costumes, carry ceremonial spears and ride bareback on ceremonial occasions, are farmers in this area. At the "Tamu" they can be seen riding buffaloes to the section of the market where the animals are traded. On their farms they raise buffaloes for meat or farm work elsewhere.

Tuaran

A pleasant little place, Tuaran is a half-hour's drive from Kota Kinabalu. The road to the town runs through farms, valleys, rubber plantations and forests. The agricultural station here is also worth a visit. Nearby is Mengkabong, a Bajau village built on stilts over the water. Transport round the village is by sampan or canoe.

Penampang

This is a Kadazan village, 13 km (8 miles) from Kota Kinabalu. The Kadazans, whose girls are particularly beautiful with long, black hair, are the rice growers of the region. Each year they have harvest festivals lasting for several days. The rejoicing and merry-making is for good harvest. They make their own potent rice-wine "Tapai" for this occasion.

Mount Kinabalu

Mt Kinabalu is set in the Kinabalu National Park. For more information see the section on National Parks.

Poring Hot Spring

Poring Hot Spring, 43 km (27 miles) from the National Park headquarters, offers a refreshing dip to the visitor.

Kudat

This is the home of the Rungus, members of the Kadazan race. It lies 238 km (148 miles) north of Kota Kinabalu and may be reached by sea or road. Every Sunday the Rungus appear at the market place in Sikuati, 23 km (14 miles) from Kudat. The women wear heavy brass bracelets, beaded necklaces and black knee-length sarongs. Nearby is a beach with surf crashing on the shore, more for photographing than for swimming. Another beach, 8 km (5 miles) away at Bak-Bak, is reached by a road lined with coconut palms.

Papar

Papar, 38 km from Kota Kinabalu, may be reached by road. This is a particularly scenic trip with green padi fields and jungle lining the roadside.

Tenom

Tenom, a Murut Area, can be reached by train from Beaufort, a journey through the spectacular Padas Gorge. From Kota Kinabalu you can travel on the main highway by an express bus passing through Papar, Bongawan and Kimanis and reaching Beaufort before taking the train to Tenom.

The Muruts continue to live in longhouses. A generous and hospitable people, they are still given to a life of song and dance.

From Tenom, excursions can be arranged for visits to other Murut settlements in the neighbouring areas.

Keningau

48 km (30 miles) by road from Tenom, Keningau can be used as a stopover point before making trips deeper into the Murut districts of Tenom. Cattle and ponies are to be seen grazing on the plains.

Tambunan

Tambunan is 48 km (30 miles) from Keningau, and the landscape is characterised by padi fields and rolling hills. The forts and graves of the Mat Salleh movement, a group that opposed British control, can be found here, but getting to these relics is a journey only for the adventurous.

Discovery Tours (Sabah), Lot 6, Shopping Arcade, Tanjung Aru Beach Hotel, ph 216 426, 216 427, have several guided tours on offer including —

City/Suburb — M$28 adult, M$20 child — 2.5 hours
KK By Night — M$65 adult, M$40 child — 4 hours
Kampong Tour — M$35 adult, M$25 child — 3.25 hours
Penampang Cultural Tour — M$35 adult, M$25 child — 4 hours
Kota Belud Sunday Market — M$45 adult, M$30 child — 5-6 hours
Trip to Kinabalu Park — M$45 adult, M$30 child — 8 hours
Kinabalu Park/Poring Hot Spring — M$95 adult, M$80 child — day
Penampang/Papar + Kadazan — M$85 adult, M$55 child — 6 hours

SANDAKAN

Lying on a bay on the north eastern coast of Sabah and facing the Sulu Seas, Sandakan is 386 km (240 miles) from Kota Kinabalu. It is a busy port, with ships loading timber, rattan, copra and birds' nests (for soups). Behind the port lies the town and beyond that are tall mountains.

The Forestry Exhibition in the centre of town has an impressive collection of flowers and plants found in Sabah as well as handicrafts and hunting weapons. The Sandakan Orchid House has a collection of rare blooms.

Three roads lead out of Sandakan, the Labuk road, the Leila road and the Sim-Sim road. The Labuk road leads back to Kota Kinabalu through palm oil, cocoa and fruit plantations, padi fields, farmlands and tropical forests.

Leila road goes along the coast offering magnificent seascapes. Off shore are islands inhabited solely by seabirds, and turtles when they come in to lay their eggs.

One of the islands off Sandakan is Berhala Island, ideal for picnicking and swimming, and within easy reach by motor launch. A lighthouse on the highest point offers interesting views for photographers.

The Sim-Sim road leads to prawn canneries, sawmills and shipyards.

Gomantong Caves
These caves can be reached by boat across the bay from Sandakan, then a 16 km (10 miles) landrover ride through jungles and plains. At the caves, swifts build their nests high on the cave walls and roof. These nests are considered delicacies and are collected by men climbing on tall bamboo poles. The stalactite and stalagmite features of the caves are also interesting to study. A visit to the caves takes a whole day and arrangements can either be made through a travel agency or the Forest Departmen in Sandakan.

Sepilok Orang-Utan Sanctuary
The Orang-Utan Sanctuary at Sepilok, about 24 km (15 miles from Sandakan, should not be missed. The only one in the world you can see the Orang-Utans being fed from a platform in the middle of the forest about 20 minutes' walk from the centre Nicknamed the "Wild man of Borneo" (arboreal anthropoid ape) the Orang-Utans are brought here for rehabilitation and late returned to the forest when they are able to fend for themselves

Tawau

Tawau has a fine mosque and avenues of shaded shops. The town lies at the south-east corner of the State on a stretch of coast. Timber, rubber, manila, hemp, copra, cocoa and palm oil are produced in the hinterland. Open air stalls along the sea front serve delicious seafood.

Semporna

An interesting old town on a peninsula. One of the tiny islands in the surrounding sea is Pulau Gayam, a volcanic island, which can be reached by motor launch from Semporna. There is a pearl culture station on this island.

SARAWAK

Sarawak lies on the north-west cost of the island of Borneo. It covers an area of approximately 124,967 km^2 (48,237 sq. miles), and has a population of 1.5 million. Kuching, the capital of Sarawak State is situated on the banks of the Sarawak River and is the gateway to a country of rain forests, unexplored ravines, plateaux and mountain ranges, rivers and exciting rapids. This is the land where fearsome head hunters once roamed until the English adventurer, James Brooke set up his private kingdom in the beginning of the 19th Century.

Now a land of the unspoiled beauty of lush tropical greenery, it is enriched by a population that comprises Iban, Chinese, Malays, Bidayuh, Melanaus, Orang Ulu and others, each having their own colourful festivals which take place throughout the year.

KUCHING

Kuching is located on the banks of the Sarawak River, approximately 32 km (20 miles) from the sea. The town has beautifully landscaped parks and gardens, historic buildings, colourful markets and an interesting waterfront.

HOW TO GET THERE

By Air

There is an international airport at Kuching, and MAS has regular services from Kuala Lumpur and Kota Kinabalu.

TOURIST INFORMATION

Tourist Development Corporation Malaysia, Sarawak Region Office, 2nd Floor, AIA Building, Jalan Song Thien Cheok, ph 56 575, 56 775.
Sarawak Tourist Association, Lot 224, L2, Sarawak Plaza, Jalan Tar, ph 240 620.

ACCOMMODATION

The rates for the hotels listed below represent those for a double room, and are in Malaysian Dollars. The Telephone Area Code is 082.

International
Aurora Hotel, Jalan McDougall, ph 240 281 — $165; Borneo Hotel, Jalan Tebuan, ph 244 121 — $105; Country View Hotel, Jalan Tan Sin Datuk Ong, ph 247 111 — $110; Ferritel Hotel, Jalan Kuching Bypass, ph 484 799 — $105; Holiday Inn, Jalan Tuanku Abdul, ph 423 111 — $350; Mayfair Hotel, 45-47 Palm Road, ph 416 380 — $168; Sheraton Damai, P.O. Box 2870, ph 20 231 — $220.

Good Tourist
Fata Hotel, Jalan McDougall, ph 248 111 — $80; Long House Hotel, Jalan Abell, Padungan, ph 249 333 — $90.

Budget
Palm Hotel, 29 Palm Road, ph 20 231 — $42.

SHOPPING

Kuching is excellent for buying tribal artifacts, and the best selection is to be found in the antique shops along Main Bazaar, Wayang Street and Temple Street. Prices are high, but bargaining is normal. Jewellery is expensive too. It is also recommended that you spend a few hours at the Sunday Open Market at Jalan Satok. Here antiques could be found on sale alongside jungle produce.

Sarawak Antique Ordinance
Visitors are reminded that under the Sarawak Antiquities Ordinance, no person may export or take away antiquity except under licence issued by the curator of Sarawak Museum. An "antiquity" is any object manufactured before 1850.

SIGHTSEEING

Sarawak Museum
This is one of the finest museums in Asia, with an excellent collection of Borneon ethnological and archaeological materials. Admission to the museum is free, and it is open weekdays from 9.30am–5.30pm (closed Friday) and Sundays and Public Holidays from 9.30am–6pm.

The Istana
This palace was built in 1870 by Rajah Charles Brooke. It is set among rolling lawns on the northern bank of the Sungei Sarawak. It is the official residence of the head of State. The best view of the palace is from Pangkalan Batu on the opposite side of the river.

Fort Margherita
Close by the Istana is the old Fort Margherita. It was built in 1879 and served as a fort of defence for the town, especially from attacks which came from down river. The fort is now renovated and has been turned into a Police Museum.

The Court House
The imposing facade of the Court building, built in 1874, has imaginative local art forms incorporated in the roof panels and the door and window grills.

Masjid Besar (Main Mosque)
This million dollar mosque was completed in 1968. The original Masjid Besar built of wood was completed in 1852.

Tua Pek Kong Temple
Kuching has many ornate temples and this, the oldest one, was built in 1876.

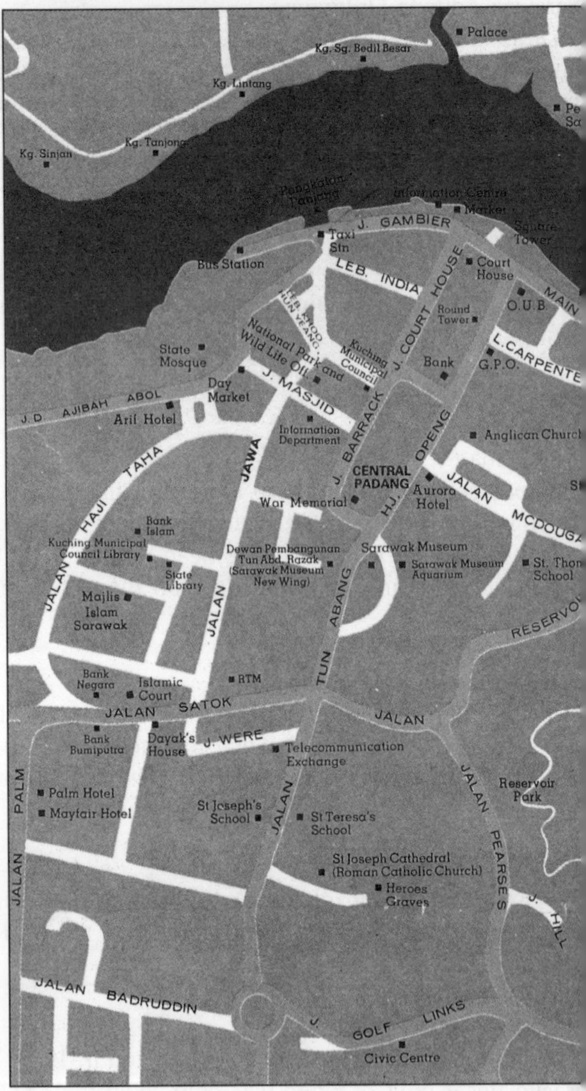
Palace
Kg. Sg. Bedil Besar
Kg. Lintang
Kg. Tanjong
Kg. Sinjan
Pangkalan Tanjung
Information Centre
Market
Square Tower
J. GAMBIER
Taxi Stn
Bus Station
LEB. INDIA
Court House
J. COURT HOUSE
O.U.B.
MAIN
Round Tower
L. CARPENTE
G.P.O.
Bank
Kuching Municipal Council
National Park and Wild Life Off.
State Mosque
Day Market
J. MASJID
J. D AJIBAH ABOL
Arif Hotel
Information Department
J. BARRACK
OPENG
Anglican Church
JALAN HAJI TAHA
JAWA
CENTRAL PADANG
Aurora Hotel
JALAN MCDOUGA
War Memorial
HJ.
Bank Islam
Kuching Municipal Council Library
Dewan Pembangunan Tun Abd. Razak (Sarawak Museum New Wing)
Sarawak Museum
Sarawak Museum Aquarium
St. Thom School
State Library
Majlis Islam Sarawak
JALAN
TUN ABANG
RESERVO
Bank Negara
Islamic Court
RTM
JALAN SATOK
JALAN
Bank Bumiputra
Dayak's House
J. WERE
Telecommunication Exchange
Reservoir Park
JALAN PALM
Palm Hotel
Mayfair Hotel
St Joseph's School
JALAN
St Teresa's School
JALAN PEARSES
St Joseph Cathedral (Roman Catholic Church)
Heroes Graves
J. HILL
JALAN
JALAN BADRUDDIN
J. GOLF LINKS
Civic Centre

SABAH AND SARAWAK 227

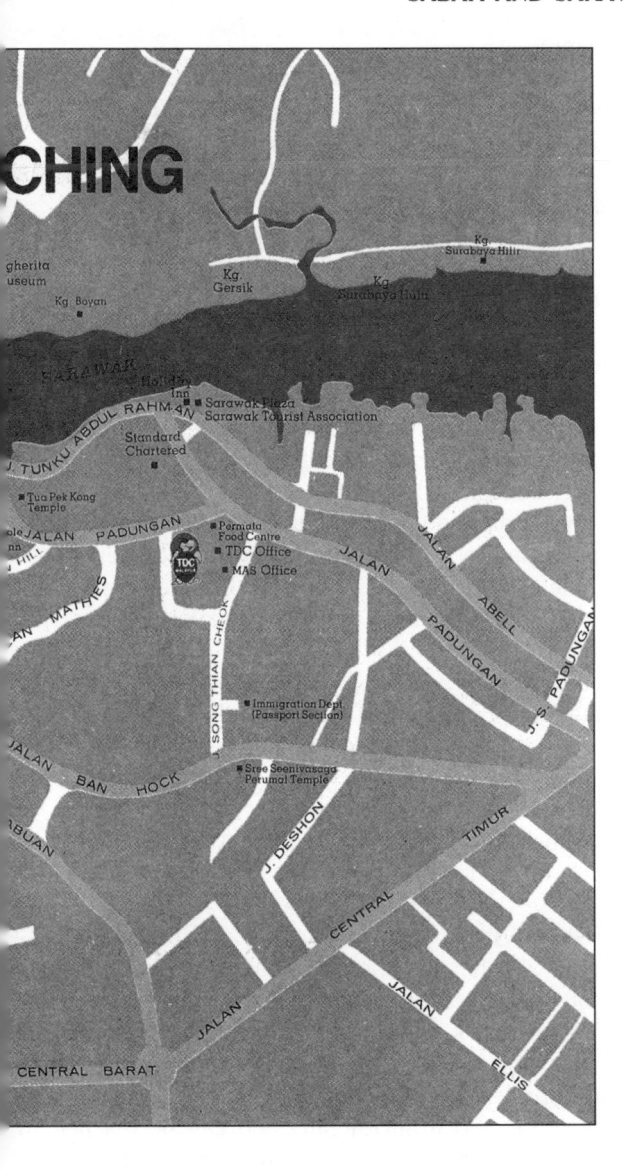

Hong San Temple
This temple was built in 1895 in honour of the God Kuek Seng Ong. Legend has it that Kuek, a native of Hokkien province, became a god over a thousand years ago.

Skrang River Safari
This safari has to be undertaken as an organised tour, It begins with a four hour drive to the banks of the Skrang River, then continues down the shallow river, by boat, occasionally shooting the rapids. The journey along this scenic river brings you to a series of Iban longhouses. These community dwellings are made of ironwood and roofed with palm leaf or ironwood shingles. All the rooms in the longhouses are side by side, facing a long communal hall used for leisure activities like wood-carving and basket weaving. Occasionally guests are invited to attend nightly ceremonies and drink rice wine, which the Ibans make. Visitors who go on organised tours are accommodated in a guest house belonging to the tour operators. These have basic amenities. For further information contact the Tourist Information Centres.

Pepper Plantations
Sarawak is the largest exporter of pepper in the country and the plantations may be seen along the Kuching-Serian Road.

The Great Cave of Niah
For more information on this cave and the Niah National Park, see the section on National Parks.

Santubong Fishing Village
The picturesque village of Santubong has good beaches and is the site of several archaeological discoveries. Hindu and Buddhist-influenced rock carvings have been found around the Santubong River delta. During the 7th and 13th Centuries, Santubong was an important trading centre.

It is 32 km (20 miles) from Kuching and can be reached by express launch. Accommodation in government chalets is available, but bookings in advance are advisable through the District Office, Kuching.

Wildlife

Sarawak is rich in wildlife with over 550 species of birds. There are also barking deer, wild pig, honey bear, biggon crocodiles, lizards, snakes and of course the orang-utan. This is the home of the orang-utan, now almost extinct, but it has become a protected species. Four species of marine turtles make Sarawak their home. One of the government conservation hatcheries for turtle eggs is at Talang-Talang Island near Kuching. The Hornbill is a protected bird and is also the official state crest.

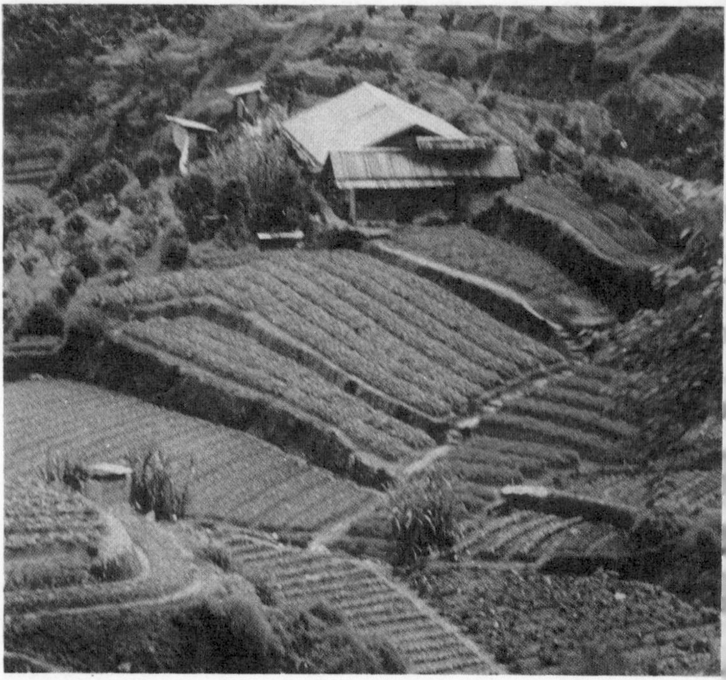

HILL RESORTS OF MALAYSIA

The Hill Resorts of Malaysia offer the visitor the opportunity to commune with nature and relax in the cool, fresh, invigorating climate. With the jungle literally at your doorstep, you may saunter along cool, peaceful jungle vales, admire the exotic flora and fauna, or simply sit and dream in front of a roaring log fire at night.

For the more energetic there is golf, hard court tennis, swimming, bowling and of course, hill-climbing on mountain peaks that rise to well over 1,829 m (5,981 ft).

CAMERON HIGHLANDS

The Cameron Highlands, 1,524 m (4,983 ft) above sea-level and with a population of 20,000, lie in the northwest corner of the State of Pahang in the centre of Peninsular Malaysia.

The Highlands are actually three districts in one. Less than 45 km (28 miles) from Tapah, in the State of Perak, is Ringlet, one of the main agricultural centres of Cameron Highlands. The soil is rich and the climate conducive to the growing of giant spring cabbages, lettuce, tomatoes and other temperate and sub-temperate vegetables and fruits.

Tanah Rata, the principal township, lies less than 13 km (8 miles) away and another thousand feet up. There, the scenery seems to suddenly shift into high gear. The air is cool and clean. There are jungle streams, lakes and waterfalls and magnificent views.

Tanah Rata's natural assets have been cleverly and wisely exploited. There are chalets, cottages and good hotels, steak houses and all the solitude you could wish. There is a bank, a post office and a busy shopping centre. There is also a bus service and taxis are available.

About 3 km (2 miles) further up from Tanah Rata is the township of Brinchang. There in front of a beautiful 18-hole golf course is the modern international-standard Merlin Hotel.

HISTORY

In 1885 a Government surveyor on a mapping expedition reported finding "a fine plateau with gentle slopes shut in by lofty mountains". The surveyor was William Cameron after whom these hills are named.

Tea planters quickly realising the suitability of these hills for their crops, hastily claimed the plateau; Chinese vegetable farmers settled in the valleys and later built a road to carry their produce to market. A wealthy planter came looking for the perfect hideaway, discovered the route and built a house there for weekend retreats. Cameron Highlands, the mountain resort, has never stopped growing since.

HOW TO GET THERE

The Cameron Highlands are easily accessible. From Kuala Lumpur or Penang proceed by car or rail to the town of Tapah. From Tapah make the ascent to Cameron Highlands by bus or taxi along a two-way traffic road that winds through jungle and hill scenery, a distance of 60 km (37 miles). The climb from Tapah is gradual and hardly noticeable except for the fall in temperature.

ACCOMMODATION

Like most holiday resorts in Malaysia, the Cameron Highlands have off and peak seasons. The latter is in April, August and December and in these months it is advisable to book accommodation well in advance.

The Merlin Hotel, ph 941 205, offers accommodation of international standard from M$80 to M$270. Several cottage-type bungalows are also available and these offer a cosy English type atmosphere, complete with log fires at hight. For those on budget holidays, there are several other hotels offering accommodation at reasonable rates. We have listed some below, with prices for a double room in Malaysian Dollars. The Telephone Area Code is 05.

International
Ye Olde Smokehouse, Tanah Rata, ph 941 214 — $60–300; Golf Course Inn, Tanah Rata, ph 941 411 — $150; Kowloon Hotel, 34–35 Brinchang, ph 941 366 — $80; Hollywood Hotel, 38 Main

Road, Tanah Rata, ph 941 633 — $80; Garden Hotel, Tanah Rata, ph 941 911 — $70.

Good Tourist
Brinchang Hotel, 36 Brinchang Town, ph 941 755 — $45; Federal Hotel, 44 Main Road, Tanah Rata, ph 941 777 — $45; Highland Hotel, 29–32 Brinchang, ph 941 588 — $40.

Budget
Town House Hotel, 41 Main Road, Tanah Rata, ph 941 666 — $22.

FLOWERS

The Cameron Highlands are famous for their large brilliantly coloured flowers. With average day temperatures hovering around 21.1C and night temperatures around 10C the Cameron Highlands have become an important flower producing centre. The much sought-after blooms find their way to all the main towns in Malaysia, and even reach as far as Singapore. Among the many varieties grown are roses, chrysanthemums, carnations, dahlias, geraniums, fuchsias, gladioli, and "everlasting flowers".

VEGETABLES

Market gardening has become an important economic activity in this district, particularly in the Ringlet and Brinchang areas. Farmers who in earlier days cultivated the valley floors have now cut tiers into the hillsides where the rich soil produces spring cabbages, lettuce, tomatoes, leeks and even rhubarb. To the visitor the simple symmetry of the tiered hillsides offers a picturesque view.

FRUITS

Strawberries, passion fruit, tangerine oranges, grapefruit — these are some of the many varieties of fruit available in the Highlands.

TEA

The tea planters who were among the first to "invade" the Cameron Highlands have now established vast acreages of high quality tea bush in various parts of the district. You can either take a drive or a walk and see the colourfully dressed women tea pickers among the bushes, or if you like, visit a factory and see the whole process of production.

MARDI STATION
Agriculture being of such economic importance in the district, an agricultural station has been established in the Cameron Highlands. This is the Malaysian Agricultural Research and Development Institute station where experiments are made with a variety of produce. The Station is located adjacent to the Tengku Ahmad Secondary School. If you plan a visit, do write in advance for an appointment.

JUNGLE TRACKS AND MOUNTAIN CLIMBING
There are numerous jungle-paths leading to such well-known hilltops as Gunung Beremban (1,841 m — 6,020 ft), Gunung Jasar (1,696 m — 5,546 ft) and Gunung Brinchang (2,032 m — 6,645 ft).

On clear days a panoramic view of Ipoh, the Straits of Malacca and other towns can be seen from most peaks.

Along most jungle paths and especially at the waterfalls — Robinson Falls and Parit Falls — brilliantly coloured butterflies flit among the trees, and butterfly nets can be purchased from the shops in Tanah Rata. If you don't have time to catch your own there are mounted displays in any of the 3 towns which you can purchase at reasonable prices.

SPORTS
For the sports-minded there is an 18-hole golf course with undulating fairways, a meandering stream and tricky greens. Visiting membership fees are reasonable and are graded according to the length of your holiday. A modern clubhouse beside the first tee offers adequate facilities. There are also tennis and badminton courts, and swimming is available in the natural jungle pool under the Parit Falls.

FRASER'S HILL
Like Rome, Fraser's Hill is built on seven hills. At 1,524 m (4,98? ft) above sea level, cool air is guaranteed. It is the closest hi

station to Kuala Lumpur and popular with visitors and residents alike.

Carving a road up through the hills was an engineering feat. In the early days bullock carts were used for the journey, but nowadays it is possible to go in perfect comfort by car or air-conditioned bus. There are several bungalows and a large hotel.

HISTORY

Fraser's Hill is named after a solitary adventurer, Louis James Fraser, who built a shack, operated a primitive mule train and traded in tin ore in the last decade of the 19th and the first decade of the 20th Century.

In 1910, Bishop Ferguson-Davie of Singapore climbed the mountain in search of Fraser who had apparently disappeared. The search was not quite fruitless for he discovered what has become one of Malaysia's most popular resorts. It was surveyed in 1919 and development of what is now Fraser's Hill commenced soon after.

HOW TO GET THERE

By Bus

There is a regular bus service from Kuala Lumpur to Kuala Kubu Bahru, and from Kuala Kubu Bahru to Fraser's Hill.
Kuala Kubu Bahru to Fraser's Hill departs 8am and 12 noon.
Fraser's Hill to Kuala Kubu Bahru departs 10am and 2pm.

Kuala Lumpur — Kuala Kubu Bahru — M$2.50
Kuala Kubu Bahru — Fraser's Hill — M$2.10.

By Taxi

Kuala Lumpur — Fraser's Hill — M$60 per taxi (M$15 per person).
Subang Airport — Fraser's Hill — M$90 per taxi (aircon), M$70 per taxi (non-aircon).

By Car

The last 8 km (5 miles) from the gap to the top of Fraser's Hill is along a narrow winding road which carries only one way traffic from 6.30am to 7pm.

Opening Times for Control Gates

Up-Going Traffic (At The Gap)	Down-Going Traffic (At Fraser's Hill)
7.00am — 7.40am	8.00am — 8.40am
9.00am — 9.40am	10.00am — 10.40am
11.00am — 11.40am	12 noon — 12.40pm
1.00pm — 1.40pm	2.00pm — 2.40pm
3.00pm — 3.40pm	4.00pm — 4.40pm
5.00pm — 5.40pm	6.00pm — 6.40pm

There is no control after 7.30pm.

ACCOMMODATION

The Fraser's Hill Development Corporation runs bungalows and chalets with full catering facilities. There is also a government run bungalow (Sri Berkat) and an international standard hotel (Hotel Merlin) right in the centre of Fraser's Hill. Peak season at this Resort is in the months of April, August and December. For accommodation during peak season and on Saturdays, Sundays and public holidays it is advisable to book well in advance. Fraser's Hill Development Corporation Bungalows range from M$25 to M$55 per night, ph 09-382 201, and the Hotel Merlin, ph 09-382 279, offers accommodation from M$80 to M$300. For enquiries about the Seri Berkat Bungalow, phone the District Officer, Ulu Selangor, on 03-804 1026.

FOOD AND DRINKS

The Arzed and the Hillview are social centres of Fraser's Hill, and no wonder. After dusk, around a roaring log fire a feeling of peace and tranquility steal over you and life is complete.

SPORTS

The Golf Course

Fraser's Hill has one of the few public golf courses in Malaysia. Contrary to popular belief, the site of the 9-hole course is not the remains of a tin mine! It was in actual fact constructed by sluicing down the hill-side into the valley of the Sungei Tras and to the dismay of the contractor, not a speck of tin was found in the process.

Playing hours: 7am till dusk daily.
Green fees: weekdays — M$15 per day.
Saturdays, Sundays, Public Holidays — M$25 per day.
Caddy fees: M$5 per round of 9 holes.

Tennis

Two hard courts are available for the use of visitors. The fee is M$5 an hour for either a morning or afternoon session, and M$7 an hour for night sessions.

Sports Complex

This complex is situated in the town centre and provides a range of facilities — changing rooms for golfers, saunas, two squash courts, a heated swimming pool, conference facilities and a coffee house and restaurant.

Opening times for pool: 9am–12 noon, 2pm–5pm weekdays and Sundays. On Saturdays and eve of public holidays the opening time will be extended to another three-hour session from 6–9pm.

Charges:
Weekdays — Adults M$5, Children M$3 per three-hour session.
Saturdays, Sundays and Public Holidays — Adults M$7, Children M$5 per three-hour session.

Swimming

The Jeriau Waterfalls are a must when visiting Fraser's Hill. The cascading falls have been cleverly cupped into a swimming pool.

Less than 5 km (3 miles) from the town centre, the waterfalls are easily accessible by car. A full paved footpath (800 m — 872 yds) leads to the pool.

Jungle Walks

The well-kept jungle paths and unusual flora are ideal for hikers. These paths lead to the peaks of the hills from which there are panoramic views of the main range of mountains.

Mini Zoo And Park

The mini zoo and park occupy 4 ha (10 acres) close to the children's playground. Attractions include a fish pond, aviary, a rose garden, chrysanthemum garden, facilities for horse-riding and camping. Entrance fee M$1.

PENANG HILL

Penang Hill is a name given collectively to a group of hills in the centre of Penang Island. A ride up the 692 m (2,263 ft) Hill is a fascinating experience. The funicular railway which plies up the Hill is rare in the Far East, the only other being in Hong Kong.

The railway operates in two sections (change trains at mid point). In just 24 minutes you can feel the temperature dropping to a cool 18C, offering a change from the tropical warmth of the lowlands.

A bus serves the Summit Station to Strawberry Hill or Tiger Hill, but most visitors prefer to walk down the Summit Road. You can follow paths branching off this main road and stroll past picturesque bungalows and beautiful gardens.

HOW TO GET THERE

You can fly from Kuala Lumpur or travel by car or rail. The bottom station of the Hill Railway can be reached by taxi or by regular scheduled bus services.

The Hill Railway service commences at 6.30am and ends a 9.30pm daily except on Wednesdays and Saturdays when it is maintained until midnight.

From the Lower Station
6.30am — 7.00am — every 15 minutes
7.15am — 9.15pm — every 30 minutes
2.00pm — 11.45pm extended hours (every 30 minutes) only or Wednesdays, Saturdays and Sundays.
From the Upper Station
6.30am — 7.15am — every 15 minutes
7.15am — 12 midnight — every 30 minutes.
Fares — M$3 return each passenger.

ACCOMMODATION

Whether you plan to spend only a day here, or stay longer, you will find a wide selection of good and ample accommodation.

There is a twelve-room hotel (Penang Hill Hotel) with all modern facilities. Room rates range from M$60 for a single to M$80 for a double — ph 04-892 256.

Apart from this hotel, there are several Government holiday bungalows which can be rented. Bookings can be made through the State Secretary, Penang (although preference is given to Government employees).

TEA KIOSK

At the summit of Penang Hill there is a little tea kiosk which caters for snacks and drinks. From here you can look down over the city nestling at the foot of the hill, and the harbour.

Looking westward, there is a wide expanse of jungle-covered slopes and foot-hills pierced by narrow cultivated valleys. Northwards lie the off-shore islands around Penang, the distant mainland and the sharply outlined Kedah Peak, while to the south are the tree-shrouded slopes of Penang's main range of hills.

OTHER FACILITIES

There is a Police Station, a Post Office with cablegram services and a children's playground. A mosque built on a level of land 808 m (2,642 ft) above sea-level provides another interesting viewpoint.

GENTING HIGHLANDS

One hour's drive from Kuala Lumpur is the latest addition to Malaysia's highland recreation spots — the Genting Highlands Resort. Opened in mid-1971, it nestles 2,000 m (6,540 ft) above sea-level. Straddling the Main Range from the State of Selangor to virgin forest in the State of Pahang, it will eventually cover an area of more than 6,000 ha (14,820 acres) when the project is fully completed.

The climate is spring-like and the cool refreshing mountain air provides a most relaxing holiday in the clouds.

HOW TO GET THERE

The centre of the Genting Highlands Resort is situated in Gunung Ulu Kali, 50 km (31 miles) from Kuala Lumpur and 1,714 m (5,605 ft) above sea-level.

By Coach
Genting operates its own air-conditioned coaches, with 8 scheduled services daily from Pudu Raya Bus Terminal in Kuala Lumpur.

By Taxi
Fare from Kuala Lumpur is M$5 per person in a shared taxi (M$20 per taxi).

By Bus
The one-way fare in an air-conditioned bus from Kuala Lumpur is M$5.

ACCOMMODATION
There are 3 attractive modern hotels which provide a total of 1,070 rooms of both international and economy classes.

The latest addition to the Genting Highlands Resort is the 18-storey, 700 room, international class Genting Hotel, which has a theatre, restaurant, a casino, heated swimming pool, 24-hour 800-capacity coffee terrace, grill room, bars, theatrette, health centre, as well as beauty salons and shopping arcade.

The Highlands Hotel has 9 storeys and offers 200 luxury rooms as well as a conference hall and a 24-hour coffee house.

Pelangi Hotel has 170 rooms with a Chinese restaurant.

Rates

Genting Hotel —	Standard Twin	M$120
	Deluxe Twin	M$160
	Superior Deluxe Twin	M$180
	Junior Suite	M$300
	Executive Suite	M$1000
	Executive Deluxe Suite	M$1200
	Presidential Suite	M$2000
	Extra Bed	M$20
Highlands Hotel —	Twin	M$80
	Triple	M$95
	Family Room	M$110
	Extra Bed	M$10

Pelangi Hotel —	Twin	M$50
	Family Room	M$70
	Extra Bed	M$10

Reservations and Enquiries — Genting Highlands Tours and Promotion Sdn. Bhd, 9th Floor, Wisma Genting, Jalan Sultan Ismail, 50250 Kuala Lumpur, ph 03-261 3833.

THE CASINO

If excitement is what you are looking for, have a little flutter at the Casino de Genting, Malaysia's first and only casino. Whether it be Roulette, Blackjack, Baccarat, Keno, French Bull, Tai Sai or just slot machines, the casino is a pleasant place for a few hours of fun.

ACTIVITIES

Boating
A 4 ha (10 acre) artificial lake in front of the Highlands Hotel provides boating facilities. The two islands within the lake contain a tea house and an aviary.

Fun and Games
A mini-railway track circles the lake to provide joyrides for children. There is also an Amusement Centre on the first floor of the Highlands Hotel.

Indoor Stadium
The indoor stadium provides facilities for basketball, table-tennis, badminton and squash.

Bowling
The Genting Hotel contains a 16-lane bowling alley.

Golf
A 18-hole course is set amidst beautiful rolling hillside scenery at the lower end of the cable car terminal and in front of the Sri Layang Hotel. The golf enthusiast can enjoy a round of golf in the cool, invigorating mountain air, or take a dip in the heated swimming pool.

Night Life
The 1,200-seater Genting Theatre Restaurant, in the Genting Hotel, features international floor-shows while you enjoy a sumptuous Chinese dinner.

Cable Car
Linking the golf course and the hotels is Malaysia's longest cable car system. This is a twin-coach 40-passenger car system which travels from 914 m (2,989 ft) to 1,768 m (5,781 ft). Fares are M$2.50 per adult and M$1.50 per child one way. Services are from 8am to 9pm on weekdays and from 8am to 11pm on weekends.

CAVE TEMPLE
The Chin Swee Cave Temple is a relatively new addition to the tourist attractions in the Resort. Situated on a slope at 1,460 m (4,774 ft) above sea-level, the cave temple commands a panoramic view of the countryside. Only 3–5 km further up is the resort proper.

MAXWELL HILL (BUKIT LARUT)
"The surrounding country with its groves of evergreens is very much like Switzerland in summer except perhaps the country is a little greener and more thickly wooded." This is how a visitor has described Bukit Larut (Maxwell Hill), Malaysia's oldest hill resort about 9 km (6 miles) out of Taiping Town in Perak State.

Access to this resort, at 1,035 m (3,384 ft) above sea-level, is by land-rover along a metalled one-way road which has several hair-pin bends and a swift-flowing mountain stream which is visible at various points along its winding course.

There is a mid-way stop at the Tea Garden House, the area around which was once an extensive tea estate. From this point there is a panoramic view of the surrounding countryside — Taiping town, a bird's eye-view of the Taiping Lake Gardens, the green suburbs of Aulong and Simpang, and the 19 km (12 miles) ruler-straight road from Taiping to Port Weld.

Most visitors go on an invigorating climb to the Cottage, the only accessible summit of Bukit Larut. From here, on a clear day, you can see the coastline from Pangkor Island to Penang.

HOW TO GET THERE
Transport up and down Maxwell Hill is by official Land Rovers only which normally run at hourly intervals from 8am to 6pm daily. The service begins from the foot of the hill. Bookings can be made at Hill Gardens Office, ph Bukit Larut 05-886 241.

Fares (Adult): M$1 to Tea Gardens; M$2 to 10th km area; M$2.50 to Hut, Treacher, Speedy Rest House, M$3 to Cottage.

ACCOMMODATION
There are a number of bungalows on Bukit Larut. You can have your pick of the Rumah Rehat Bukit Larut (Maxwell Rest House) 1,036 m (3,388 ft); Rumah Beringin (Watson Bungalow) 1,036 m (3,388 ft); Rumah Cendana (the Hut) 1,097 m (3,587 ft); Rumah Rehat Gunong Hijau (Speedy Rest House) 1,113 m (3,639 ft); Rumah Cempaka (Hugh Low) 1,139 m (3,724 ft); Rumah Tempinis (Treacher Bungalow) 1,143 m (3,737). Bookings can be made through the Superintendent, Maxwell Hill, Taiping, ph 05-886 241.

Except the last 2 VIP Bungalows, the Speedy (now known by its Malaysian name) and Bukit Larut, Rest House rates range from M$8 for a single room to M$15 for a double. Rates for the bungalows range around M$100 per bungalow.

Malaysian and European food is available at the Rest Houses, while at the bungalows you can either make arrangements for meals with the caretaker or do your own cooking.

All these rest houses and bungalows are accessible by metalled roads.

KOTA TINGGI
At 634 m (2,073 ft) above sea-level, Gunung Muntahak, in Johor State, makes a fitting end to the Main Range of mountains which forms the "backbone" of Peninsular Malaysia. In its lower reaches 91 m (298 ft) above sea-level, is a catchment area which supplies water to Kota Tinggi Town, and from it the Waterfalls thunder down the slope of the hill, passing huge boulders, weeping ferns and hanging vines. At 37 m (121 ft) the waters of the falls flow over a weir, pass rapids, tumble down a 24 m (78 ft)

slope of rocks and finally flow placidly through two natural pools into Sungei Pelepah.

There are good foot-bridges and concrete steps with railings to ease the climb to the Falls.

This holiday resort, 56 km (35 miles) from Johor Bahru, is a favourite picnicking and bathing spot.

HOW TO GET THERE
There are regular bus and taxi services from Johor Bahru to Kota Tinggi town and from the town to the Waterfall.

By Bus
From Johor Bahru to Kota Tinggi (Bus no. 41) — every 15 min — M$2 per person
From Kota Tinggi to Waterfalls (Bus no. 43) — every hour — M$0.90 per person.

By Taxi
From Johor Bahru to Kota Tinggi (41.6 km) — M$2.50 per person.
From Kota Tinggi to Waterfalls (14.4 km) — M$2 per person.

ACCOMMODATION
Seven fully-furnished, self-contained chalets are conveniently situated near the Waterfalls. Each chalet has one bedroom, sitting/dining hall and a kitchen equipped with cooking utensils, crockery, cutlery, gas, gas rings and a refrigerator.

The rent per night is M$42 and the rent for a day chalet is M$26.25.

Chalets should be booked two weeks in advance, through the Assistant State Secretary, Local Government State Secretariat, Johor Bahru, ph 07-241 957, ext. 30.
Entrance Fees: Adult M$1, Children M$0.20/0.40.
Parking Fees: Bus M$5; Car M$2; Motorcycle M$1.

FACILITIES
The 2-storey restaurant on the hillside, facing the waterfalls and chalets, serves European, Muslim and Chinese dishes, while a cluster of stalls offer a variety of Malaysian foods.

A spacious car park and changing rooms are also part of the modern amenities provided for the convenience of visitors.

SIGHTSEEING

Apart from a refreshing dip in one of the clear pools, the visitor can also climb to the top of the mountain.

An added attraction to a visit here is that it is a perfect base to explore the historical sites of Johor Lama, the famous fortified capital of the Johor Kingdom, built by Sultan Alauddin Ri'ayat Shah (between 1547 and 1587).

It is also a convenient base for swimming at Teluk Mahkota (37 km — 23 miles away) where a sandy bay lies sheltered from the waves of the South China Sea for a stretch of 10 km (6 miles).

NATIONAL PARKS OF MALAYSIA

While the Ice Ages were effecting far-reaching climatic changes across the northern hemisphere and afflicting the flora and fauna of the rest of the world, the Malaysian jungles remained untouched by nature or man for an estimated 100 million years — believed to be older than the jungles of the Congo or the Amazon.

Amongst the many splendid gorges, rivers and towering hills, Malaysia's National Parks provide an adventure tour with a full quota of thrills — boating through swirling rapids, stalking big game with a camera, fly-fishing for giant carp, bird-watching, mountain-climbing, exploring limestone caves, swimming in placid river waters, and camping amidst the majesty of giant tropical trees.

TAMAN NEGARA

Taman Negara comprises 4,343 km^2 (1,676 sq. miles) and is situated partly in Pahang State, partly in Kelantan State and partly in Trengganu State. The National Park, accessible to visitors, is contained in the State of Pahang, bounded on the south-east by the Tembeling River. The Headquarters of the Park is at Kuala Tahan and it is invariably the first point of call for all visitors to the park.

HOW TO GET THERE

By car
Travel to Jerantut by way of Mentakab or Raub (3–4 hours from Kuala Lumpur). From Jerantut, Kuala Tembeling is a further 16 km (10 miles) to the north, along a narrow, steep road. Follow the signs from Kuala Tembeling.

By Bus
Services leave from the bus station at Jalan Tun Razak in Kuala Lumpur to Temerioh. The journey is then continued by another bus or by taxi.

There is also a bus service that operates from Kuantan direct to Jerantut, from where you can pick up a bus or taxi.

By Train
A night train leaves Singapore at 10pm and arrives at Tembeling Halt at 7.57am next morning. From Tembeling Halt it is a half-hour walk to the jetty.
From Kota Bahru a south-bound train leaves from Tumpat at 10am and reaches Jerantut by 7.30pm.

By Taxi
Taxis from Kuala Lumpur leave for Temerloh and Jerantut from Puduraya Bus Terminal on Jalan Pudu.

By Boat
The journey by boat from Kuala Tembeling to Kuala Tahan takes from 2 to 2.5 hours, depending on the condition of the river.

ACCOMMODATION

A modern Rest House, 6 chalets and a hostel are available from the Park Headquarters at Kuala Tahan. Each room has a bathroom attached, modern sanitation and piped water. There is also electricity. Hostel accommodation is of the dormitory style, with bunk beds.

There are Visitor Lodges at Kuala Atok, Kuala Terenggan and Kuala Kenyam and Fishing Lodges at Lata Berkoh and Kuala Perkai. At Visitor and Fishing Lodges, beds, bedding, sheets and pillow slips are provided as well as crockery, cutlery, cooking utensils, water and firewood.

Accommodation at Visitor and Fishing Lodges consists of two rooms, each containing two single beds, and for a large party, extra persons can be accommodated in camp beds on the verandah. All beds are fitted with bedding and mosquito nets.

Camp equipment for visitors who wish to live under canvas includes tent, a camp bed and lamps with fuel.

For all bookings and further information, contact:
Wildlife and National Park Department,
KM10, Jalan Cheras 56100 Kuala Lumpur.
Ph 03-905 2872/3/5.

TRAVEL WITHIN THE PARK

This is mainly by river, but there are numerous jungle paths for the more energetic to follow. Between Kuala Tahan and Kuala Terenggan there is a series of seven rapids which, if there is sufficient water, may be negotiated non-stop by outboard, but when the water is low, passengers are required to get out and walk along the river bank until the boatmen push the boat into deeper water. Visitors are requested not to attempt to assist in any way with the handling of the boat, since the stones of the river bed are slippery and inexperienced help is generally more of a hindrance to men who are used to the work.

On the downward trip through the rapids, one should expect to ship a certain quantity of water, as the boat negotiates rough water at speed. It should also be remembered that early morning travel in a fast boat can be rather chilly.

CLOTHING

For everyday trips in the Park, the ubiquitous jungle green or khaki drill is excellent, and that together with jungle boots, or short rubber-soled boots and puttees should be sufficient. One or two changes, of course, are essential for comfort.

For normal wear around camp ordinary shirts and slacks suffice. A jacket, cardigan or pullover is handy if early morning travel by boat is envisaged, as the air at that time of the day is very cold.

Each visitor should provide himself with a good torch (flashlight).

For jungle travel on foot, especially in the wetter months, one should be dressed in as leech-proof a manner as possible. The most practical is the normal jungle green or khaki slacks and shirt with jungle boots closely laced up, the socks inside and underneath the trouser leg. For the most part, however, leeches are seldom troublesome enough to give rise to concern and can be dealt with quite easily.

STORES

It is not necessary for visitors to bring their own food to Taman Negara as there are full catering facilities at the Kuala Tahan Rest

House, and tinned food for journeys further afield may be purchased at the Rest House Shop. No catering facilities are provided at the outlying lodges and halting bungalows, and visitors must undertake their own cooking there.

PHOTOGRAPHY

Photography of river scenery and wild life in salt licks is the most popular attraction. For still cameras two types of film should be brought — a fast panchromatic film for use in poor light, and a much slower one for out-door photography in the sun. A telephoto lens is essential if good pictures of wild life are required, as is flash equipment.

Colour film may be used, but it is generally difficult to obtain enough light for animal photography at salt licks.

SALT LICKS

There are seven salt-licks within easy reach of Kuala Tahan and Kuala Terenggan. A large variety of wild life come to these salt licks to drink the water and eat the chemically impregnated soil. At Jenut Belau, sambar, barding deer, wild pigs and tapir are visitors, and the same animals may be seen at Jenut Tabing salt lick. These two licks are within easy reach of the Park Headquarters at Kuala Tahan. Observation hides have been built at 4 of these licks so that the visitor may watch unseen. At Jenut Kumbang and Jenut Belau there are high hides in which visitors may stay overnight.

ANGLING

The rivers in Taman Negara are well-stocked with fish, those most frequently encountered being members of the Carp family, which includes the well-known Mahseer of India, known locally as Kelah. The Kelah can be found in the swifter reaches and a line of about 12 lb breaking strain will give the best results since they run up to 20 lbs.

The Kelasa (Sceleropages formosus) will put on a wonderful fighting display leaping high out of the water and moving at amazing speed. They are to be found in the fast flowing rivers at points where the water is deep and relatively quiet. To add to the angler's difficulties, they particularly enjoy those small dents along river banks where old driftwood collects.

All these fish can be taken on artificial bait, the most successful being 1" to 1.5" silver and silver/copper spoons. The ordinary treble hooks, however, should be changed for special mahseer hooks as the crushing power of the jaws of these fish is enormous. The line should be at least 91 m (100 yds) in length, although 137 m (150 yds) is a safer length particularly when progress along the river bank is impossible due to boulders and high steep shores.

Fishing can be undertaken from a slowly paddled boat or from the bank, which also includes wading as long stretches of boulders do not permit progress along the water's edge.

Fishing Areas

Probably the most spectacular river in the Park is the Sungei Tahan, which falls some 152 m (497 ft) from Kuala Teku at the foot of the Gunung Tahan massif, to its mouth at Kuala Tahan. The lower reaches up to the barrier of Lata Berkoh are reasonably placid and there are many large pools containing plenty of fish. Above Lata Berkoh cataract, there is a seemingly endless succession of pools and rapids, all excellent fishing water but seldom fished. A week's camping holiday up there at the right time should be a worthwhile experience.

Sungei Kenyam so far has been the most patronised fishing river, and some very good catches have been made. The further one goes beyond Kuala Kenyam Kechil, the better the water seems to be. To reach the best fishing water you normally need a two-day trip. Thus the visitor who wishes to avail himself of a week's good fishing in the Kenyam requires no less than a 10-day stay.

The most suitable times of the year for fishing are the months of February–March, and July–August. During the other months, sport is liable to be spasmodic owing to local rainfall.

SWIMMING

About 10 minutes' walk from Kuala Tahan, at Lubok Simpon, there is a fine swimming pool. The short trip may also be made by boat.

GUNUNG TAHAN
Many people have climbed this mountain (2,187 m — 7,151 ft) which is the highest in Peninsular Malaysia. The main obstacle is time. From Kuala Tahan to Kuala Teku (at the base of the mountain) it takes two-and-a-half days on foot. From Kuala Teku to the summit, the journey must be done in two stages owing to the scarcity of water. Thus to reach the top, travelling time is 5 days. The return journey takes roughly one day less. Guides must be hired. The ascent of Gunung Tahan is nevertheless a memorable experience and well worthwhile to anyone who is really interested.

OTHER INTERESTING POINTS
Within the area of the Park there are many limestone hills and outcrops. Anyone interested in speleology will be well rewarded by a visit to the limestone caves that were used by aborigines and elephants; some have crude drawings on the walls, and in addition there is the challenge of rock climbing. It takes about two-and-a-half days of travel by boat and on foot.

Not so far afield is the solitary peak of Guling Gendang which gives a fine view of the Park from its summit. It is 590 m (1,929 ft) in height, and the return trip from Kuala Tahan can be made in a full day. Camping in the vicinity can also be arranged.

TEMPLER PARK
Covering an area of 1,214 ha (2,998 acres), Templer Park is a cool haven, profusely green, with tumbling cascades and rushing streams. Set like a jade amidst forested hills, the Park abounds with an enormous variety of flora.

Located about 21 km (13 miles) from Kuala Lumpur on the North/South Highway, the Park was named after Tan Sri Gerald Templer, the last British High Commissioner in the former Federation of Malaya and was opened in May, 1954. For the urban population, it offers the young and old a place to relax and enjoy themselves after a hard and busy week.

HOW TO GET THERE
By car from Kuala Lumpur it is a half hour drive.

NATIONAL PARKS OF MALAYSIA 253

ACCOMMODATION
There is no accommodation in the Park.

ATTRACTIONS
On arrival at the Park a canteen close to the road awaits the thirsty and hungry. Well-kept paths along the rushing streams lead to the interior where you may explore and admire Nature's beauty. Almost as soon as the Park is reached, monkeys are waiting to welcome visitors to their jungle lair, and of course to accept the nuts or fruits they are used to receiving.

As the paths wind higher and higher up the forested hill, they are flanked by bamboo clumps, tree ferns and tangled flowering creepers, and there is a never-ending chorus of birds and insects. A large variety of butterflies are found in this Park, among them one of the world's most attractive species, the Raja Brooke's Birdwing.

Other paths lead further into the interior to the fascinating limestone outcrops at Bukit Takun and Anak Takun, which rise to 305 m (997 ft) and are of great interest to naturalists. Anak Takun contains a network of caves with geological formations and living fossils which remain largely intact. The caves and limestone escarpment also throw a challenge to the adventurous climber.

The natural charm of Templer Park has always enthralled visitors, and it was here that a Hollywood film team shot the jungle scenes for the movie "The Seventh Dawn".

KINABALU NATIONAL PARK
86 km (53 miles) from Kota Kinabalu, capital of Sabah State, rises the 4,101 m (13,410 ft) Mount Kinabalu, one of the highest mountains in South-East Asia. The Park extends from an elevation of 152 m (497 ft) above sea-level to the summit.

A reserve of some 767 km^2 (296 sq. miles) encircling Mount Kinabalu, the Park represents a fascinating panorama of North Bornean flora and fauna.

This "revered place of the dead", as believed by the Kadazan people, is not only a resting-place for spirits but also has long been a challenge to mountaineers and a favourite haunt of ardent zoologists, ornithologists and naturalists.

254 SINGAPORE AND MALAYSIA AT COST

HOW TO GET THERE

By Bus
The Tuaran United Transport Co. runs a daily mini bus service between Kota Kinabalu and Ranau. It departs Kota Kinabalu bus station at 8am and the journey to the Park takes about 3 hours, at M$10.50 per person. The return trip to Kota Kinabalu passes the Park Headquarters at 9am.

Numerous charter mini buses are available and are recommended for groups. Rates are approximately M$224 from Kota Kinabalu to the Park. Charter information and arrangements can be obtained through the National Park Office, Kota Kinabalu.

By Air
Ranau has a short airstrip. A helicopter landing pad is available at the Park Headquarters.

ACCESS AND ASCENT

Kinabalu Park Headquarters is at Simpangan Kinabalu, 50 km (3 miles) from Tamparuli. At 1560 m (5,101 ft) above sea-level it can be reached by any vehicle in about 2 hours from Kota Kinabalu or 30 minutes from Ranau air-field.

From Simpangan Kinabalu, another 15 minutes drive will take you to the Power Station at 1,829 m (5,981 ft). From here travelling is on foot.

The ascent begins with a graded trail joining a jungle track which is followed to the first of the shelters. This stretch of 2.8 km (2 miles) takes about 3 hours depending upon the climbing ability. The next stop will be at Sayat-Sayat which is another hour walk. From here, Low's Peak, the summit can be reached in about an hour.

An early start should be made for the ascent, as clouds often obscure the view after 9am. The summit can be reached and a return made to the Park Headquarters from either Panar Laban or Sayat-Sayat but the descent should commence before noon if the Power Station is to be reached before nightfall.

Visitors must utilise the services of an authorised guide for the ascent to the summit. The rates for the guide range from M$25 to M$30 per day for a normal 2-day trip depending upon the size o the group. All arrangements for the climb, including the booking of guides and porters, should be made well in advance through the Park Warden.

ACCOMMODATION

The Park provides overnight facilities at Park Headquarters at the 50th kilometre on the Ranau Road and at Poring Hot Springs, 19 km (12 miles) north of Ranau.

At the Headquarters there are 2 hostels, 4 deluxe cabins, 10 twin bed cabins and 2 luxury chalets. Rates for the hostel are M$8 to M$15 per night per person (students at M$2 to M$4.50).

The luxury chalets have facilities of a higher standard of comfort and convenience at a daily rate of M$80 for a two-bedroom cabin and M$100 to M$150 for a three-bedroom chalet (plus 5% Government tax).

Accommodation at Poring include two cabins and a campground. Visitors are reminded to bring their own food. Rates for the campground which has prepared tent sites, a communal cookhouse, bathrooms and a recreation/dining room are M$1 per person, students M$0.50, per night. Cost for the cabin is M$21 per person per night.

For reserving hostel accommodation, procuring guides and other necessary arrangements, write to the Director, Sabah Parks, P.O. Box 10626, 88806 Kota Kinabalu, Sabah, Malaysia, or phone 08-211 588, 211 881, 211 652.

ORNITHOLOGICAL AND ZOOLOGICAL INTERESTS

The birds of Mt Kinabalu are unusually tame. Although some birds such as the Argus Pheasant are shy, the Mountain Blackeye and the Friendly Warbler Blackbird will hop around your feet.

More than 250 varieties of birds have been recorded. Lizards, tree shrews, bats and squirrels, amongst other small mammals, dart around unconcerned. Fish have also been identified in little rock pools at 3,962 m (12,986 ft).

FLORA

Kinabalu is the hub of the oak-beech kingdom. One can discover the Trigonobalanus forest tree which has oak-like leaves, beechnuts in acorn and suggests that it connects the southern beeches

(Northofagus) of New Guinea, Australia, New Zealand and the extremity of South America with the northern hemisphere's togoceal.

Rhododendrons and over 800 orchids add extra colour and the reddish Rafflesia, the largest flower in the world, spreads its metre-wide blooms on the floor of the primary forest between 609 and 1,219 m (3,986 ft) above sea-level.

It is possible to find the huge Hepenthes rajas, a species of the Pitcher plant, the bowl of which can hold up to four pints of water.

TUNKU ABDUL RAHMAN NATIONAL PARK

The Park, comprising the five islands of Pulau Gaya, Pulau Sapi Pulau Mamutik, Pulau Manukan and Pulau Sulug and the surrounding seas, covers a total area of approximately 4,931 ha (12,180 acres).

Being so close to Kota Kinabalu, the Park is a great tourist attraction for visitors from overseas as well as local pelple. It also offers snorkellers and scuba-divers an opportunity to view the underwater world of coral life. For non-swimmers going to the Park, the excellent nature trail system provides many happy hours of hiking and studying the flora and fauna typical of tropical islands.

HOW TO GET THERE

Boat services to the islands are provided by private firms and the rates are as follows:
Sunday and Public Holidays — Return trip to Pulau Sapi, M$12 per head. Return trip to Police Beach, M$15 per head.
Weekdays — Charter for one boat, M$185 per head (maximum 12 persons).
Prices quoted are subject to revision and those interested can contact the Sabah Parks Office for further information, ph 088-21 585, 211 881.

ACCOMMODATION

The accommodation available is included in the information of the various islands.

PULAU GAYA

Pulau Gaya, some 1,483 ha (3,663 acres) in size, is the biggest island in the Park and the site of its Headquarters.

An attractive island for swimming, snorkelling, picnicking and camping, it also has interesting beach flora. The forest is typical of the lowland rain forest. It has a good beach at Bulijong Bay — called Police Beach because the police used to have target practice there before the Park was gazetted. The water in the bay is crystal clear and calm except during the monsoon periods. Casuarina trees provide excellent shade for picnickers. Day-use facilities include a large public shelter, toilets and changing rooms. Fresh water is available.

There are some 21 km (13 miles) of graded nature trails with gentle slopes on the island for visitors who are interested in exploring.

PULAU SAPI

Only about 25 minutes away boat, this small island is the most popular and best developed in the Tunku Abdul Rahman National Park.

It has a clean sandy beach and crystal clear waters. Day-use facilities provided on the island include a jetty with a shelter and diving board, public toilets, barbecue stands, beach shelters and picnic tables. Camping is permitted but visitors must bring their own food and camping equipment.

PULAU MAMUTIK

This island is quite rich in corals especially on the eastern reef on the north-eastern tip of the island. Interesting sights are the delicate white colonies of Distichopora and clusters of red Dendrophyllia corals, both fairly rare.

Work is currently underway to develop this beautiful island into a good camping ground for visitors who would like to experience a Robinson Crusoe style camping trip. Basic facilities such as water, electricity and picnic tables are available. A Jetty and other beach facilities will be built soon. A rest house is available for rent (accommodation for 12 persons) for M$60 per night.

PULAU MANUKAN
About 21 ha (52 acres) in size, this island resembles a big whale basking in the sun. It has a long beach on the eastern side. Public shelters, picnic tables and barbecue stands will be provided for picnickers. A nature trail system will also be developed on the island.

PULAU SULUG
Pulau Sulug is the furthest from Kota Kinabalu. However, some of the best coral reefs in the park are found here. There are beautiful shallow coral beds and several large coral heads along the reef rim. Fish are plentiful. The reef here is extensive, varied and densely packed with Acropora, Montipora, Seriatopora, Pocillopora and Echinopora corals.

Pulau Sulug, however, is still being developed and visitors who wish to go to the island are advised to bring with them all the necessary items such as food and drinks. If an overnight camping trip is intended, permission must first be obtained from the National Park Office in Kota Kinabalu.

FLORA
The vegetation on the islands is extremely varied. You can stroll from the beach-front across a boardwalk through a mangrove swamp and end up in a tropical rainforest.

FAUNA
Mammals such as monkeys, squirrels, rats and pangolins (anteaters) are common along the trails. You may see the Bearded Pig, which has a very long snout with a tuft of hair half way down.

A large number of birds inhabit the islands — the sky Megopode, the white-bellied Sea Eagle, Pied Hornbill, Pink-necked Green Pigeon and many species of bulbuls, babblers, flycatchers, swiftlets and sunbirds.

Lizards and insects of fascinating varieties can also be spotted.

MARINE LIFE
The Park provides excellent opportunity for exploration of an underwater coral reef wonder world. There are several coral beds

close to the beaches of all islands as well as two platform reefs which can be viewed from a glass-bottomed boat.

The corals also provide a house and hiding place for myriads of colourful sea creatures.

BAKO NATIONAL PARK

Situated on a peninsula at the mouth of the Bako River, these 26 km^2 (10 sq. miles) of primary forest are accessible by boat from Kuching, by way of the Sarawak, Santubong and Bako Rivers.

HOW TO GET THERE

Arrangements for a trip to the Park can be made through commercial launch operators or tourist agencies. A popular way is to catch a bus from the Kuching Bus Station to Bako Fishing Village, and from there by longboat to the Park. The bus fare is M$1.90 one way and M$2.50 return, while the boat fare is M$6 depending on the boatload.

Boats can be hired from Kampung Bako to Telok Assam at the following rates:

Number of passengers per boat	Charge per Trip M$
1 to 5	25.00
6 to 10	30.00
more than 10	3.00 per person

Note: All rates quoted may be subject to change from time to time.

ACCOMMODATION

Booking of accommodation has to be made at the National Parks and Wildlife Office, Ground Floor, Jalan Gartak, Kuching, Sarawak. The telephone number is Kuching 082-248 088. All bookings must be confirmed at least 3 days before travelling to the Park. Permits to stay at Bako National Park will be issued once various charges have been settled.

Resthouses: These can accommodate 13 people in 2 resthouses at M$31.50 resthouse/night. Refrigerator, gas stove, bed linen, easy chairs, cutlery and cooking utensils are all provided. There are also 4 units of resthouses that can accommodate 10 people in one unit at M$42 per unit/night.

Hostels: About 30 people can be accommodated in 4 hostels at M$1.05 person/night. Facilities include bunks with mattresses, tables, kerosene stoves and benches. Visitors are advised to bring blankets and some cooking utensils.

Camping: Plastic flysheets (size 4.6 m × 3.6 m) are available for hire at M$1 tent/night. Camping is restricted to specially prepared camping areas unless prior approval from the Park Warden is obtained.

Food: All visitors must bring their own food and drink to the Park, although a limited supply of snacks and soft drinks are on sale at the canteen.

VEGETATION

The land is moderately hilly, rising from sea level to about 244 m (798 ft). The coastline of the park is indented by many sandy bays often backed by steep cliffs beyond which a gentle plateau spreads into the wooded interior.

Within this relatively small area at least 7 major types of vegetation typical of Sarawak are found. They are the Mangrove forest, Sandy beach forest, Sandstone cliff vegetation, Alluvial forest, Peat swamp forest, Lowland dipterocarp forest and Kerangas (Heath) forest. The sand stone cliff vegetation and kerangas scrub on the plateau are characteristic of the Park.

Visitors will find of great interest the ant plants and carnivorous plants whose peculiar characteristics afford an insight into some fascinating aspects of nature at work. The carnivorous pitcher plant (Nepenthes), sundew (Drosera) and bladderwort (Utricularia) are abundant on the kerangas scrub. The ant plants or Mrymecophytes live in association with colonies of ants. They include baboon's head (Hydnophytum formicarium), samboko (Myrmecodia tuberosa), Pitis-pitis kecil (Dischidia) and the fern Phymatodes sinuosa which frequently drape stunted bonsai-like trees on the padang vegetation.

The various vegetation types offer an excellent opportunity for scientific studies in tropical rainforest particularly on the adaptations of the many plant species under different ecological conditions.

FAUNA
Longtailed macaques, monitor lizards, pigs and sambar deer are common. The long-nosed monkey or orang blanda (Nasalis larvatus) can sometimes be spotted along the coast. It is endemic to Borneo and is protected in Sarawak. Reptiles and amphibians nose in and out of the water in the interior.

BEACHES
Beaches at Telok Assam (hostel area), Telok Paku and Telok Pandan Kechil provide good safe bathing at mid and high tides. Telok Paku and Telok Pandan Kechil are about 45 and 90 minutes' walk respectively from Telok Assam.

JUNGLE PATHS
There is a well-demarcated system of paths within the park which may be followed without difficulty or fear of getting lost. Maps in the Interpretation Centre and resthouses show the layout of trails through various vegetation type. The main paths are Lintang, Tanjong Sapi, Telok Paku, Telok Pandan Kechil, Telok Tajor, Bukit Kerning Gondol and Ulu Serait.

WEATHER
As the sea can be rough from October to March, it may not be possible to visit the park during this period. The park warden will advise whether visits are possible.

NIAH NATIONAL PARK
The Niah National Park encompasses 3,102 ha (7,662 acres) of forest and limestone, situated in the Miri District of Sarawak. Here it is possible to explore the great number of limestone caves, observe the collection of edible birds nests, and view prehistoric wall paintings as well as the preserved remains of the artists themselves. This is also the site of archeological excavations carried out by the Sarawak Museum in the late fifties.

HOW TO GET THERE

By Taxi
The Niah National Park can be reached from Miri or Bintulu by first going to Batu Niah. The taxi fare from Bintulu to Batu Niah is

M$25 per person, while from Miri to Batu Niah it costs M$15 per person.

By Bus
There are bus services between Bintulu and Batu Niah.
The bus departs Bintulu at 7.30am and 12 noon, and the return trip departs at 7am and 12 noon.

By Boat
From Batu Niah you can use a longboat to go to the Park Hostel. The fee is negotiable.

Alternatively you can follow the footpath from Batu Niah down the Niah River to the Bungalow, which takes 45 minutes. Otherwise, if you have your own transport, you can drive along the Sim Kheng Hong Road right to the Park Headquarters.

ACCOMMODATION
The Park Hostel has 3 rooms and can accommodate a total of 36 people. A fee of M$2.50 per person is charged per night. Bookings for accommodation at the Park Hostel should be made through the National Parks Office in Miri. There are also hotels available at Batu Niah.

JUNGLE TRAILS
From the Park hostel you can use the plankwalk trail to reach the Great Cave. In good weather the journey takes 45 minutes. Good footwear is essential as the planks can be slippery when they are wet. Other hiking trails are also found in the Park.

WILDLIFE
Three species of swiftlets and 12 species of bats are found in the caves. The thing to watch for is the bats rushing out of the entrance to the Great Cave in their millions, yet never colliding with each other. Other wildlife found in the cave include earwigs, the naked bats, lizards, centipedes, scorpions and snakes. In the surrounding forests you can find long-tailed macaques, hornbills, squirrels, flying lizards and many species of butterflies.

NATIONAL PARKS OF MALAYSIA 263

PLEASE NOTE: The Great Cave is a historical monument within the Niah National Park. As such, visitors to the caves are required to observe certain regulations prohibiting the digging, collecting or removing of any object, natural or man-made, from the caves. Similar regulations are also enforced in the park.

Also please note that it is dangerous to walk inside the caves on your own as you can easily get lost or fall into deep gullies, some measuring hundreds of metres deep. Only with an experienced local guide and a good torch (flashlight) will you be able to move about safely in the darkness.

INDEX

A Famosa 115
Air Hitam 212
Air Itam Dam 137
Alor Setar 147–150
Ayer Keroh 119

Bako Nat. Park 259–261
Batu Caves 95–96
Beserah 199–202
Bujang Valley 150
Bukit China 117–118
Bukit Keluang 195
Bukit Larut 173, 242–243
Bukit Takum 96

Cameron Highlands 231–234
Cape Rachado 121
CN West Leisure Park 33

Dendong Beach Park 195
Desaru 213
Dutch Fort 121

East Coast Park 33
East Coast, Malaysia 175–184

Forest Reserve, Lenggeng 105
Fort Cornwallis 137
Fraser's Hill 234–238

Gadek Hot Spring 120
Genting Highlands 239–242
Georgetown 132–137
Gomantong Caves 222
Gunung Ledang 212

Gunung Tahan 252

Haw Par Villa 36

Ipoh 165–166

Johor 205–214
Johor Bahru 205–212
Johor Lama 212
Jurong Bird Park 32

Kampung Dalam Kota 193
Kedah 147–154
Kedah Peak 149
Kelantan 175–184
Keningau 221
Kenong Rimba Park 202
Kinabalu Nat. Park 253–256
Kota Belud 219
Kota Bharu 175–182
Kota Kinabalu 215–221
Kota Tinggi 243–245
Kranji War Memorial 36
Kuah 152
Kuala Besar 184
Kuala Kangsar 167–169
Kuala Kedah 150
Kuala Lumpur 79–94
Kuala Perlis 144
Kuala Terengganu 187–194
Kuantan 197–199
Kuching 223–228
Kudat 220

Langkawi 150–154

INDEX

Lumut 171

Malacca 107–119
Malaysia 55–263
Malaysia-in-Miniature 119
Marang Village 193
Mardi Station 234
Maxwell Hill 242–243
Melaka 107–119
Mengkuang Dam 141
Mersing 213
Mimaland 95
Mount Kinabalu 220

Negeri Selangor Darul Ehsan 94–96
Negeri Sembilan 99–105
New Ming Village 36
Niah Nat. Park 261–263

Padang Besar 144
Padas Hot Spring 104
Panching Cave 202
Pantai Bisikan Bayu 183
Pantai Dasat Sabak 183
Pantai Irama 183
Pantai Kuda 183
Pantai Puteri Dewi 172
Pantai Rhu 152
Papar 220
Pasir Bogak 172
Penampang 220
Penang 125–137
Penang Hill 139, 238–239
Pengkalan Kempas 104
Perak 157–173
Peranakan Place 36
Perlis 143–144
Poring Hot Springs 220

Port Dickson 104
Porta De Santiago 115
Portuguese Square 118
Pulau Besar 121
Pulau Gaya 257
Pulau Kapas 194
Pulau Mamutik 257
Pulau Manukan 258
Pulau Pangkor 172–173
Pulau Perhentian 195
Pulau Rawa 213–214
Pulau Sapi 257
Pulau Sibu 214
Pulau Sulug 258

Sabah 215–223
Sandakan 221–222
Santubong 228
Sarawak 223–229
Seberang Jaya 140
Sekayu Waterfalls 194
Semporna 223
Sentosa 33–34
Sepilok 222
Seremban 99–104
Serkam 120
Singapore 1–50
Singapore Experience 36
Singapore Mint Coin Gallery 36–37
Singapore River 37
Singapore Science Centre 37
Skrang River 228
Southern Islands, Singapore 34–35
Sri Menanti 105

Taiping 169–171
Taman Negara 203, 247–252

Tambun Hot Springs 166
Tambunan 221
Tanah Rata 231
Tanjong Lumpur 199
Tapah 231
Tawau 223
Telok Chempedak 202
Teluk Batik 172
Teluk Intan 171
Templer Park 96, 252–253
Tenom 220

Terengganu 187–195
Tioman Island 202
Tuaran 219
Tumpat 183
Tunku Abdul Rahman Nat. Park 256–259

Ulu Bendol 104

Van Kleef Aquarium 37